LISTENING FOR A MIDNIGHT TRAM

John Junor was born in Shannon Street, Glasgow, in 1919. Before the war he read English at Glasgow University, where he was also President of the University Liberal Club. During the war he served first in armed merchant cruisers in the Royal Navy and then as a pilot in the Fleet Air Arm, founding and editing the Air Arm's magazine *Flight Deck*. In 1947 he joined Beaverbrook Newspapers, rising to become the Assistant Editor of the *Daily Express* from 1951 to 1953, the Deputy Editor of the *Evening Standard* from 1953 to 1954 and the Editor of the *Sunday Express* from 1954 to 1986, a Fleet Street record. In 1989 he joined Associated Newspapers where he now writes a hugely popular column for the *Mail on Sunday*. John Junor has one son, Roderick, and a daughter, Penny, who are both journalists. He was knighted in 1980.

D1136947

To: Dan

From: Rachel

Christmas 1991!

JOHN JUNOR

Memoirs

---

*Listening
for a Midnight Tram*

PAN BOOKS
IN ASSOCIATION WITH CHAPMANS

First published 1990 by Chapmans Publishers Ltd
This edition first published 1991 by Pan Books Ltd,
Cavaye Place, London SW10 9PG
in association with Chapmans Publishers Ltd

1 3 5 7 9 8 6 4 2

ISBN 0 330 31862 4

© John Junor 1990

The right of John Junor to be identified as the author of this work has
been asserted by him in accordance with the Copyright, Designs, and
Patents Act 1988.

Printed in England by Clays Ltd, St Ives plc

This book is sold subject to the condition that it
shall not, by way of trade or otherwise, be lent, re-sold,
hired out, or otherwise circulated without the publisher's prior
consent in any form of binding or cover other than that in which
it is published and without a similar condition including this
condition being imposed on the subsequent purchaser.

For
Roderick and Penelope

I would like to thank
JAMES KINLAY
for reading my manuscript and at times correcting my memory

ILLUSTRATIONS

John Junor, 1945 (*Mail on Sunday*)

The Sports Staff of the *Sunday Express* (*Sunday Express*)

With Lyndon Johnson, 1968

Alongside the quay at Barfleur

The President of the Gambia spends a day aboard *Outcast* (*Sunday Express*)

With Reginald Maudling, 1970 (*Sunday Express*)

The Prime Minister and Lord Hailsham at the dinner to celebrate JJ's twenty-five years as Editor of the *Sunday Express* (*Sunday Express*)

I

THERE ARE NOT too many people who in complete health and in good control of their intellectual faculties have known that they have just seventeen more minutes to live.

I am one of them.

On 13 April 1941 I took off from the airstrip at Kingston, Ontario in Canada in a Fairey Battle on a routine night-flying exercise.

The purpose was to perform circuits and landings round the airstrip – a simple exercise for trainee pilots. All one had to do was to take off, climb on zero by the directional giro to 500 feet, turn left on to zero nine zero, then on to 180 zero, then on to 270, turn left again and there were the lights of the runway waiting to meet you.

The technique was to wait at right angles to the end of the take-off runway for a green light. One then turned on to the runway and unlocked the directional giro. The idea was to keep the directional giro on zero throughout take-off, keeping one's head in the cockpit as much as possible to make sure that it was. On this particular night I unlocked the directional giro and opened the throttle and to my delight and surprise throughout the take-off the giro stayed constantly on zero. Normally one expected it to drift maybe 5 or 10 degrees.

At 500 feet I began my climbing turn to the left on to zero

nine zero. Half-way through the turn I looked at the giro. It was still firmly on zero. It had failed to unlock.

When I did succeed in unlocking it it simply spun round and round.

I looked out of the cockpit for the airfield. There was nothing to be seen. No airfield, no landing lights. Nothing. I realised that I must have drifted badly on take-off, but which way? To the right? To the left? I had no idea.

All I knew was that there was not a light on the ground to be seen anywhere.

And on a dark night in Canada without stars, without moon, the blackness is impenetrable.

I knew that on take-off to the left of me had been Lake Ontario, one hundred miles long, thirty miles wide and for all I knew perhaps twenty miles deep. Towards the right, beyond the narrow coastal strip, was an impenetrable forest of trees 150 feet high.

But I had no way of telling in which direction I had drifted on take-off. I might be over Lake Ontario. I might be over forest. And I had no radio, no Mae West and no inflatable dinghy. I had a parachute and petrol for precisely 2 hours and 47 minutes.

For 2 hours and 30 minutes I flew in circles trying desperately to find the airfield, utterly without success.

With just 17 minutes to go I had a simple choice: either parachute into the unknown or stay with the plane when it crashed. I knew in my own mind that I was going to stay with the plane when it crashed. Partly because I was shit scared. Partly because I knew that if I bailed out the chances of being hit by the tailplane were high. I also knew that my chances of survival were almost zero.

So I prayed. My mouth was quite dry. The exhaust fumes of the aeroplane belched blue out into the Canadian night.

And then suddenly as if in answer to my prayer I saw two lights – a red light and a green light, some 1000 feet below me.

It was another aeroplane on the same circuit from the same aerodrome. I followed it down and landed. My engine coughed and died from lack of petrol as I parked the aircraft.

I told no one what had happened.

Not until now.

Do you wonder why, as someone brought up in the Calvinistic faith, and a firm believer in predestination, I came to the conclusion that someone up there had decided I had some purpose still to serve in life?

Even though, after a lifetime in Fleet Street, I still do not know what that purpose was?

I was born on 15 January 1919 in a red-stone tenement in Shannon Street, Maryhill, Glasgow, a two-roomed flat without indoor sanitation. The midwife was a Mrs McNaught. I have few memories of that first home, although I can recall being held out of a window as a toddler by a young woman (I have no idea who she was) and being terrified of being dropped into the street far below. I remember also being awakened at night, around Christmas time, to receive a gift from a friend of my father who was visiting the house. It was a toy horse about twelve inches high, hollow and filled with chocolates. I can still feel it in my hands. And I recall with distaste and fear the smell of the isolation hospital in which I spent my fifth birthday suffering from diphtheria and scarlet fever, diseases now almost unknown but vicious killers then. I must have been near to death.

I have no memory at all of being taken to hospital. When I recovered consciousness the first thing the boy in the next bed said to me was, 'Are you a cup or a plate?' I did not know what he meant but replied 'a plate' – an answer which met with his approval. It was quite some time before I discovered, and he could not have been much older than myself, that he had been asking whether I was Catholic or Protestant. Religious feelings ran high and early in working-class Glasgow. Soon afterwards Millie Clyde, the seventeen-year-old daughter of a friend of my parents, found herself pregnant and committed suicide by putting her head in a gas oven. Such was the shame of an illegitimate birth she felt she had no alternative. I suppose the only greater sin she could have committed would have been to have married a Catholic.

When I left hospital it was to a new home in Springburn, a

council house with two rooms downstairs, three rooms upstairs and a garden. It was like paradise. My mother had bought a shop selling milk and groceries close to my first school, Elmbank Public.

We moved house once again when I was thirteen, this time to a flat with three rooms and a kitchen at a rental of £32 per year and close to my second school, North Kelvinside Secondary. It was a humble enough home but compared with many other children in the area, I had a privileged upbringing. For my father was never on the dole. We always had enough to eat. I had two brothers, one twelve years, the other ten years older than myself. The three of us had a priceless advantage in life, a mother who was determined to send us all to university. And she did. My eldest brother became a schoolmaster, the second a doctor. Being so much younger than them I was brought up in effect as an only child. I was always happy, although looking back there was not always that much to be happy about.

My mother was a fanatical whist player and in Glasgow at that time there were whist drives everywhere. Every night my mother would attend one, often in a part of the city far from our home. She was a good player and frequently came home carrying the evening's first prize, which might be a bag of groceries. But she always came home late and many a night at the age of ten I lay awake in bed, worrying, until nearly midnight.

There were few motor cars anywhere in those days. Often the only sound as I lay in the stillness of the night was a tramcar clattering along the rails. My mother would be on one of those trams. As the night drew on, their sound would become less frequent. It was with some relief that I heard the sound of a key in the door. Only then could I sleep.

My father was a good man, an honest man, a hard-working man. But I never, and now I regret it bitterly, felt any affection for him. The deafness he suffered as a result of his job as a steelworker made communication with him difficult. Indeed, I do not recollect ever having a real conversation with him.

His own mother had died when he was a child of eight. His father, a farm grieve or manager and later a crofter in Easter Ross, then married again. His wife must have been a hard

4

woman, for before he was fourteen my father had to leave home. He came to Glasgow and found employment in a steelworks. Every Friday night, after he had handed over the weekly house-keeping allowance to my mother, he would use the few shillings left in his pocket to go to the pub and get drunk, as did many working-class Scotsmen of the time.

I hated Friday nights. I hated the shouting, the rowing, the cursing monster my father became, although looking back my mother probably gave him cause for anger. He never drank the housekeeping money or said a word in anger for the rest of the week, but even into early adulthood, Friday night was a night on which I dared not bring my friends home. Perhaps if my mother had devoted a bit more time to her husband and a little less to pushing her sons ever upwards, my father's life would have been different. But then so would have been mine. For even under the marvellous Scottish educational system and the beneficence of the Carnegie Trust which contributed substantially to the fees of every Scottish boy going to university, the sacrifice my parents made was extraordinary.

And yet, Friday nights apart, life was good. In the evenings after school I would play football with my chums on ash and cinder pitches – because there were no such things as grass ones. On Saturday afternoons from the age of eleven onwards I would go alone to watch my favourite football team, Partick Thistle. Even today, so many years later, the Thistle result is the first I look for on a Saturday night.

Then there were the joyous school holidays. My mother was one of a large family and had sisters living in various parts of the Scottish countryside. On the first day of my school holidays she would dispatch me to one of them and there I would stay until the time came for me to return to school. Mary, my favourite aunt, lived in Turnberry in Ayrshire, a place famous for its golf course and luxury hotel. She had a little shop there which sold everything from chocolate and ice-cream to rice and tapioca. There were two sons, one two years older than myself and another two years younger.

I loved my holidays in Turnberry. The long-distance bus from Glasgow stopped close to my aunt's front door and the only snag about the journey was that until the age of fifteen I would be violently sick about ten miles short of my destination. Thereafter instead of becoming sick I was studying any young girls who happened to be fellow passengers.

My Turnberry cousins and I were great chums. When at the age of ten or twelve I became strong enough to carry a golf bag, I used to caddy two rounds a day and then play myself in the evening. Some of the people I caddied for were among the richest in the land – the Salmon family of Lyons Corner House fame, for instance, or the Mackintosh family who had become mega-rich from toffee. Carrying their bags for 17 pence a round gave me a glimpse of another world. Sometimes at night I would wait outside the hotel until the orchestra struck up. I would then press my nose against the ballroom window and watch the dancers, the men in black ties, the women in elegant ball gowns. But I never felt envious. I just wanted to join them.

Back home in Glasgow, I used to put out the lights in the evening and listen to the late-night dance music from such glamorous far-away places as the Dorchester and the Savoy in London. The Savoy's bandleader, Carrol Gibbons, was my idol. In the darkness, with the only light coming from the windows, I would dream happily of what lay ahead. It never occurred to me that I might fail to conquer the world.

Many years later, driving to work one lovely spring morning in a brand-new car, I was whistling happily as I passed a council estate and thinking how wonderful life was – because in addition to a new car, I had just acquired a nine-ton Bermudan sloop and would be spending my summer holiday cruising in her. Then I felt a pang of guilt. 'What about the poor sods in these council houses? Would you still be whistling if things had gone the other way and you had grown up to be one of them?'

My feeling of guilt passed just as quickly as it had come. For I knew damned well that if things had indeed gone the other way and I had failed to make the grade, I would still have been optimistically filling in football-pool coupons or working on a novel, which even although it had already been rejected by twenty-seven publishers I would be quite certain would still make the grade.

All my life I have been utterly, stupidly certain that the best day of my life is going to be tomorrow.

As in most universities, political feelings ran high when I enrolled at Glasgow University to read English Literature in 1936. It was the time of the Franco revolution in Spain, of the terror-bombing of Guernica, of the ever-increasing posturing of Hitler and Mussolini. I was violently anti-Fascist, anti-Franco, above all anti-Hitler.

But it was the University Liberal Club I joined, not any of the societies further to the Left, because although I could not support the Tory government, I did not like the socialists either.

Then, as now, there were not too many Liberals in Scotland. So few, in fact, that I was immediately appointed Assistant Secretary of the Club; two years later I was its President. But by then we had one of the biggest memberships among the political societies and had come to the notice of the Scottish Liberal Party. For I discovered that I had a talent not only for speaking in Union debates and on public platforms but also for persuading other people to share my views.

I found myself attending conferences, being invited to make speeches and generally being treated almost as a celebrity by Liberals in Edinburgh and elsewhere. I was once even invited to open a sale of work in West Perthshire by the Liberal candidate in the West Perth by-election, a Church of Scotland Minister's wife called Mrs Coll McDonald. That was one invitation I turned down. I felt that nineteen was just a little too young to be opening church bazaars and sales of work.

But I did accept another invitation.

The newly selected prospective Liberal candidate for Orkney and Shetland was a member of the fantastically rich Coats cotton family, Lady Glen-Coats. She invited the President of the Edinburgh University Liberal Club, whose name was Ivor Davies, and myself to come to Orkney and Shetland during the summer vacation of 1938 to accompany her on a tour of the constituency and to make speeches on her behalf. All our hotel expenses would be paid and, in addition, we were each given a cheque for £30 for any incidental expenses we might incur.

7

Thirty pounds! I had never seen such a large amount of money before. I don't imagine anyone else in my family had either.

And Orkney and Shetland was a wonderful experience. We lived in first-class hotels, ate almost unlimited local lobster and spoke every night to what I was then convinced, and indeed still am, must be the most intelligent electorate in the world. Even though no election was in prospect, all our meetings were packed out.

There was, of course, no counter-attraction from television in those days, but even so it must have taken quite a lot of determination to walk miles, as many people did, to a meeting in a village schoolhouse. The Orkney trip also gave me my first experience of flying. For we flew to many of the outlying islands when the distance was too far to make a boat trip convenient.

In the Shetlands, Lady Glen-Coats' Liberal agent was a local solicitor called Peter Goodlad. He was a delightful man and at that time, I suppose, would have been in his early forties.

One Sunday afternoon he took me to tea in his parents' home in Lerwick. In Scottish fashion the whole family always gathered there on a Sunday. I surveyed the gathering – the parents in their late seventies, the children all middle-aged. My eye was caught by a painting on the wall above the fireplace. It was a portrait of a young man in uniform. His face looked so full of life and vitality, in stark contrast to the dull people around me.

'Who is that?' I asked Peter Goodlad.

'That was my brother,' he replied. 'He was killed in the war.'

I reflected then and have often reflected since on the truth of Laurence Binyon's lines: 'They shall grow not old, as we that are left grow old.' The whole experience had opened my eyes to a new way of life.

They were opened wider when I was invited to spend week-ends at the Ayrshire home of Lady Glen-Coats and her husband. Hollybush House was some four or five miles from the town of Ayr and on the banks of the Doon. There was a butler, Davis, a chauffeur, a host of maids and a small army of gardeners. For me it was like being transported into fairyland. But I remember one thing with horror. When I went to my room on my first night I discovered that a valet had unpacked my battered cardboard suitcase. There on the dressing-table were laid out – one tatty toothbrush, one tube of toothpaste and a Woolworth's safety razor.

Although I regarded Lady Glen-Coats as being somewhat elderly, I now realise that she could only have been in her mid-forties. She was an attractive, vivacious woman, half French in origin, and when young had been beautiful enough to model for the society painter Sir John Lavery.

I would have been very surprised, again looking back, if she had ever had marital relations with her husband. The fabulously rich Sir Thomas Glen-Coats, who was much older than his wife, was a shy, diffident man with a pronounced stammer.

And extraordinarily naive.

One night in Orkney after our meetings were over, Ivor Davies and I were playing Monopoly with two other guests in the hotel in Stromness. Sir Thomas watched us for a while, saw us bid for properties like Park Lane and Mayfair, then said to his wife, 'Do you really think that John Junor and Ivor Davies can afford to play for such vast amounts of money?' Reality for me was still thirty miles away in a Glasgow tenement flat.

Soon afterwards, however, I was able to try my hand at politics again, for in March 1939 a crucial by-election took place in Kincardine and West Aberdeenshire.

The Liberal candidate was a London barrister, A. J. Irvine, a man whom Lord Chief Justice Hewart had tipped as a future prime minister and who, after he converted to socialism, did indeed become a Labour MP and a law officer in Harold Wilson's government. Irvine was an engaging character and enormously superstitious. So superstitious that on freezing March nights he used to drive round the constituency with his car windows open rather than run the risk of seeing the new moon through glass.

There was only one issue in the by-election, coming as it did only a few months after the Munich Agreement when Neville Chamberlain had returned to London triumphantly holding up a piece of paper and saying 'I have won peace in our time'. The issue was whether Chamberlain had secured a lasting peace by the Munich Agreement, as the Tory candidate, Colin

Thornton-Kemsley, argued or whether Hitler would tear up the scrap of paper whenever it suited him, as Irvine argued.

The by-election took place during the university Easter vacation and, as President of the Glasgow University Liberal Club, I was invited to help A. J. Irvine.

It was a most exciting experience. Since the candidate would address perhaps six different meetings in one night and might from time to time be delayed, other speakers had to go ahead and keep the audience entertained until the candidate arrived. I was one of those speakers. On one occasion I had to stay on the platform speaking for two hours until the arrival of the star speaker. On that particular occasion it was Dingle Foot, then a Liberal MP.

Right in the middle of our campaign, on 15 March 1939, Hitler invaded what remained of Czechoslovakia. Every point we had been making on our political platform had been proved.

It seemed inevitable to me that we would now win the election, but we didn't. The Tory candidate changed tack. Far from defending the Munich Agreement, he now insisted we must all unite in rallying behind the prime minister. My faith in the common sense of the British people came pretty close to being shattered when he emerged the victor from the count of votes.

When the next university long vacation arrived the following June, Lady Glen-Coats invited me to spend it as her private secretary. I was to be provided with a car and a salary of £4 a week until I returned to university in October to complete my Honours course in English. A brief time, perhaps, but it was a wonderful one. I met and became friendly with some leading Scottish journalists – Tom Chalmers of the Outram Group, Eric de Banzie of the Glasgow *Evening News*, Willie Hunt of the *Scotsman*. In my capacity as President of the University Liberal Club I even tried my hand at the occasional political article and, to my joy, had one accepted by the Glasgow *Evening Times*.

Then, in July, Lady Glen-Coats decided that she wanted to see what was going on in Berlin and to visit the contested Polish port of Gdynia, now Gdansk. She asked me to accompany her.

We travelled by a small German ship from Hull to Bremen. We arrived at the mouth of the River Weser on a brilliant sunny morning, travelling upriver to Bremen. All the way we passed pleasure yachts travelling in the opposite direction, with some of the most beautiful-looking blondes I have ever seen sunbathing on their decks. It was an enchanting sight. But on the banks of the river there was something that made me tingle with apprehension. There seemed to be field after field absolutely stacked with grey warplanes.

We travelled from Bremen to Berlin by train and stayed in the Bristol Hotel in the famous Unter den Linden. The atmosphere in Berlin that autumn was electric. We were taken to see the Olympic Stadium and our German guide proudly told us that it could seat 90,000 people.

'Really?' I replied. 'Back home in Glasgow we have Hampden Park, a stadium which holds 130,000 people. But we keep it only for football.'

At night we ate in the hotel's roof-garden surrounded by the richest Germans in the land. In the background we could hear the roar of the lions from the neighbouring Tiergarten zoo.

As we had a few days before continuing to Gdynia, I decided to visit the *Daily Telegraph*'s Berlin office. Their correspondent, Michael Nairn, ushered me in, offered me a drink and said that he would help us in any way he could.

The next morning I awoke to the sound of a military band parading down the Unter den Linden, led by an officer on a white horse. Just before leaving Glasgow, I had read an article in the *Evening Times* explaining that one could always tell when the Germans were on the point of war. Military bands started to parade through the streets led by officers on white chargers.

It was idiotic to take it seriously, but I did. I rushed to the *Daily Telegraph*'s office to consult with Michael Nairn and found him packing. He stopped his packing only long enough to say to me, 'If I were you I'd get the hell out of here. The balloon is about to go up.'

I dashed back to the Bristol Hotel and told Lady Glen-Coats. I must have sounded pretty convincing because two hours later we were in a train on our way to the Dutch border. Trains going the other way were packed with German soldiers, many of them leaning out of the window and singing happily.

Michael Nairn had been a little premature in his warning – but only a little. We arrived back in London on the first of September. Two days later I listened to Neville Chamberlain announcing in sombre tones that we were at war with Germany.

Within a week of the announcement I had discovered that liners on the Clyde were being converted into armed merchant-cruisers.

I learned of this from Ronnie Mackay. Ronnie lived in the next street to mine in Glasgow, but belonged to a different social class. His father, a widower, was a lawyer and unlike me Ronnie had been to Kelvinside Academy, a fee-paying and quite expensive day school, before going on to Glasgow University to read Law. We used to walk together to lectures every morning and became friends.

Ronnie had found out that most of the civilian crews were remaining on board the ships, but were changing into naval uniform and under an agreement known as T124 were being given naval ranks as wartime members of the Royal Naval Reserve. The Royal Navy supplied the Captain, gunnery officers and some other key posts.

Apparently there were a few vacancies for midshipmen and Ronnie had wangled himself a commission as a Midshipman RNR (T124) and had been assigned to HMS *Forfar*, an armed merchant-cruiser. He was thrilled. So was I. I immediately applied myself and, to my delight, was accepted. I became Midshipman RNR (T124) on board HMS *Canton*, a newly converted P&O liner soon to go on northern patrol in the Denmark Straits.

Ronnie's ship was torpedoed in that first winter of the war. Ronnie was among the dead. He was just nineteen and it must have broken his father's heart. Some years later, I visited a country cottage the family had owned and discovered hanging behind the door the Kelvinside Academy blazer which Ronnie had worn on his very first day at school. It was just about the only thing the father had left to remind him of his son.

My ship, HMS *Canton*, took over the northern patrol from HMS *Rawalpindi*, the armed merchant-cruiser commanded by Captain Edward Kennedy, Ludovic Kennedy's father, which had been blasted out of the sea by the German battle-cruisers *Scharnhorst* and *Gneisenau*. But on the only two northern patrols HMS *Canton* made we did not see any enemy action. On our second patrol we barely saw anything at all, the visibility was so poor.

And on our way home we ran into a reef off the west coast of Scotland and ripped a hole 125 feet long in our hull. The ship went down heavily by the bow, all the holds flooding with water. In the main hold it was two and a half feet deep. But the bulkhead was still holding. As long as it kept holding, we might stay afloat. If it gave, and there was more than a fifty-fifty chance that it would, we would sink like a stone.

The First Lieutenant asked for a volunteer to help him check the hold. I volunteered to accompany him. It was my first and only act of wartime bravery. The ship could not go forwards since the pressure of water would have burst the bulkhead. So we went astern at three knots until three days later we finally crawled into the Clyde and ran ourselves on to a sandbank in the Holy Loch. I celebrated my twenty-first birthday there, in the *Canton*'s gunroom.

With the *Canton* out of action, I transferred to another armed merchant-cruiser, HMS *Salopian*. Before the war she had been the Bibby Line ship *Shropshire* but had been unable to keep that name since there already was an HMS *Shropshire*. She was a very happy ship and I enjoyed my stay on board. France was on the verge of falling, though, and the phoney war had ended. I wanted something more active. After a couple of months I applied for a transfer to the Fleet Air Arm and was accepted for training as a pilot. But it meant that I had to give up my temporary RNR commission and start again as a naval airman in sailor's uniform. On the very next patrol, HMS *Salopian* was torpedoed.

Life in the Fleet Air Arm began with an eight-week preliminary training course at HMS *St Vincent* in Gosport, currently under heavy attack by the Luftwaffe. Many of our nights we spent underground in air raid shelters. During the day we were put through our paces by Chief Petty Officer Wilmot, a magnificent man who although a strong disciplinarian endeared himself to all of us and instilled in us a love of the Royal Navy which I have never lost.

My neighbour in the dormitory at *St Vincent* was Clare Murphy, the son of a Presbyterian Minister from Northern Ireland. Before turning in on our first night, he knelt beside his bed and prayed. This action caused a great deal of ribaldry, to which Murphy paid not the slightest bit of attention, so firm was his faith.

But his faith began to waver when night after night he stayed in while the rest of us went our wicked ways in Portsmouth in search of pleasure. One day, two or three weeks into the course, he came to me. The previous night he had been beset by lust and wanted desperately to find a woman. He had been walking in the black-out and had heard footsteps in front of him and realised they were those of a woman. Hurrying to catch up in order to proposition her, he realised just as he was about to open his mouth that she was a tottering old lady out exercising her dog. His remorse was pitiful.

After eight weeks at *St Vincent*, most of us were sent to RAF Elmdon, now Birmingham airport, for pilot training. I soon found that I was very far from being a world-beater as a pilot. At one stage during our advanced training, we were visited by a chief instructor from headquarters. In order to assess how good we were, he picked three trainees at random from the class and took them up into the air. I had the bad luck to be one of those he chose.

During our half-hour flight he made no comment at all on my handling of the aircraft. Back on the ground he asked me what my job had been in civilian life. I replied that I had been a university student.

'Oh,' he said, 'I thought you might have been a bus driver.'

His assessment was dead accurate. I was just good enough to earn my wings, but not good enough to be anything other than a mediocre pilot.

That Christmas at Elmdon we had a New Year's Eve party. One of our instructors, a Flight Lieutenant in the RAF, had brought his eighteen-year-old daughter, Pamela, along to join in the festivities, and I found myself standing next to this gorgeous blonde at the singing of 'Auld Lang Syne'. 'I am going to marry you,' I said to her.

I did, too. But not before I had criss-crossed the Atlantic and spent more than four months in Ontario completing my flying training. I was a member of number 19 Fleet Air Arm Pilots' Course and we travelled to Canada for our advanced training in a Polish ship called the SS *Batory*.

One of the passengers on board the *Batory*, although travelling in accommodation rather grander than the four-tier bunks which housed us, was an American called Penny Rogers. We were given to understand that he was a relative of the famous film actor Will Rogers. He was civilian and his job was to deliver aeroplanes across the Atlantic to Britain from the United States which was then still neutral. It was a hazardous operation. After each delivery he would then travel back to the US by ship.

He was a source of great hero-worship for us. I remember a group of us clustering around him one day and asking him what it was like to fly the Atlantic single-handed. I still remember his hands shaking as he broke a Hershey chocolate bar and told us, 'It's like this boys. I take off, climb to ten thousand feet and hand over to Jesus Christ.'

When we arrived in Halifax, Nova Scotia we had to stay on board the ship for one more night before taking our train to Kingston, Ontario. Only one of us had any Canadian money. A New Zealand member of our course, Des Bourke, had one single Canadian dollar.

With this one single dollar four of us left the ship in search of something to eat. We found a restaurant not far from the docks, went in and sat down. To our delight every main course was just 25 cents and with the main course a starter and dessert were included as well as coffee. The four of us ate like we had not eaten for years in England. It was a wonderful welcome to Canada.

The food was equally abundant when we arrived at RAF Kingston. On every table in our mess there was a huge mound of butter and a seven-pound jar of honey – and the RAF cooks served up unlimited amounts of bacon and eggs. The only snag was they ruined it all with their cooking.

And if I had come in close to death in the air over Kingston in 1941, I came almost as close in December later that year. I was in Trinidad, where I had been flying with an observer training squadron. With two other Fleet Air Arm officers and a Dutch naval officer, I was to take passage from Port of Spain via New York to Liverpool in a Norwegian freighter, the SS *Thalassa*. She was right down to the Plimsoll line, laden with six thousand tons of sugar for a wartime Britain never very far from hunger.

For the hazardous trip from Trinidad to New York we were on our own. From New York our convoy was the slowest possible, a four-knot convoy. In the warm Caribbean waters, if we had been torpedoed, the fear of having to abandon ship would have been of sharks. In the North Atlantic beyond New York the fear was of the intense cold. That December it was reckoned that not even the fittest of men could survive for more than five minutes in the freezing water.

Five days out of New York our convoy was attacked by a U-boat pack. It was around 11 p.m. When action stations sounded the four of us who were passengers put on our great-coats and strapped our flimsy Mae West life-jackets on top before going out on deck. There we found the Norwegian crew, all of them completely encased in heavy one-piece rubber suits with a whistle, torch and knife all attached to the belt. They at least had a chance of survival in the water. We had none.

The *Thalassa* was not a big ship. The deck on which we were standing was only a few feet above the icy water.

All around us ships were exploding into flames.

The next torpedo could be for us.

I prayed. And quite extraordinarily I suddenly knew that everything was going to be all right. If before that night I had had any doubts about the existence of God, I never had thereafter.

There is one other thing about that night which I will never forget. Before the U-boat action started, the ship's cook had prepared a huge plate of ham sandwiches and placed them in the saloon for the late-night comfort of the passengers.

The moment the U-boat attack ended and we were able to go below into the warmth and comfort of the saloon, the most senior of us, a Lieutenant Commander RN called Harrison, hungrily grabbed one of the sandwiches. As he did so, a huge cockroach jumped out of the middle of it.

'Sod off you little bugger,' said Harrison, waving an angry fist at it. And then he began to devour the sandwich without a second's hesitation and without even taking a look to see if the cockroach's mate might still be inside.

We arrived in Liverpool on a bitter January morning. The whole country was rationed, battered, seemingly surrounded. And yet no one I met ever contemplated the possibility of defeat. The tide was already turning – a couple of months before, General Montgomery had smashed the German army at Alamein. But my arrival home coincided with the loss of all my close personal friends in quick succession. Terry Cooper, a New Zealander who flew into a 'stuffed' cloud near Oban. Charlie Don, aged just nineteen, who was killed in a Seafire, the Fleet Air Arm version of the Spitfire. Graham 'Paddy' Irvine, killed by the French in a raid on Madagascar. I had with them a comradeship which perhaps because of the dangers we all knew we faced I have never since had with anyone else.

And then something happened which changed my life.

It was at the beginning of 1944. I was stationed at HMS *Ringtail*, a Naval Air Station in Burscough, Lancashire, and was at a mess party in which the drink was flowing freely. I found myself in the company of the Station Commander, a four-ringed Captain RN, and I suddenly found myself saying: 'Don't you think it would be a good idea, Sir, if we had a Station magazine?'

The next morning I had forgotten all about my idea. He hadn't. I was summoned to his presence and given the job of producing the magazine.

When it eventually appeared a copy of it was sent to the Admiralty in London. By an extraordinary coincidence, Admiral Sir Denis Boyd, the Fifth Sea Lord and commander of the Fleet Air Arm, was at that very moment planning a Fleet Air Arm magazine which he hoped would rival the RAF magazine *T.M.* He had invited the famous writer, independent MP and wartime Naval Petty Officer, Alan Herbert, to edit it. They were looking for a young pilot who actually knew something about the Fleet Air Arm, which Herbert didn't, to be Assistant Editor. I was summoned to London to be interviewed by the Fifth Sea Lord himself.

A few days later, I presented myself on the fifth floor of Rex House in Lower Regent Street in the office of the Admiral's secretary, a Paymaster-Commander. He questioned me for a few minutes, said he would tell the Admiral I was there and disappeared through a connecting door into the Admiral's office.

Just then an air raid warning went. It was at a time when London was being attacked by doodle-bugs. I sat there alone in that fifth-floor office, marvelling at the courage of the Fifth Sea Lord who was next door to me carrying on quietly with his work, despite the dangers of being on a top floor during an air raid.

I sat there for perhaps half-an-hour before the door opened and in came the Paymaster-Commander. 'Good God!' he said, 'Are you still here? I had forgotten about you. We've been in the air raid shelter for the last half-hour.'

I not only got the job as Assistant Editor. I got the job as Editor. For Alan Herbert had turned down the editorship and Sir Denis Boyd, who I suspect was losing a little of his earlier enthusiasm for the project, handed over the task of producing the magazine to me. It turned out to be a quite sparkling success. I named it *Flight Deck* and it ran until the end of the war.

From then on, during the last critical year of hostilities, I was in London. In the evening after my day's work was finished, I would repair to Fleet Street where I made many good friends in the Press Club. I also secured, quite illegally, a job moonlighting as a sub-editor for an Australian news agency, Australia Associated Press. My task was to condense stories from the British press and send them over the wire to Sydney. That was why, when the war finished, I had a job to go to.

But the war was not yet finished, even though like so many thousands of others I was soon to exchange my service uniform for civvy street. And it was as the Editor of *Flight Deck* and still a Lieutenant in the Fleet Air Arm that I fought the July 1945 general election.

I must have made a reasonably good impression as a speaker in the Kincardine and West Aberdeenshire by-election of 1939. For the Liberal Association, whose Chairman was one of the most splendid men I have ever met, a village blacksmith, Mr James C. Forbes of Glassel, Aberdeenshire, invited me to be their new parliamentary candidate in place of A. J. Irvine who had moved on elsewhere.

It was the most exhilarating three weeks of my life. My wife Pam and our baby son Roderick accompanied me. Kincardine and West Aberdeenshire was a far-flung constituency and there were only two candidates – myself and the sitting Tory member, Colin Thornton-Kemsley, whose last-minute change of tack had defeated A. J. Irvine six years previously.

Before the war, Thornton-Kemsley had been violently anti-Churchill. He had been the Chairman of the Epping Conservative Association, Churchill's constituency, and had led a campaign to have Churchill ousted from the seat because of Churchill's opposition to Chamberlain. Now he was campaigning as a Churchill supporter.

In meeting after meeting I pointed this out. All to rousing cheers. But Churchill sent him a message of support and I failed to win the seat by just 642 votes. Had the result gone the other way, my whole life would have been changed and I would have been perhaps the youngest MP in the House of Commons. Now that dream for the time being was finished. All I wanted in July 1945 was to make enough money to support my wife and child while waiting for another chance to get into Parliament.

In the Fleet Air Arm I had lived on my pay. I never got into debt and at the end of the month usually had a few shillings left in my pocket. But as far as money was concerned, I was in a different social class from most of my fellow officers.

One of them, Stephen Vercoe, himself the product of a good public school and upper middle-class family, once asked me: 'If you were put to it, how much money could you raise?' Not wishing to appear poverty-stricken I exaggerated wildly. 'About a hundred, I guess.' He looked at me with interest. 'A hundred thousand pounds?' he asked. His face registered incredulity when I explained I had meant just one hundred pounds.

In fact in April 1942, when I married Pam, at the end of our first month we had had just one pound, a brand new one pound note, left in the whole wide world. I made my wife smear it with her lipstick and we placed it in a tiny tapestry purse. 'We must never, never spend this pound,' I said. 'We must keep it forever.'

It was never spent by me. Nor I am sure by Pam either. For she has never been interested in money. Unhappily, and it is all my fault, for some years she has not been much interested in me either.

But on my first day as a civilian in the summer of 1945, I felt quite well off. In the Bank of Scotland safely rested my gratuity for six years of war service – ninety-nine pounds and fifteen shillings, by far the largest capital sum I had ever raised. I walked out of the demob centre at Olympia wearing a sports jacket and a pair of grey flannel slacks and I hopped on to a Number 11 bus.

As I jumped off the bus half an hour later, outside the *Daily Telegraph* and Hancock's the Chemists, I thought that in the sunshine Fleet Street was the most wonderful place I had ever seen.

II

I WAS SACKED two weeks before Christmas 1947.

In retrospect it turned out to be the luckiest thing that ever happened to me. At the time it seemed a major disaster.

I was married with a four-year-old son. We had no place of our own and lived in a furnished house. My total capital, give or take a few shillings, amounted to the £99 I had received as a wartime gratuity. And at the time in Fleet Street, because of paper rationing, papers were only four pages in size and the chances of getting a job as a reporter or as a sub-editor in any of the dailies was generally regarded as mighty slim.

The job from which I was sacked was with the London office of the *Sydney Sun*, where I had been taken on full-time after freelancing for them while still in the Fleet Air Arm. The paper's London Editor was an agreeable drunk called Gordon Gilmour, and as part of his duties he had to write a London diary for the *Sydney Sun* called 'Gordon Gilmour's London Diary'.

In fact, the diary was written by me. It wasn't a specially good one. When the people in Sydney woke up to the fact that Gilmour was not writing his own copy and spent all his time drinking, they sent one of their bosses to London who sacked both Gilmour and me. Otherwise, no doubt, I would still be writing 'Gordon Gilmour's London Diary'. For I am a conservative chap and always very unwilling to change. As dismissal money I collected three months' pay in lieu of notice which meant that my total capital came to somewhere near £400.

Nor was that all my misfortune. The lease on our furnished house was ending. As an unemployed man I was unable to supply sufficiently satisfactory references to secure the lease on another for which we had been negotiating. So my wife, small son and I moved into a modest hotel which charged £4.50 a week including board for adults and just half that for Roderick.

My only hope lay in a letter I had written to Christiansen, the Editor of the *Daily Express*.

I had couched my letter in the most flattering terms and to my intense pleasure 'Chris' agreed to see me. He was a tubby little man with bright twinkling eyes, gold-rimmed spectacles and rosy-pink cheeks. He was widely regarded as the greatest editor of his time and it was the ambition of every young newspaperman to work for him. There was a glamour about the *Daily Express*, in itself by far the greatest newspaper of the time, with which no other paper could begin to compete.

Chris seemed to like me and to my delight offered me a job as a reporter at eighteen guineas a week. It was less than I had been getting on the *Sydney Sun* but to me it was as if I had suddenly been plucked from the middle of an Atlantic storm.

Everyone I knew in Fleet Street warned me that it was difficult to survive on this volatile and exciting paper, that the rate of hire and fire was fast and that I would be lucky if I lasted three months. The reality was different. On my first day on the paper some of my new colleagues in the newsroom came and introduced themselves to me. I found them a friendly, helpful bunch. When I asked one of them how long he had been with the *Daily Express*, he replied 'Twenty years'. I was soon to discover that the hire-and-fire stories were very much a myth.

Fleet Street itself was a place of bustling magic. The saloon bars of the pubs were full of journalists and the public bars full of print workers.

Christiansen held court in a pub called Poppins in a lane which ran from Fleet Street adjacent to the *Express* building. Every evening after the daily conference would find him at the bar surrounded by his acolytes. Further up Fleet Street, in El

Vino, the leader writers and feature writers mingled with barristers from the Courts of Justice. It was an entire community dedicated to journalism; the vicar of St Bride's was the rector of what was our parish church. There was an immense sense of belonging to a very special world – a world which alas has now disintegrated.

I soon discovered that if Christiansen had not been a great editor he would have been a great figure in show business. He conducted editorial conferences as if he were a master of ceremonies on a glittering Palladium stage. He had an enormous capacity to enthuse and inspire his editorial staff.

Every day his secretary would put up on the notice-board a bulletin containing the editor's views on the previous day's paper. It was a wonderful system. Chris administered praise and criticism in equal measure, and everyone read and absorbed. If a reporter got a favourable mention in the bulletin, he was so pleased that he put off asking for the rise he had been intending to seek. When he got a bad mention, he was then too scared to ask for the same rise.

One day in his bulletin, Christiansen announced that he wanted to start a new column on current affairs and called for volunteers and for suggestions as to what the column should contain. I immediately volunteered and wrote a long memorandum describing what I would put in my column if I were given the job.

But I wasn't. Instead, the great reporter James Cameron was appointed to a tremendous fanfare of trumpets. The column survived only a very few weeks. I have often wondered what would have happened to me if I had been given the job then of writing the same sort of column which I was to take up so many years later.

Another reporter and a splendid writer on the paper was James Leasor. He was just four years younger than me and had already published his first novel. Leasor remained with the *Daily Express* until 1955. He travelled with Beaverbrook and worked quite closely with him. But he never got any promotion. Then in 1956 he wrote a book, *The One That Got Away* – the story of the one German prisoner of war who escaped from Britain.

It was a brilliant success. A film was made of it. Leasor made a pot of money and went on to write innumerable other books. Today I would guess him a millionaire two or three times over. And yet when I last met him, I had the extraordinary feeling that the only career James Leasor had desperately wanted to succeed in was as a journalist.

I discovered early on that I would not have made a very good hard news reporter. In my very early days as a general run-of-the-mill reporter on the *Daily Express*, I was sent out to cover a story in South London. I have forgotten what the story was about, but on the way I saw a crowd gathered round a red double-decker bus. A fire engine was there too. I pushed to the front of the crowd, eager to see whether there was a story for the *Express*.

What I saw made me almost sick. Under the rear nearside wheel of the bus was the body of a little boy about the same age as my own son. I walked away. There was no way in which I could have asked any questions. Afterwards I felt guilty about having let down the paper, but I need not have worried. For I was to find out that the death of a child in a routine accident was not national news anyway.

Some years later, when I was on the *Evening Standard*, a horse-box carrying a Derby winner called Dante knocked down and killed a child. The *Standard* ran the story under the headline DANTE IN ROAD ACCIDENT. The little boy's name was not even mentioned. His grief-stricken mother wrote to the editor, protesting that it would seem a horse was more important than her child. And the terrible thing is that in terms of news it was.

Chris had other ideas for me, however. Hearing that I had been a Liberal parliamentary candidate, he very adroitly decided to try me out on by-election reports.

My first by-election was at Camlachie in Glasgow where I met Charles Wintour for the first time. He was reporting the by-election for the *Evening Standard*. We both sent out reports on the same day from the Glasgow office of the *Daily Express*, but mine had the good luck to be subbed by a brilliant sub-editor called Mather. It created a bit of a stir and from that time onwards I was the by-election reporter of the *Daily Express*.

One day, some three months later, I picked up my phone and there was the voice of Max Aitken, Lord Beaverbrook's son, at the other end. The *Sunday Express*'s Cross-Bencher parliamentary column, he explained, wanted to include a piece about Philip Fothergill, then President of the Liberal Party. Would I like to send over a piece describing Fothergill? I did so and it appeared duly the next week in Cross-Bencher. I also received a call of thanks and praise from Max.

Another month or two passed. Summer was with us and the Olympic Torch was due to land at Dover en route for the Olympic Games at Wembley Stadium. Christiansen sent me down to cover the Torch's arrival. On the same day, an Italian had arrived in Dover claiming to have swum the Channel. He asked me to report that story too.

Since swimming the Channel seemed an event of entire non-consequence to me and since it never occurred to me that anyone would fraudulently claim such a feat, I reported the story straight. I also reported, with what I thought was a bit of panache, the arrival of the Olympic Torch with its perpetual flame. For, as it happened, when the runner with the Torch arrived in Dover, the Torch went out. I stepped forward and relit it with my cigarette lighter.

Unhappily, relighting the Olympic Torch failed to make up for the other sin I committed. The next day the *Daily Mail*, in a report by Laurence Wilkinson, ran a magnificent exposé of the fraudulent Italian. Chris devoted an entire bulletin to telling the rest of the office what an absolute mess I had made of this vital story.

I was despondent. But not for long.

Shortly after this I received a telephone call from E. J. Robertson, the Canadian who was then Chairman of the Beaverbrook Newspapers. It was a telephone call which excited me enormously. Lord Beaverbrook, he told me, was planning to leave for Canada in a week's time. It was his custom to take a young journalist with him as companion. I was one of the young journalists whose name had been put forward by Mr Christiansen. Would I be prepared to go? I said that of course

I would. I was then told to present myself the following afternoon at 3.30 p.m. at Lord Beaverbrook's London home, Arlington House in Piccadilly, to be interviewed by the great man himself.

I arrived at Arlington House in a state of pent-up excitement. After a ten-minute wait I was taken up to the roof-garden where Lord Beaverbrook was sitting in the sun. I already knew, of course, what Beaverbrook looked like. His photograph was constantly in the newspapers and he was frequently caricatured by cartoonists. To me, he seemed exactly as I had imagined him to be. He was then seventy years old but vigorous and active and bubbling with energy. On my way in I tripped over a telephone cord. Beaverbrook rose anxiously. Anxious not about my welfare, but whether I had disturbed the telephone. Despite this initial mishap, it seemed to me that the interview went very well indeed. He laughed a lot and we had a vigorous and amiable discussion. Afterwards I walked along Piccadilly in the afternoon sunshine, absolutely certain that the following week I would be on my way to the United States and Canada.

The next day E. J. Robertson brought me back down to earth. 'I'm terribly sorry, Junor,' he said to me on the telephone. 'Do not take this as any reflection on yourself, but Lord Beaverbrook has decided that he will take an older man on this trip.' I took out my diary and made just about the only entry I have ever made in a diary. I wrote, 'Some day I am going to prove him wrong.'

To this day it is a mystery to me as to whether, in fact, there was any proving which needed to be done. For within three weeks of my failure to land the American trip I was called into Christiansen's office where he told me that Cross-Bencher of the *Sunday Express* was going on holiday. He suggested that I stand in for him during the three weeks Cross-Bencher would be away.

Was this indeed Chris's idea? He always afterwards claimed that it was. Or was it Lord Beaverbrook who, on the basis of my interview with him and on my by-election reports, had decided that I should be Cross-Bencher? I shall never know.

I reported for duty on the *Sunday Express* on the following Tuesday morning. I had never been in the Lobby of the House of Commons. I had no political contacts apart from the people

I had personally fought against in elections and I hadn't the slightest conception of what to write in the Cross-Bencher column.

But that first morning in the *Sunday Express* I received quick reassurance. A man called Garbett who occupied the same largish room as me came to my desk and whispered conspiratorially, 'You'll be all right. I handle Cross-Bencher.' I deduced from this that perhaps he took my material and rewrote the whole column in the polished *Sunday Express* style. How wrong I was. I discovered afterwards that all he did was put the typesetting instructions on the copy.

In my first week of Cross-Bencher luck came my way via my old rival in Camlachie, Charles Wintour. He had stumbled across a booklet issued by the Transport and General Workers' Union which listed the amount of money it paid in grants to Members of Parliament. I seized on this and my first Cross-Bencher column headed 'Pennies from Heaven' duly appeared and was warmly received. It seemed that I had made the grade.

It then transpired that not one but two Cross-Benchers were due to return from holiday. Beverley Baxter and Anthony Marlow, the Conservative MP for Brighton, wrote the column together and had been packed off on holiday at exactly the same time. Marlow never returned. Once again I was called in by Christiansen who suggested that I take his place.

Baxter's return turned out to be confined to Friday afternoons in a supervisory role. At this stage in my career he could have done me enormous harm. As it was, Beverley Baxter showed me the greatest goodwill and limited himself to beaming benevolently around the office. One day he put his head round the door and said to me, 'Laddie, I can't help you. You are doing me out of a job.' He turned out to be right.

I then had another stroke of luck. Now I was established as Cross-Bencher I was entitled to a secretary, and so it was that Miss Henrietta Mackay, a Scots girl whose parents had moved south, came to join the *Sunday Express*.

She was small and did not look particularly robust. Indeed, when in only her second week in the job her mother phoned one morning to say that Henrietta had a cold and would not be in that day, I feared the worst. I need not have worried. It was just about the last day off for sickness that Mac, as she came to be known on the *Sunday Express*, ever had. Long after I had moved on to other things she remained the sheet-anchor of the Cross-Bencher column and the right-hand, protector, nanny and friend of successive Cross-Benchers for the next thirty-seven years. Her job was to check and cross-check the accuracy of every item, every quote, even every line of poetry that appeared. And she was never once in error.

I had been writing the Cross-Bencher column for perhaps four weeks when Max Aitken rang me again. His father was back in England and wanted to see me at Cherkley Court, his home near Leatherhead, on the next Sunday morning. Max assured me that he, too, would be present.

The meeting took place in the library at Cherkley. Beaverbrook had there, as he had in all his homes, a podium or desk at which he could stand and read his newspapers.

He began by making some friendly comments about my column. From there he went on to a discussion of the political scene and moved over to his desk looking for a newspaper which had published an item he wanted to discuss. Apparently it was not there. Suddenly he barked, 'Get me Wednesday's *News Chronicle*.' I immediately jumped to my feet, assuming that he was speaking to me. But someone else was even quicker off the mark. Max was already trotting along the corridor in search of that newspaper.

It was a revelation to me.

Here was Max Aitken, DSO, DFC, one of the great war heroes, handsome beyond measure, chased by every gorgeous-looking girl in London, acting like a frightened little boy in front of his father. Yet that is precisely what he was. He so adored that father and Beaverbrook adored him, although he would speak about him disparagingly and often treat him with contempt. Deep down there was deep love, and Max tried so desperately and, so often, unsuccessfully to imitate his father.

Christmas Day of 1948 fell on a Sunday and there was to be no newspaper in London. There was, however, to be a newspaper

28

in Scotland and I therefore had to write a Cross-Bencher for use by the Glasgow office alone. I spent all week on this task, completed it on the Friday morning and then rushed out to do Christmas shopping for my wife and son. I went to Hamleys and bought a fairy-cycle for Roderick.

When I returned to the office all hell was let loose. Max Aitken had been calling for me. Would I get in touch with him the moment I returned?

I went down to see Max who looked at me in relief.

'Thank God you are not tight,' he said. 'I thought you had been out drinking.'

'No,' I replied with a touch of acid in my voice. 'I have been out taking one hour to do my Christmas shopping.'

Max was not listening. 'Lord Beaverbrook wants to see you at Cherkley right away. Take a train down there and a car will meet you at the station.'

I groaned. This meant only one thing. Beaverbrook had not liked my column for Scotland and wanted me to rewrite it. I was furious beyond measure.

When I arrived at Cherkley, Beaverbrook straight away invited me to join him in a small open Hillman Minx in which he was about to make a tour of his estate, with himself at the wheel. I sat beside him, impatiently waiting to be told where my column had gone wrong and how it should be rewritten.

Beaverbrook said nothing. He stopped the car and we got out and looked round an uninhabited house on the estate – a gardener's cottage. He made no comment of any kind. We got into the car again and drove off to another part of the estate. Once again the same procedure – only this time there was an old lady in bed in the cottage who looked visibly alarmed as we walked round.

Still no comment on the column. Then a visit to a third house at the end of a walled garden at Mickleham. A semi-detached house and empty.

We went back into the car and returned to Cherkley. By now I was almost in despair at the length of time I had been kept waiting for the bad news about my column. Instead Beaverbrook beamed at me and said, 'Would you like one of these houses?

Which one would you like? You can have it rent free and you can have it whenever you like.'

I almost collapsed. I had not even looked at the houses on the way round. I stammered I would accept the first house. 'Good,' said Beaverbrook. 'Bring your wife over on Sunday so that she can see it.' But it was clear that he would have been quite happy for me to have had the second house even if it meant turfing out a sick old lady.

I took Pam over on the Sunday and, in fact, she chose the third house – a house in which we spent ten very happy years, even though for the first few years we did not have electricity.

For a Sunday columnist, Friday is the moment of truth. There were many times during my early months on Cross-Bencher when Friday ideas for the column were difficult. I used to have nightmares about waking up on Friday morning with nothing to write about. One Friday the nightmare came true. I went to Max and told him that I had no ideas for the column.

I will never forget his kindness.

'Don't worry,' he said. 'There's plenty of time. Why don't you go home and write it there? And I will look in tonight to see how it is going.'

I went home but no ideas came. At nine o'clock, when Max arrived in a large black Bentley convertible, I had still not written a word. Max poured some black coffee while I stared gloomily out of the window. Max had once given me a lift into town in that black Bentley with his quite breathtakingly beautiful wife Jane. As we crossed Waterloo Bridge, the conductor of a red double-decker bus, leaning against the pole at the rear, surveyed the Bentley with enormous interest.

'Do you see that conductor looking at us?' said Max. 'Do you know what he's thinking? Sod that rich chap in his Bentley!'

'I don't think he is,' I said from the back seat. 'I think he's just wishing that he could win the pools and buy one like it.'

Max would have none of it. But I know that I was right.

By half-past ten and several cups of black coffee later, Cross-Bencher still remained unwritten. 'Don't worry,' said Max standing up to go, 'you'll be all right in the morning.'

After Max left I went to the typewriter and then like magic

the words came. By one o'clock in the morning I had a good presentable Cross-Bencher. Satisfied, I went to bed and tried unsuccessfully to sleep. Thanks to having drunk so much coffee, I tossed and turned all night. The next morning I found that Max had not slept a wink either.

Although his official job at that time was managing the *Sunday Express*, it was Max who had control of the Cross-Bencher column. It was to him that I reported and delivered my column each week and not to the newspaper's Editor, John Gordon. For Gordon, it must have been humiliating not to have been in control of a vital part of the paper's content. But the fact was that Beaverbrook did not trust Gordon's political judgement and he regarded the Cross-Bencher column as being his own personal voice. Besides, he had no compunction about humiliating him or any other editor.

It was therefore Max whom I approached in May of the following year concerning my holiday entitlement. Pam was pregnant, the baby was due in October and Max was completely agreeable to our taking a two-week break. But he was also solicitous on my behalf about what might happen in my absence.

'You must be aware,' he pointed out, 'that you now have one of the most sought-after jobs in Fleet Street. It would be terrible if, while you were away, your stand-in made such a good impression that he was given the job on a permanent basis. After all, the only reason you were given Cross-Bencher was that you stood in for Beverley Baxter and Anthony Marlow when they were on holiday. And I would hate to see that. So why bother with a stand-in? Why not just write two columns in advance?'

I looked at him in genuine astonishment.

'There is just no way I could write two topical political columns in advance. And besides, if you find a stand-in who is better than me, shouldn't he be doing the job anyway?'

As it turned out John Prebble, then a *Sunday Express* features writer and later a distinguished author, stood in for me. And my job was still waiting for me when we returned from our two weeks in Villerville.

Just over two months later, on the first Sunday in August, the telephone rang in our cottage at Mickleham. Lord Beaverbrook was at the other end speaking from Cap d'Ail in the South of France where he had a marvellous villa, La Capponcina.

'Would you like to come and spend the Bank Holiday weekend with me in the South of France?' he asked. 'And bring your wife with you?'

I explained that Pam was pregnant and would not be able to travel, but I would be delighted to come on my own.

'Good,' he said. 'I will expect you to travel on Friday morning and I will arrange to have you met in Nice.'

'What shall I bring to wear?' I asked. 'Do you want me to bring a dinner jacket?'

'Not at all,' he said. 'Just bring a sports jacket and a pair of trousers.'

No doubt he suspected – with good reason – that on the money he was paying me I didn't have a dinner jacket. I was earning no more than £25 a week. As E. J. Robertson, the company Chairman, explained to me before I left, it was illegal at that time to take more than £50 out of the country unless one was on a business trip, which I was. Beaverbrook required money to run his villa, and since he would be providing me with bed and board I should not be surprised, said Robertson, if he asked me for my business allowance. He had, it appeared, done just that to Robertson himself and to such an extent that Robertson had not enough left over even to buy himself a drink.

But in the event it did not happen to me. I set off at the end of August for the South of France with a tiny suitcase and wearing a pair of grey flannel trousers and a utility sports jacket.

Lord Beaverbrook's villa commanded the cliff at Cap d'Ail. Behind it, on the landward side, the Alpes-Maritimes formed a magnificent backdrop. I had never been anywhere like it and was immediately captivated by the splendour and the beauty of the place.

The rooms were large and airy and elegantly furnished and the gardens leading down to the sea were fragrant with the scent of orange and lemon blossom. Beaverbrook had a magnificent library in which, he explained, the books had been chosen not for their contents but for the colour of their bindings. The previous owner of the villa had been Edward Molyneux, the great dress designer, and while he never read anything he had a keen eye for the beauty of coloured bindings.

I had no idea, when I arrived on Friday evening, why I had been invited or whom I was expected to meet. But on Saturday in the afternoon I met someone whom Lord Beaverbrook had not intended me to meet, nor indeed had expected to see again himself.

The Aga Khan, who must then have been in his middle seventies and who seemed a very old man to me, arrived unexpectedly. It was the first he had seen of Beaverbrook since before the war, and, as I afterwards learned, he had come to make his peace. Beaverbrook did not approve of the way in which, during the war, the Aga Khan had tended to be neutral and had failed to support Britain.

The Aga, gross, fat and aged, sat on the veranda, but when he began to speak I realised that he was clearly a very wise old man. He said, for instance, that in the East communism was the same word in most dialects as the word for hunger. So communism was clearly the politics of the hungry.

He also spoke about his son, Ali, and his son's marriage to Rita Hayworth.

'I don't like her,' he said. 'She is a dirty girl.' And quite clearly when he used the word 'dirty' he was not speaking about her morals, but about her lack of personal hygiene.

On the Saturday night the reason for my invitation to the South of France became apparent. Again absolutely without warning to me, the Duke and Duchess of Windsor arrived for dinner accompanied by the Duchess's Aunt Bessie, an old lady from Baltimore. The Duke was wearing what looked like an American engine-driver's boiler suit, striped blue and white. The Duchess looked as if she had stepped out of a Dior salon.

I can report with absolute accuracy the first words the former King of England spoke to me. He crooked his finger, beckoned me towards him and whispered, 'Tell me, where's the boys' room?'

The other guests included Daisy Fellowes, the Singer sewing-machine heiress, her husband Reggie and Beaverbrook's nurse whose name was Christine, who was about twenty-five and very beautiful, and not I guessed entirely employed in the capacity of nurse.

Beaverbrook had arranged a table, a refectory table, outdoors in the hot, black, warm evening, the stars shining in the South of France sky. He had so arranged the table that I was at one end of it with the Duchess of Windsor on my right and a blank space on my left. Beaverbrook explained that someone he had invited had failed to arrive. The result was that all evening the only person the Duchess of Windsor could speak to – since Beaverbrook on her right largely ignored her – was me, and in turn the only person I could speak to was the Duchess.

I found her absolutely fascinating and enchanting. She made a man feel as if he, at that moment, were the only man in her life. She allowed me to do the talking, even prompted me to, and she seemed fascinated by whatever I had to say. I found myself thinking, as the evening drew on, that she was a beautiful woman and enormously sensible – no doubt because of the flattery of her listening to me.

At one stage in the evening, the Duke wanted some bread or biscuits to eat with his cheese. In the Beaverbrook household no such thing as bread was ever supplied at the dinner table. The Duchess had clearly anticipated this. Fetching a tin from under her chair, she dashed up to the other end of the table to provide the Duke with his necessary sustenance.

I discovered long afterwards the reason for the whole performance. Beaverbrook, in conjunction with Time-Life of New York, had bought the Duchess of Windsor's memoirs. It had been arranged that an American writer, an employee of Time-Life called Charles Murphy, would ghost the writing. Murphy and the Duchess did not get on, however, mainly because he persisted in treating her as a fellow and ordinary American, whereas she wanted to be treated as a Royal Highness.

Beaverbrook was fearful that there would be such a row between them that the memoirs, in which he had invested a great deal of money, would never be completed. He had invited me to the South of France for only one purpose – to see whether the Duchess and I got along well together. In the event of Murphy failing to produce the memoirs, he could use me instead to ghost them for the Duchess. Luckily, Murphy and the Duchess came on to good terms and my services were never required.

There is one sequel to this weekend. At that time, in 1949, food was scarce in England and most products were rationed. I determined that I must bring back some French ham for my own family. This I bought in Monte Carlo – a piece of ham of perhaps two or two-and-half pounds in weight – and I put it on top of my pitiful belongings in my pitiful little suitcase.

We travelled back to London in a specially chartered aircraft. As the plane came in to land, Lord Beaverbrook began lustily to sing 'The Lord's My Shepherd'. Being a devout coward myself, I joined him in doing so.

When we arrived at London airport, we proceeded into an empty Customs hall. All our luggage – that is the luggage of Beaverbrook, his valet, his secretary and myself – was lined up for Customs inspection. There must have been perhaps thirty suitcases, of which perhaps twenty-six belonged to Beaverbrook and all or most of which contained books, papers and manuscripts.

The Customs officer was a young man and quite clearly did not recognise Beaverbrook, then at the very height of his power and influence in England. To my consternation, he held up that idiotic piece of cardboard which described the regulations appertaining to goods being brought into the country and asked Beaverbrook whether he had read it. 'Have you anything to declare, Sir?' he then said.

Beaverbrook's hair stood on end with anger. 'These are my cases and there's nothing in them but papers,' he barked. 'There is nothing to declare in that lot.'

I looked askance at my own little suitcase with its two-and-a-half pounds of uncooked ham – it was illegal to bring uncooked food into England – and trembled. If the Customs officer demanded that every case be opened, it would be the end of my career.

I was saved by the arrival of a senior officer who took the whole prospect in at a glance and whispered suddenly and urgently in the young officer's ear. The young man blushed, stammered 'All right, Sir', genuflected and we all went through – with my precious uncooked ham.

I was to meet the Duke of Windsor on one further occasion.

Beaverbrook's doctor was Sir Daniel Davies, perhaps the most distinguished physician of the time. He had been Lloyd George's doctor, Beaverbrook's, King George VI's and was also the Duke of Windsor's. When I collapsed from a duodenal ulcer a few years later, he became mine too at Beaverbrook's behest. He also became a friend. Sir Daniel was the last of the really grand doctors and he and his wife Vera lived in Wimpole Street. I spent many a happy hour there with them.

Although the Duke of Windsor lived in Paris he came to London occasionally without the Duchess on fleeting, unrecorded, unofficial visits. On this occasion he had come for a medical check-up and Dan had suggested that afterwards he stay for lunch. Dan then telephoned me and asked me to join them – a fact which I guessed he had cleared in advance with the Duke.

There were only four of us at the lunch table – the Duke, Dan, Vera and myself – and the conversation was low-key but agreeable. The Duke spoke more about golf than any other single subject. I was confirmed in my view that he was a pleasant if rather a shallow man and certainly very far from being an intellectual.

Dan, who was always discreet, was a rich source of information about the aristocratic and the famous. He told me of one patient, a Duke who I suspect was the then Duke of Westminster, now long dead, who had a drink problem. Dan was trying to ascertain how much alcohol he consumed a day.

'Would you say that perhaps you drank as much as a bottle a day, Your Grace?' he enquired.

The Duke looked at him indignantly and held out a shaking hand. 'Bottle a day? I spill that much.'

And when Dan suggested that he might at least cut out his pre-breakfast snifter the Duke's reply was brusque. 'How the hell do you think I could shave?'

Dan was also fascinating about Jack Kennedy, then emerging as the Democrats' candidate for the Presidency of the United

States. Dan told me that before the war, when Joseph Kennedy had been the American Ambassador in London, he had sent his young son Jack to see him. Dan had diagnosed Addison's disease, for which there was then no cure. The boy was sent back to the US on a liner sailing from Liverpool, Dan assuming that he was being returned to die. But in fact while the boy was on his way across the Atlantic cortisone was discovered. As a result of that discovery, Jack Kennedy lived for many more years until he was assassinated in Dallas.

Back in England from the South of France, life on the Cherkley Estate continued to be a fascinating experience. And often a very hard experience. For when Beaverbrook was in the country, which was perhaps for four or five months of the year, I could not count on having any time at all away from work.

Every weekend, often on a Sunday morning, Beaverbrook would invite me to come and have lunch. There at lunch I would find the most extraordinary collection of celebrities. Brendan Bracken, Michael Foot, Sir Patrick Hennessy, Pamela Churchill – every one who mattered in London would be found round Beaverbrook's table. Very often after lunch, instead of being dismissed – one always waited until one was told to go and that applied to every Beaverbrook employee from the Chairman downwards – one would hang around and finally end up having dinner there.

On one Sunday, Pam and I had invited some friends and their children over for the afternoon to play cricket on our little home-made pitch at Mickleham. Beaverbrook happened to be on his own that weekend. He rang me, not in the morning, but just after lunch and about an hour before our friends were due to arrive. 'Will you come and take a walk with me?' he asked. 'I'm on my own. If you like I will set off walking from Cherkley and you can meet me half-way.'

Grumblingly, I agreed. In fact I reached Cherkley just as Beaverbrook was on the point of starting. 'Let's walk back your way,' he said. As we approached our house we heard laughter and the sound of bat and ball.

'What's all this?' Beaverbrook asked. I explained that some

friends had come to play cricket with the children and, no doubt, this was what we were hearing. He looked at me and said, 'You should have told me. Just walk back with me and then you can go home.'

I felt enormously grateful to him, but it was just a little bit early for gratitude. For when we got back to Cherkley I didn't immediately get away, not by a long shot. To begin with, there was that day's paper Beaverbrook wanted to discuss. Then there was a film that he was going to see that night. Would I look at it with him for just a few minutes to see whether it was suitable for the dinner guests? And if by chance I didn't like it I could just walk out in the middle.

We went in to see the film and after ten minutes Beaverbrook was sound asleep. Silently I got to my feet and tiptoed towards the exit. Quickly he wakened and said, 'I don't think it's any good either.'

It was eight o'clock in the evening before I got home that summer afternoon and jolly lucky to be home that early. Beaverbrook was a most complex character, perhaps the most complex character I have ever met.

On Christmas Eve of 1949, Douglas Bader, whom I then regarded as being little short of God, and I were sitting having a Christmas Eve drink with Max at his house, Wellbottom Cottage, which was also on the Cherkley Estate and not far from our house.

As Max turned to pour out another drink, Douglas, with the familiarity of an old friend said, 'By God! What a beautifully cut suit you're wearing, Max. I wish I could afford a tailor like yours.'

Max turned and said, 'Do you like it? Guess how much it cost?'

Douglas thought for a second. 'It must have cost you at least sixty quid.'

Sixty pounds was a small fortune for a suit in those days.

Max looked quite delighted. 'I paid twenty pounds for it with two pairs of trousers and I got it from Moss Bros in Covent Garden.'

I was fascinated by this information. The price he had mentioned was within even my range. As soon as Christmas was over, I took myself to Moss Bros, went into their tailoring department and shuffled around among patterns until I came across what I was sure was the identical piece of material – grey flannel.

'How much would this cost with two pairs of trousers?' I asked an assistant.

'Fifty pounds, Sir,' he replied.

My amazement showed. 'But I have a friend who bought a suit just like this from you with two pairs of trousers for only twenty pounds,' I said.

'What was your friend's name?' asked the tailor. I told him, whereupon he took me into an office, turned over an order book and showed me Max's name. The price was fifty pounds.

It was not a question of Max having misled us or having deliberately told an untruth. It was simply that Moss Bros of Covent Garden were a step out of his normal high world of Savile Row and Cork Street and he had not bothered too much about the price or about remembering the price.

When I first became Cross-Bencher I was anti-Tory.

That was natural. As a Liberal I had fought Tory candidates, and indeed if I had not been defeated by one by 642 votes in Kincardine and West Aberdeenshire in 1945 I would have spent my career in politics, not journalism.

But the more I got to know MPs and ministers in the House of Commons, the more I got to like the Tories. Perhaps I was just lucky. The ones I met were straightforward, simple and on the whole honourable men. They might be cheating on their wives but, at least at that time, they never tried to stab a colleague in the back. With the Labour Party, it was absolutely different. All my best stories came from socialist MPs or ministers ratting on their colleagues. I quickly came to the conclusion that very few of them could be trusted. They had a tendency to turn on you too.

But Manny Shinwell? Manny was different. Manny was quite prepared to rat on his enemies. But, by God, he was loyal to his friends.

39

At that time, four or five years after the war, there was a restaurant in Fleet Street called the Wellington owned by a Frenchman called Emil. Under the restaurant was a cellar with butts of wine and sherry. Occasionally, a few of Emil's chosen friends were invited down.

Although I was not a friend of Emil's I found myself there one morning and to my surprise there was Manny Shinwell, then Secretary of State for War. His host was the late and great John Carvel, then political correspondent of the *Star* and father of the distinguished *Evening Standard* political correspondent, Robert Carvel.

Shinwell was by this time a legendary figure. He had been one of the original Red Clydesiders jailed for urging revolution. He had ended the career of Ramsay MacDonald by sensationally defeating him in the famous Seaham by-election. He had once crossed the floor of the House of Commons and thumped a Tory MP, Commander Bower, who had suggested that he 'go back home to Poland'. And he was certainly one of the giants of the Labour Party.

I took an immediate shine to Manny Shinwell and he happily to me. We arranged at that first meeting to lunch soon, and indeed from that time we lunched together on Fridays for many years.

Manny was a delightful man, unostentatious and frugal in his habits. He drank little at that time – a gin and Italian was his favourite drink. Later it was to become whisky – never wine – or perhaps a glass of beer. He did not eat very much and preferred simple dishes. His favourite restaurant was the modest Russell Hotel in Russell Square.

This was in strong contrast to Herbert Morrison, another fabulous character of the period but who was far from frugal. He liked the Caprice and he liked the most expensive things on the menu. 'This is Beaverbrook who is paying for it, of course, isn't it?' he used to say to me. But unlike many of his colleagues, Manny would not accept hospitality unless he was allowed to offer hospitality in return. And he was extremely generous with what little money he had.

Often when I had no ideas for Cross-Bencher or the column

was going badly, Manny would console me and offer me political titbits – frequently ones which showed the Attlee government of the time in a poor light. For there were many members of his own party whom Manny disliked far more cordially than ever he did the Tories.

Once, when he was Secretary of State for War, he summoned me to the War Office on a Friday afternoon to tell me what at the time was a most exciting story. In Parliament, he confided to me, there was a group of influential socialist intellectuals called the XYZ Club. At a meeting of the club, Douglas Jay in anger had picked up a jug of water and poured it over Christopher Mayhew's head. I gleefully told the story in next week's Cross-Bencher. Since both Mayhew and Jay were ministers it made quite a splash.

At this time Colonel George Wigg, the MP for Dudley, was Manny Shinwell's Parliamentary Private Secretary. Wigg, who was utterly devoted to him, was a real ferret when it came to sniffing out news of events in government circles. He once told me, when Sir Stafford Cripps was Chancellor, that he was absolutely convinced that Cripps was going to devalue the pound the following weekend. It was not a question of there being a leak. It was simply that Wigg had made certain deductions from things that were happening around the place and had reached conclusions.

As it happened Beaverbrook paid one of his exceedingly rare visits to the office that Friday and I was summoned from my Cross-Bencher desk to see him in the Chairman's office. When Beaverbrook asked me his usual question, 'What's the news?' I replied with utter certainty, 'Cripps is going to devalue the pound on Sunday.'

At that time shares and currency dealings were quite out of my ken, but I often afterwards wondered whether Beaverbrook had taken heed of what I had said and profited hugely from it. What is for sure is that on the Sunday devaluation duly took place. It could all have done my standing with Beaverbrook no harm at all.

George Wigg was to become a close confidant of mine, although later he went into a huff with me from which he never really recovered. But that was much later, over the Profumo affair when I dared to criticise George for some of the things he had done.

After the general election of 1950, Manny was appointed Minister of Defence and I went to see him on his first day in office in his great room in the House of Commons. He was clearly delighted with his position and showed off to me the splendour of his surroundings.

I asked him what had happened to A. V. Alexander, Lord Alexander, the Co-operative Socialist who had been the previous Minister of Defence. And injudiciously I added, 'Is he still knocking off Frances Day?'

Manny looked at me in what I thought was anger. 'What do you mean?' he demanded.

I stammered that I only meant that it was common gossip that Frances Day, then a famous actress, was A. V. Alexander's lover and I wondered whether she still was now that he had fallen from power.

Manny looked at me astounded. 'You don't really mean that a beautiful girl like that went to bed with a toothless old wreck like Alexander?'

'But I do,' I said. 'Everyone knows it. After all, some women like power. And as Minister of Defence, Alexander had a lot of power.'

Manny thought about this for a second and then said, 'Yes, I see what you mean. But I'm Minister of Defence now and why don't I have a bird like Frances Day?' He did get Field Marshal Montgomery's whisky, though. For Montgomery recognised Shinwell as someone who stood up for the Army and indeed in some ways they were not all that dissimilar. Manny used to recount with pride how Monty, a tee-totaller, on his visits to England always gave to Manny his personal allowance of duty-free tobacco and whisky.

Manny, however, was to have his problems as Minister of Defence. When Mossadegh, the Prime Minister of Iran, seized control of the BP oil fields at Abadan, Manny Shinwell and Herbert Morrison wanted to send in paratroopers to protect British interests. They were overruled in Cabinet. It was the beginning of the end of British influence in the Middle East.

But my friendship with Manny endured. He told me that after he had lost his parliamentary seat in 1929, he still stumped the country as a Labour speaker but had to depend on the local constituency party for his travelling expenses and for board and lodging for the night. Normally he would be put up in the home of one of the committee members. But on one occasion in Wales no hospitality was offered and no expenses were suggested.

Manny was too proud to ask and spent the night in a modest hotel. First thing in the morning, he went to the Post Office and sent a telegram to his wife asking her to wire him £2 by return. He then hung around outside the hotel until he saw a telegram boy arrive, accosted him and asked him if he had a telegram for Emanuel Shinwell. To his relief, the boy had. So Manny was able to pay his hotel bill.

He had so little in his early life. In the East End of London as a child he had lived in utter poverty. When his father, a tailor, moved to Glasgow Manny was put on a train with a label tied round his neck and sent to join him. So in childhood Manny had no privileges, not even education. But ironically he loved this country with absolute passion and hated anyone who tried to do Britain down.

In 1919, Manny was sentenced to five months' imprisonment for his alleged part in the George Square riot, when an angry mob in Glasgow had tried to overturn a tramcar. The authorities were terrified that it might be the beginning of a Russian-type revolution and looked upon Manny as the ringleader.

Manny was sent to Calton Prison in Edinburgh, where his experiences must have been crucifying. For the first six weeks he was not even allowed to leave his cell – apparently on the grounds that workers demonstrating for his release outside the prison gates might be incited to acts of violence by the knowledge that he had left it. Even at the time there were many who regarded his sentence as vindictive, but afterwards Manny never showed malice towards anyone.

During his time at Calton, Manny made friends with one warder, a man who seemed much more humane than the others. He was interested in the prison rose garden and told Manny that he grew roses himself. When Manny asked him if he intended to remain a prison warder, the man replied, 'By no means. I am hoping for another job. I am applying to become public hangman.'

Manny was to marry three times. When his first wife died he was desolate, but in time he married again – a charming Jewish lady who worked in a City merchant bank. She had, I suspect, a modest amount of money and she knew about investment. Manny began to prosper slightly, but then she, too, died and once again he was left alone. But not for long. There came a third wife whom I never met but who would seem to have been a slightly odd character.

She was apparently quite well off and I suspect that her family were terrified that her money might end up with Manny. So she and Manny entered into a covenant with each other whereby neither would benefit from the other's death. Manny suspected that this was all arranged in advance by her family, although he protested that the last thing he wanted was any of her money.

When his wife died in 1978, Manny discovered that she had kept diaries of the most intimate nature detailing every day of her life. And that she had left these diaries in her will to her family. Manny read them and was horrified to discover that she had described every act of love-making that had ever taken place between them. He burned the whole lot.

Throughout the many, many years of our friendship, Manny's vigour and love of life remained unabated. His contributions in the House of Lords almost always made headline news. And, until late in life, he always travelled pipe in mouth on the top deck of a red London bus. I ocassionally saw him, brown snap-brim hat on his head, running after and catching a bus in his eighties.

Then, on 23 October 1984, came the lunch party to celebrate his hundreth birthday. Unfortunately, it was also the day of a visit to London by President Mitterrand. The police had closed off Parliament Square and most of the adjoining streets.

So I turned up half an hour late at 1.15. As it happened, Manny was even later and arrived by taxi complaining that what was normally a £4 trip from his home in Oslo Court had soared to such an extent because of all the waiting in traffic jams that he did not have enough money to pay for it. He had handed the taxi driver £9 and explained that that was every penny he had in his pocket.

The attendance at the lunch was fantastic. There were two ex-prime ministers, Harold Wilson and Alec Douglas-Home. I had to be just about the least consequential person among the thirty-six present, yet to my delight Manny had chosen to have me sit beside him.

In the last years of his life, Manny for some extraordinary reason was quite determined to get me into the House of Lords. And he went to great lengths and spent a good deal of money in furthering the project. To my embarrassment he would give little lunch parties in the House of Lords to which he would invite peers whom he thought would be helpful in advancing my cause – Lord Nugent of Guildford, the Earl of Selkirk, people of that order.

The late Lord McAlpine of Moffat was one of them.

Late in 1985 Lord McAlpine, Manny and I arranged to have lunch at the Howard Hotel, but when the day came I had some doubt as to whether Manny, now aged 101, would arrive at all.

The previous day Lord McAlpine's secretary had telephoned me saying that McAlpine had a cold and was afraid that his germ might be a danger to Manny. He wondered whether he should come to lunch. I suggested she ring Lord Shinwell, explain the situation and abide by his decision.

She rang me back half an hour later saying that she had spoken to Lord Shinwell but had been unable to make herself understood. He had seemed in a state of confusion. I suggested that in the event we simply let the lunch go ahead. I arrived at the Howard Hotel to find Lord McAlpine waiting.

Manny arrived spot on time. He was very fragile. He had to be helped down the two steps into the foyer and he walked like a frail sparrow supported on Lord McAlpine's arm into the dining-room. But that was the only thing that was frail about him. His mind was crystal clear.

He had clearly one objective. To do myself, a friend of some thirty-six years' standing, a service. And he was out to woo and manipulate Lord McAlpine into his bidding.

He confessed that he had always had difficulty in remembering Lord McAlpine's first name.

'I keep calling you Wendy,' he said, 'when of course it is Edwin.'

He enquired after Lord McAlpine's wife.

'What would she like for Christmas?' Manny asked. 'I know what I am going to do. I am going to go to Harrods or Fortnum & Mason's and send her one of these great wickerwork hampers. I expect it will cost me about £140 but I would like to please her.'

Lord McAlpine gurgled with delight. 'I am sure she would like a present of any kind. All girls do.'

'And don't you think John would make a good member of the Lords?' Manny then asked.

'Yes,' McAlpine replied. 'But we've got to get his Chairman in first.'

Not very long afterwards David Stevens, Chairman of United Newspapers, became Lord Stevens of Ludgate.

After a while I began to quiz Manny about his finances. He replied that only recently his bank manager had been on to him suggesting that he kept far too much in his current account – some £7000. He also told us that he had £159,000 in securities and he thought his flat was worth another £44,000.

'I found myself worrying last night about what I was going to give all the grandchildren for Christmas,' he said. 'Then I asked myself, "Why are you worrying? They never give you anything."'

Manny told us he'd had a dreadful night. 'Sometimes I don't know whether I'm alive or dead. I live in a sort of twilight world.'

I asked him whether in these twilight hours, when he did not know if he were alive or dead, he ever thought he had been wrong in his atheism. Perhaps he now had come to believe in God?

Manny's eyes lit up. 'No, I will never change. But I do not want to destroy anyone else's faith. I do not want to disturb people who do believe in God. But for myself, no, I cannot believe.'

46

Afterwards, when I drove with him as far as Fleet Street on his way home, I found myself marvelling at the brilliant lucidity of his brain and the loyalty of his friendship.

When Manny died, his son telephoned me and said that his father's wish had been that I should give the address at his funeral. And this I did at Golders Green Crematorium. I felt humble beyond measure that he should have wanted me to do so.

On 2 March 1950 I was responsible for a furore although my part in it has not until now been disclosed.

Beaverbrook and I were sitting in cane chairs by the lily pond at Cherkley and Beaverbrook was speaking on the telephone to Herbert Gunn, then Editor of the *Evening Standard*. The subject under discussion was the case of the atomic scientist, Klaus Fuchs, who had passed over vital and secret information concerning the atom bomb to the Russians. Fuchs had been sentenced the previous day to fourteen years' imprisonment. There was a hue and cry over MI5's failure to probe his past.

Beaverbrook was discussing with Gunn how best the story could be handled when suddenly a thought occurred to me. I realised that the then Secretary of State for War, John Strachey, appointed only the previous day, had in the past been a communist and had never, in fact, disavowed his communism.

While Beaverbrook was still speaking on the telephone, I wrote down on a piece of paper, 'Do you realise that the Head of MI5 and, therefore, responsible in Fuchs' case, is John Strachey, himself a communist?'

Beaverbrook, with that enormously agile brain, took in the message instantaneously and straight away suggested to Gunn that he should look into the association between Fuchs and Strachey. That same day, the *Evening Standard* published a banner headline: 'FUCHS AND STRACHEY: A Great New Crisis – War Minister Has Never Disavowed Communism. Now Involved In MI5 Efficiency Probe.'

The story was sensational. Herbert Gunn was widely criticised for having published it and there were some suggestions that the *Evening Standard* might even be sued for criminal libel. But

47

no action was ever taken. Gunn suffered greatly because of the story and it may be that he was rather brash with his headlines.

The interesting thing is that it was virtually the end of John Strachey. His biographer, Hugh Thomas, wrote in 1973 that Strachey never recovered from the attack on him.

Early the following year, I was to come into more personal contact with Strachey when I fought him in Dundee West in the general election of 1951. In fact I should have fought him earlier, for I travelled north to Dundee to fight the 1950 general election as a Liberal candidate. On arrival I found enormous pressure being exerted upon the Tory candidate, a man called Anstruther Gray, and myself, for one of us to step down so that there could be a straight fight against the socialist, John Strachey. In the event I was forced to stand down, but I exacted a return promise that I would have a clear run at the next election if the Tory failed to capture the seat.

On arrival back in London I joined Beaverbrook and was with him the night the 1950 election results started to come in. Confidently, in my role as political expert, I had assured him that Attlee's government would be returned with a sizeable majority. That first night, a Thursday night, it seemed as if my prophecy was going to come true. The *Daily Express* were running their usual election party at Claridge's and Beaverbrook had agreed to put in an appearance. We travelled in his Rolls-Royce listening to the results being broadcast over the car's loudspeaker and result after result gave the same sad story, Labour win, Labour win. Beaverbrook became more and more depressed.

We arrived in the lobby of Claridge's to be greeted by Albert Asher, then the *Express*'s Director of Publicity. Beaverbrook looked over Asher's shoulder and saw a scantily clad girl in the background.

'Who is that?' he demanded. Asher explained that she was one of the cabaret put on to entertain the guests in between results.

'I can't stay here with entertainment of that kind,' Beaverbrook snapped. 'Don't you know I'm in mourning for my brother?'

Beaverbrook stumped back to Arlington House, me behind him, to listen to more desolating results.

Of course, if the Tories had been winning Beaverbrook wouldn't have given a damn about his brother who had died in Canada a few weeks previously. But the next day everything changed. The counties began to bring in their results. Excitement mounted in the flat at Arlington House, Pam Churchill and a host of others following the Tory wins which came in one after another. In the end the Labour Party held power by only six seats and it was clear that soon I would have to go again to Dundee.

In the new Labour government which was formed Harold Wilson, whom I had met only once or twice, became President of the Board of Trade. In the previous Parliament his Parliamentary Private Secretary had been a Labour MP called Tom Cook who was, in fact, Labour MP for Dundee East and a friend of mine.

Cook was a very nice chap, a bit naive and red-faced, with fuzzy hair and a broad Scots accent, and Wilson secured his promotion to the post of Under-Secretary of State for Colonial Affairs. Wilson then suggested to me that Beaverbrook ought to meet Tom Cook. A dinner was arranged at Arlington House for Wilson, the new President of the Board of Trade, Tom Cook, the Under-Secretary of State for the Colonies, Lord Beaverbrook and myself.

Now Tom Cook, although charming, had one fault and that was that he had an enormous capacity to flatter people. He never liked contradicting anyone and always seemed to agree with everything you said.

The night of the dinner came. Harold Wilson, Tom Cook and I met in the Reform Club. We had a couple of sherries and then went to Arlington House.

The dinner was an absolute disaster. Every time Beaverbrook opened his mouth, Tom Cook, acting quite out of character, expressed disagreement with everything he said. I could see what was happening. Clearly Cook was determined to prove to Beaverbrook, whom he actually revered, that he was not a yes man. Wilson and I looked at each other in growing confusion.

Poor Tom Cook. He never met Beaverbrook again and, in

fact, he did not meet many more people. One night not very long afterwards his car went off the road in Scotland and crashed into a tree.

The next election soon came and I went back to fight Dundee in 1951 unopposed this time by a Conservative. It was a three-cornered fight among myself, John Strachey and a communist candidate, Dave Bowman.

Bowman was an admirable chap, an engine driver with a fine sense of humour and a friendly disposition. He and I became good friends. Once, long afterwards, he joined some of us for a drink in the Press Club on an evening in Fleet Street. At ten o'clock he looked at his watch and said, 'Well, I've got to go now, the train leaves at 10.30.' Fred Ellis, the *Daily Express*'s City Editor, who was with us said, 'What train are you catching?' Dave replied, 'I'm not catching a train. I'm driving one.'

But in Dundee in 1951 there were no such pleasantries during the election. It was a marvellous fight, a wonderful constituency, a great electorate.

I lost by 33,000 votes to 36,000.

And at the end of the campaign, some thirty of my supporters came to the station to see me on to the night-sleeper to London. In the dining-car I found Bob Boothby, whom I had met once before when I had fought Kincardine and West Aberdeenshire in 1945.

Bob seized upon me and we spent much of the night drinking. In that deep, wonderful voice of his he told me of his hopes and aspirations in the new government which Churchill would be setting up on the morrow. He knew that I would be seeing Beaverbrook in the morning. He pleaded with me to urge his case with Beaverbrook, who in turn would urge it with Churchill, to be the next Minister of Labour.

I listened entranced to his arguments. I knew of his eloquence, I knew of his common touch and I thought he would make a splendid Minister of Labour. The next morning, as promised, I advanced my arguments and Bob's to Beaverbrook.

Beaverbrook listened to me and shook his head sadly. 'Go and look up Hansard for the Czech gold debate,' he said. 'Read how Boothby swindled. He can never ever become a minister in any administration in this country.'

I went back to the office to read Hansard and I realised that Beaverbrook was right. The fact is that in the early years of the war Bob was found guilty of sharp practice, to say the very least, in the manipulation of the Czech gold deposits in London. There was even a move to impeach him. It would have been virtually the first time in history that a minister – because Bob was then a junior minister – had been impeached.

But the war was on. Boothby had been a friend and supporter of Churchill before the war and Churchill magnanimously remembered.

David Margesson, who during the war was Tory Chief Whip, told me long afterwards of how Boothby had been brought into Churchill's room in the House of Commons and Churchill had said to him, 'I am going to take no action against you. There is a war on. You have a chance to go out and sponge the slate clean.' Another Tory MP who had been a member of the pro-Hitler Anglo–German LINK movement, Sir Arnold Wilson, had already done so by being killed, aged fifty-five, while serving as a tail-gunner in a British bomber.

According to Margesson, Boothby stood to attention and said, 'Thank you, Sir. I will sponge the slate clean. Tomorrow I am going to join the RAF.'

'And so he did,' said Margesson. 'He went the very next day and joined the Air Force as a Public Relations Officer.'

It is difficult to envisage today just how popular and public a figure Bob Boothby was. He was a brilliant orator with a capacity for attracting headlines every time he spoke. He was also a frequent performer on the *Any Questions?* radio programme and had a large public following.

I came to like him very much indeed, but the more I knew him the more I became aware of his defects. Everyone in the Establishment knew that at one stage he had been the lover of Harold Macmillan's wife, Dorothy, and the father of Sara, one of her children. Certainly, I once went to lunch with Boothby and found Sara Macmillan there. She acted towards Boothby in a way one could imagine a daughter acting towards her father.

Sara was an attractive and vivacious young woman as she sat that day on the arm of Bob Boothby's chair. But her life was to end in tragedy. She became pregnant while still unmarried and while Macmillan was still Prime Minister. Quentin Crewe told me that Sara had never been sure whether he, Quentin Crewe, or another of her boyfriends called Andrew Heath was the father. Quentin may have been boasting, but I do not think so. The Macmillans had been good to him and had treated him almost like a son after the illness which confined him to a wheelchair.

Sara wanted to have the child, but her father insisted that she have an abortion. She had the abortion and was never able to have a child thereafter. She married Heath and in the end became a hopeless alcoholic. At one stage she tried to adopt a baby and her application was turned down on the grounds that she would not be a fit parent. Sara died a very sad woman.

Macmillan's son, Maurice, who later became MP for Farnham, was also an alcoholic but he took the cure. His other daughter, who married Julian Amery, was an alcoholic too. Whether that was all due to the fact that their father was Prime Minister or that their mother had a lover is a matter for conjecture.

But Bob Boothby was not in truth a woman-chaser. He might have been chased by women and he might occasionally have succumbed. Unhappily, Bob's predilection was for boys.

Over the years more and more stories came in. There was one story much later of a youngster from Aberdeen who was charged by the police on suspicion of theft because he was found waving a bottle of champagne and in his pocket was a gold watch with Boothby's name engraved on it. In court the boy was conditionally discharged and put on a train for Scotland.

I took the trouble to have him traced on his arrival in Scotland and found out the background to the story. The boy, a constituent of Boothby's from East Aberdeen, had arrived in London and been taken, this working-class boy, to the restaurant Quo Vadis where he had been wined and dined excesssively by Bob. He had then gone back to Bob's flat. He swore blind, and I believe truthfully, that the champagne and the gold watch had been given to him by Bob, clearly in return for services rendered.

There was another case of a youngster who was charged with having stolen a cheque-book and with having tried to cash a cheque in a bank on Sloane Square. The boy maintained that he had found the cheque-book in the street, but there were many who suspected that he had taken it from Bob's hip-pocket as Bob's trousers lay over his bed.

In 1951 I had of course no idea that Bob Boothby was a homosexual. Nor had I any idea that Richard Crossman, whom I liked and respected, had, at least when young, a track record in that direction too. Stephen Spender always claimed that his own homosexualism started when Crossman had seduced him when they were both students.

But I knew nothing about that on the night I took Boothby and Crossman to dinner at the Reform Club.

Over dinner Boothby told with great glee a wonderful story concerning Tom Driberg. Driberg, Boothby and Lady Violet Bonham-Carter were all scheduled to take part in an *Any Questions?* programme in the West Country on Good Friday. Boothby had thought the sensible thing to do was for him to drive the other two down by car. He telephoned Driberg to finalise the arrangements but Driberg was appalled that Lady Violet should be travelling with them.

'Why do we have to have her with us, Bob?' Driberg protested. 'If she is there it means I can't talk to you. And I want to talk to you. I want to tell you about this marvellous new boyfriend of mine.' I was told subsequently that the new boyfriend was American singer Johnny Ray. 'It is the most wonderful thing that has ever happened to me. I must talk to you about him.'

Whereupon Boothby, according to Boothby, said that he couldn't possibly go back on his arrangement to give Lady Violet a lift and that Driberg would just have to keep silent on the subject of his boyfriend.

On the Friday morning on their way down to the West Country, they were passing through a village when Driberg saw a church and shouted, 'Stop, Bob! I want to go into that church. I want to make the Stations of the Cross.'

Boothby stopped the car. And Driberg went into the church

leaving Boothby and Lady Violet Bonham-Carter sitting twiddling their thumbs. But it was what Driberg said to them when finally he emerged from the church that had Boothby rocking with laughter.

'You may like to know,' Driberg said, 'that I have said a prayer for both of you.'

Back in London after the election, Beaverbrook put the choice squarely before me. Did I want to go on playing around with politics, or did I want to make myself a career in journalism with all the treasures that journalism could provide?

'If it is politics,' he said, 'you will reach the highest echelon. But if it is journalism, I will put on your head a golden crown.'

I had a wife and two children, I had no financial resources and I was a member of a political party which did not seem as if it could ever win a seat in Parliament. I was still determined to become an MP. I judged it wise, however, to say that I was prepared and willing to become a journalist.

III

BEAVERBROOK SENT ME to the *Daily Express* as chief leader writer and Assistant Editor in the autumn of 1951.

I was one of four leader writers on the paper. There was a charming chap called Jack Sewell who, although an agnostic, was able to write one brilliant leader a year at Easter on the Christian message. Unhappily, he was never able during the rest of the year to write another leader which was even coherent.

Another was Harold Jaffa, a splendid man who smoked a large pipe, had a long face and horn-rimmed glasses, wore what he called lucky suits and sat behind what he called a lucky desk, but seldom alas had a leader in the newspaper. Yet Harold earned himself a reputation for wisdom at Christiansen's daily conference. Because, whenever Chris said 'What do you think, Jaffa?' Harold would move his pipe from one side of his mouth to the other and say, 'Well, I must consider that, Sir.'

The third was a dear man called Willie Williams, grey-haired, intense, middle-aged and I have no doubt utterly faithful to his wife. Even so, when he bent over his desk one could see the shape of a Durex packet in his hip-pocket. Willie was a good leader writer, but on my arrival Chris decided to sack him. Unfairly, I thought. And I was happy that, long afterwards, too long afterwards, I was able to arrange a job for Willie on the *Evening Standard*.

With Christiansen again, I realised how like a woman he was – madly jealous of Beaverbrook's favours. Sometimes Beaverbrook, if he wished to annoy Chris, would just avoid telephoning him for days on end. When that happened, Chris became more and more desolate and would remain hunched over his desk. And, of course, sadistically, Beaverbrook during that period would telephone me incessantly, giving me messages to pass on to Chris as to how the newspaper should be conducted.

It was a cruel business, but then Chris in a way was cruel, too. Knowing how jealous he was, I once took him out to dinner and explained to him frankly that my real ambitions were not in journalism but in politics and that he had nothing to fear from me.

'I can't understand you,' he said, looking at me with incredulity. 'All I ever want to do is to make Lord Beaverbrook happy.'

With Willie Williams having left and Sewell and Jaffa failing to produce, I soon found myself writing the leader column every day entirely on my own and getting pretty fed up at doing so. Fortunately, whenever Beaverbrook was in town he would take me walking every morning and there was an enormous flow of ideas. For Beaverbrook had plenty of ideas and he always encouraged other people to have them. He stimulated.

Beverley Baxter, my predecessor on Cross-Bencher, had also worked for Lord Kemsley, then owner of the *Sunday Times* and *Sunday Graphic* and a great provincial newspaper empire.

He once explained to me the difference between the two men.

'It's like this, Johnny,' he said. 'When you work for Beaverbrook and he kills an idea, he replaces it with another and better idea. But with Kemsley, the old boy comes down in the morning and says, 'Bax, I've got a marvellous idea. You know that feature we are running on page three? Let's kill it.'

Shortly after my arrival at the *Daily Express*, it was announced that Hugh Cudlipp had been appointed the Managing Editor of the *Sunday Express*. Cudlipp was an extraordinary journalist of great talent, but he never really fitted in at the *Express*. At the end of his time he had not left even one little fingerprint on the newspaper. He was outmanoeuvred at every turn by the then Editor, John Gordon. It may have been frustration at his lack of success that made him such an irritable character at the time.

On one occasion Beaverbrook gave what was euphemistically known as a tea party for all his employees at the Savoy Hotel. There was plenty of everything to drink except tea.

At the party I found myself in the company of Cudlipp, his charming wife Eileen Ascroft who later committed suicide, and Tudor Jenkins, then Editor of the *Evening Standard* Londoner's Diary, and his wife. Cudlipp suggested that we all go on and have dinner with him. He took us to a restaurant in Charlotte Street.

We'd all had a fair amount to drink, myself rather less than the others. Suddenly in the middle of dinner Cudlipp leaned across and said to me, 'How old are you?' I replied that I was thirty-one. This threw him into an absolute fury. He refused to believe that I was only thirty-one.

'Come on, tell me the truth,' he sneered.

Politely I repeated that I was thirty-one as indeed I was. I kept my cool, however, partly because the Cudlipps had promised to drive me back to Waterloo for my train to Leatherhead and I wanted to make sure that I got there. Cudlipp continued to abuse me for the rest of the meal.

But once in the back of their car, a Jowett Javelin, I unleashed my own anger the moment I reached the safety of Waterloo Bridge, knowing that even on foot I could get my train on time. I told Cudlipp exactly what I thought of his rudeness.

The next morning when I arrived in the *Daily Express* building there was Cudlipp in a lightweight oatmeal-coloured suit waiting to apologise to me.

I felt afterwards that the reason he got so nettled about my age and the reason he continued so abusively and so embarrassingly throughout dinner on the subject was that he could not bear the thought of anyone being younger than he was.

There was another curious incident during Cudlipp's time on the *Sunday Express*. Beaverbrook had given him the right to fire and hire, and he used this right on one occasion to sack a man called Sidney Rodin who had refused to work a late-night turn of duty on the grounds that too much pressure might be put on his health. Rodin appealed to the Editor, John Gordon. John

Gordon succeeded in humiliating Cudlipp entirely by having Rodin reinstated.

A few weeks later, Cudlipp left the *Sunday Express* to go back to the *Mirror*. And the first appointment he made when he reached the *Mirror* was that of Sidney Rodin. He took the man who had been the cause of his humiliation on the *Sunday Express* and gave him a new job. The irony of it is that very shortly afterwards Rodin collapsed and died from a cerebral haemorrhage.

One day, I was hammering out the leader column during my lunch hour when I heard voices in the corridor. Chris was showing Lord McGowan, Chairman of ICI, around the *Express* and in a loud, booming voice as he passed my office – unaware that I was in there – he said to Lord McGowan, 'and that's where the leader writers sit. But the truth is, of course, that I myself write the leader column every day.'

I was hopping mad. When, eventually Chris came back from his lunch, I took the completed leader column into his office, threw it on his desk and said, 'There's the leader column that you say you write every day. From tomorrow you can write the bloody thing yourself.'

Chris immediately accused me of having eavesdropped on his conversation. But in the end he apologised and the affair was patched up.

It was during my first few months of writing leaders that Lord Beaverbrook again invited me to the South of France. This time I stayed for four weeks, writing leaders every day which were telephoned through to London and absorbing wisdom at the feet of the master. It was a most agreeable experience. I did not stay in the great house but in a hotel in Monte Carlo, which suited me very well indeed.

Beaverbrook's house-guest was Frederick Lonsdale, the great playwright and author of so many glittering pre-war hits. Lonsdale, I suspect, really disliked Beaverbrook intensely and Beaverbrook disliked him, too. But the two of them were the only survivors of a pre-war gang which had included Lady Maureen Stanley, Arnold Bennett, H. G. Wells and a host of other celebrities.

Lonsdale and I became good friends. He would never travel by air and when he crossed the Atlantic it was always on a French ship, since he took the view that 'on French ships there is none of this bloody nonsense about women and children first'. In his early days, he told me, he had worked as a boot-black in Canada and had jumped trains because he had no money for the fare. He had finished up in Essex, in Westcliffe-on-Sea, utterly broke but determined to be a playwright. He began by making a few bob patching up the plays of others.

One day he received a telegram from Daly's Theatre in London asking him to come and see the Manager. Lonsdale borrowed ten shillings from the milkman and journeyed to London.

He found there that the Manager had a problem. Seymour Hicks was due to open in a play at Daly's in ten days' time. The Manager had doubts about the second act. He offered Lonsdale £50 if Lonsdale would put the second act right. Lonsdale agreed to read the play while the Manager went out to lunch. When the Manager returned Lonsdale, in a grandiloquent gesture, threw the play at him and said, 'I wouldn't touch that with a barge-pole. No one could save that play.' He stalked out of the Manager's office and went back to Westcliffe-on-Sea to face an angry wife and an even angrier milkman.

The Seymour Hicks play opened and closed within three days. Another telegram came from the Manager of the theatre: Would Lonsdale like to come back to London? Lonsdale went back to London and this time the Manager said: 'You were right about the play. Now the theatre is empty. Have you any play of your own that you would like to submit?'

Lonsdale pulled out of his pocket a manuscript that had been round almost every theatrical management in London and said, 'Here you are.' It was *Maid of the Mountains* and it made Lonsdale £200,000.

But alas, poor Freddy. The end of the war and the arrival of kitchen sink theatre was also the end of Lonsdale.

I continued to see him and was aware that he was getting more and more hard up. He always protested that he had plenty of money, but by now he lived in a single room in Claridge's.

Now when he took me to lunch in the Savoy and I offered to pay he would say, 'No, nonsense. I've got plenty of money.' And he would bring out a fistful of fivers. But one suspected that that fistful of fivers represented all his money.

Freddy was always planning the new play that was going to restore him to fame and wealth. And one day, happily, walking down Hill Street, he collapsed and died before that fistful of fivers had finally run out.

As the *Daily Express* leader writer, I never had any difficulty, either then or later, reconciling my conscience with the leaders I was writing. For, in the main, the *Daily Express* and Beaverbrook stood for a form of rugged, radical imperialism – very much my own point of view. In fact, it is my belief that newspapers tend to attract journalists who believe in that newspaper's policy. So it certainly was on the *Express*.

Beaverbrook in his newspapers was basically on the side, as I saw it, of good. He had an enormous disregard of the Establishment and a contempt for privilege. I was walking along the Mall with him one morning at this time and he said to me, 'Do you realise that the only reason the Mall is open to public transport is that I conducted a campaign to have it opened? For many, many years it was a private Royal thoroughfare and I thought that this was ridiculous with London bursting at the seams. So I pursued a campaign to have it opened. And do you know what the Palace did? They came to me and said that if I desisted from my campaign I could have personal rights to use the Mall. I told them to go to hell.'

The only difficulty with a leader I ever had was during the Korean War, when General MacArthur was chasing the North Koreans up to the Yalu River and there were suggestions that he should proceed beyond it.

At this stage in my career, I was avoiding the office in the morning and working from the Reform Club instead. I found it much easier in the club's contemplative calm to read the newspapers and to think up my leader ideas. My custom was to telephone Chris around about 12.30 and tell him what my ideas were going to be for the afternoon, when I would come back to the office and write the column.

On this particular day Chris listened to my ideas and then told me that Beaverbrook wanted leaders supporting General MacArthur. It was a small testing point for me. I explained firmly to Chris that in no circumstances could I write a leader in which I did not believe. And nor did I.

That policy I have followed throughout my journalistic career and with my own leader and article writers. I have never asked anyone to write anything which was against his own beliefs. Douglas Clark, for instance, a great *Sunday Express* writer, was an abolitionist. So he was never asked to write a leader supporting capital punishment. When it was necessary to do so I either wrote it myself or found someone who believed in it. This is not simply a question of ethics. It is also a question of getting the best leader in the newspaper. For my experience is that people write well only when they write about the things in which they believe.

And I learned another thing while working for Beaverbrook. He once said to me, 'If you walk over a man once you can walk over him again any time you want to.' He was absolutely right. I watched him do that so often to people who crumpled before him.

I made up my mind early on that I would never allow it to happen to me and, to the best of my knowledge, it never has. No editor lasts for long unless he is prepared to quit rather than ever accept humiliation.

One morning, I was sitting with Beaverbrook in Arlington House discussing a leader. The telephone rang. It was his financial adviser in Montreal discussing stocks and shares. Beaverbrook gave swift, sharp instructions, put the telephone down and returned to discuss the leader at the very sentence on which he'd been cut off.

The telephone rang again. This time it was his farm manager calling from Cricket Malherbie, his farm in Somerset. Beaverbrook began to discuss the milk round and wanted to know how many pints had been sold that morning. Were the electric milk floats adequate? What was the current butterfat content of his herd of Ayrshires? Then right back into the leader again at the precise point he had left off.

Beaverbrook was quite the most remarkable man I'd ever met. And no one I have ever met could match him for quickness of brain and breadth of knowledge. His reading was encyclopaedic. There was virtually no subject except perhaps for sport of which he did not have a deep understanding.

Every day he would take me walking through Hyde Park, quizzing me closely about the day's news and what possible leaders or leader-page articles could be written on that news. Out of sheer self-defence I always made sure that I had read the papers thoroughly and formulated some ideas of my own. It was all part of my training.

I never knew where we were going when we went walking. One day we left the park and marched for what seemed miles. Then Beaverbrook entered a jeweller's shop, inspected a piece of jewellery which clearly he had arranged in advance to be ready for him, looked the manager straight in the eye and said 'How much?' The manager mentioned some £200 or £300. Beaverbrook again looked him straight in the eye and said 'How much discount?'

Without blinking, the manager replied '10 per cent, my Lord'. I so admired the technique that I have used it myself ever since – usually with a good deal less success than Beaverbrook.

Another morning, with me padding along beside him, he stopped by the back of the Hyde Park Hotel and pointed up to the third floor.

'That's where I lived when I first came to London,' he said.

'Are you pointing at the actual room?' I asked.

'Oh no,' he replied. 'We had the whole floor. And the next year I bought the whole hotel.'

Once, when for some reason our morning walk took us near Battersea Park, Beaverbrook told me how F. E. Smith, later Lord Birkenhead, had been caught there with a prostitute. He had telephoned Beaverbrook immediately after the arrest desperately seeking his help in keeping the matter secret. Part of Smith's problem was that he had committed the cardinal sin of giving a false name to the police.

Had Beaverbrook been able to help? Beaverbrook had – although he didn't tell me how. Was Beaverbrook telling the truth? All I can say is that I never knew him lie.

He was quite the master journalist, quicker off the mark than anyone. I only knew him to fail once and that failure endeared him further to me. He had given me an idea for an article designed for the leader page of the *Sunday Express*. But I had failed to make anything of it. I just could not get it to work out.

We sat on the porch at Cherkley in wicker chairs looking over the Cherkley Valley and he said, 'Give me some paper and a pencil and I will show you to how to write this article.' He began to write and I thought to myself that I was really going to see the brilliance of the old master. But after a few sentences he stopped. 'You're quite right,' he said, 'this idea won't work.' Beaverbrook certainly kept his leader writers on their toes.

George Malcolm Thomson, who had been Beaverbrook's secretary during the war, was when I met him in effect a rather superior leader writer for the *Daily Express*. He was also book critic of the *Evening Standard*. He was a most engaging fellow, although he did have an enormous capacity for speaking in witty-bitter fashion about Beaverbrook in private but of never, never disagreeing with Beaverbrook in public.

Indeed I remember Lord Lambton many years later coming to lunch in the office at one of the few luncheon parties, perhaps the only luncheon party, Beaverbrook gave there in my time and after lunch saying to me, 'Tell me, who is that man who always laughed first every time Beaverbrook said anything remotely funny?' It was, of course, George Malcolm Thomson.

Before the war, when Beaverbrook took a party to Russia, I believe that the great cartoonist Low, in a cartoon based on Napoleon's retreat from Moscow, caricatured the Beaverbrook party themselves retreating from Moscow. On a horse close by Beaverbrook was the figure of George Malcolm Thomson, whom Low picked out as Marshal Yea. But Thomson had a great brain and a good turn of phrase, and he was vastly underpaid during all his service with the *Express*.

Beaverbrook once told me a story about Thomson and I

afterwards heard it from Thomson himself, so it is checked from both points.

Beaverbrook liked swimming and had a swimming pool at Cherkley. Thomson hated swimming and Thomson's duty was to tell Beaverbrook each morning what news there was in the newspapers – of course Beaverbrook read every page himself. This was merely a ploy to get discussion going on leader-writing subjects.

Knowing that Thomson hated swimming, Beaverbrook used to take joy in making him swim in the swimming pool.

One day when Thomson, blue and shivering, came out of the pool Beaverbrook said, 'Good, isn't it, Thomson?'

Wearily, Thomson replied, 'I like it very much, Sir. If only I didn't find that I had to micturate every time I enter the water.'

He never swam in that swimming pool again.

Not long after joining the *Express*, I tried to repair the gap on our leader-writing front by taking on a man about the same age as myself from the *Yorkshire Post*. His name was Derek Marks. I had met him at the National Liberal Club and was impressed by this fat, bouncy young man who wore, in typical *Yorkshire Post* fashion, striped trousers and a black jacket.

Derek started badly. At the end of the first fortnight not one line he had written had appeared in the newspaper. And he still came into the office every day in a black jacket and striped trousers. He began to become irritable. He complained to me that I had taken him away from the *Yorkshire Post* and that he felt he was at a complete dead end on the *Daily Express*.

I reasoned with him, explaining that it took a great deal of time to change style. I suggested that he might be more relaxed if he dressed in a more relaxed fashion; if, for instance, instead of wearing his black jacket and striped trousers, he came to the office in a blazer and flannels. This he agreed to do.

Soon afterwards at Beaverbrook's request I wrote a leader-page article for the *Sunday Express* on the Dean of Canterbury who had been making some extraordinary pronouncements in North Korea about the Americans and about his belief that the Americans had been practising germ warfare. I began the article with the words 'With his gold cross of Christ glinting in the sun the Dean of Canterbury comes home, home to trouble such as not even he has ever known before.'

The article appeared on the Sunday and on the Monday I was making my way from Waterloo to the *Daily Express* offices when in the Aldwych I met an Australian journalist called Peter Gladwyn, later a director of the *News of the World*. He said to me, 'Are you going to the press conference?' I replied, 'What press conference?'

'The Dean of Canterbury's, of course,' he said. 'He's giving a press conference at eleven o'clock at the Imperial Hotel.'

When I got to the office Derek Marks was already there and on the spur of the moment I suggested that he go along to the Dean of Canterbury's press conference and write a piece on it. This he did. In fact he wrote the most brilliant piece which, even though we already had a professional reporter at the conference, made the lead story in the next day's *Daily Express*. Beaverbrook was entranced.

'Who wrote that lead story?' he demanded of me.

'My boy Derek Marks,' I replied.

'Send him to see me this morning,' said Beaverbrook.

I duly sent Derek Marks. By this time he was wearing the most dilapidated blazer and the dirtiest old pair of slacks you have ever seen in your life. But from that point Derek Marks never, ever looked back.

In addition to my morning walks with Beaverbrook, I also found myself a frequent guest at his table. Beaverbrook's dinner parties were glittering affairs. The men were either leading figures in the world of politics or brilliant conversationalists. The women were all beautiful and wise enough to keep their mouths shut unless, like Pam Churchill, they had something interesting to say. Ladies who offended were never invited again, as some wives of top Beaverbrook executives indignantly found to their cost.

Brendan Bracken, who was so devoted to Churchill that he liked it to be thought, absolutely falsely, that he was Churchill's illegitimate son, was a frequent guest. He ate almost nothing. Two mouthfuls of food and his plate was pushed aside in favour of a huge cigar which he clamped between his teeth. He had been far and away the closest of Churchill's wartime henchmen and was still close in peacetime.

Bracken's background fascinated me. Far from being Churchill's son, he had been born in poverty in Ireland, had gone as a boy to South Africa and in a very short time had made enough money to be able to return to England and present himself at Sedburgh, the public school, where he must have been the only pupil in history to pay his own fees.

Sir Patrick Hennessy, Chairman of Ford and at that time one of the most important industrialists in Britain, had been Beaverbrook's right-hand man at the Ministry of Aircraft Production during the war and he adored the old boy. Much of the glory which went to Beaverbrook for his part in producing Spitfires at a critical time in the Battle of Britain might have been fairly claimed by Hennessy.

Michael Foot was also often at the dinner table and in fact had been given the use of a weekend cottage on the Beaverbrook estate at Cherkley.

Another guest was Lord Grantley. He was at that time in his late sixties – gentle, stooped-backed and most agreeable to speak to. He once said something to me which I have never forgotten. Explaining why he loved gardening, he said, 'It keeps the jaws of the coffin open because you are always looking forward to the next season.' I did not realise, however, that his wife, Jean, had been Beaverbrook's great love for many years and indeed had died on Lord Beaverbrook's estate. It has always fascinated me the way in which the rich are able to remain on friendly terms with the lovers of their wives.

Grantley, who had begun life as plain Richard Norton, was a descendant of Richard Sheridan. He was an executive at Pinewood Film Studios and it is said that on the morning he inherited his title he was out walking when he saw that some Pinewood workers had chalked on a wall 'Richard Norton is a shit'. The new Lord Grantley immediately rubbed out Richard Norton and chalked in instead 'Lord Grantley'.

He inherited his father's money, but only just and after a most amusing court case. The old Lord Grantley had late in life taken up with the wife of a chef at the Savoy and had installed himself with this much younger woman in a flat. The old Lord was at this time in his eighties.

His son did not object to the liaison until catastrophe happened. The Savoy chef sued for divorce, which meant that if it were granted Lord Grantley would be free to marry the woman. The son was furious. For, if the marriage took place, then the wife would inherit his father's money at least for her lifetime. In anger against the chef he immediately boycotted the hotel restaurant.

The case came to court and the judge refused to believe that a man of Lord Grantley's age could have sexual intercourse. Lord Grantley was called to the witness box and asked if it were true that he had sex with his mistress.

'Yes, m'Lord,' he piped up. 'Every Saturday night.'

The divorce was granted but, happily for his son, the old Lord Grantley died before the decree nisi became absolute.

I remember the night Roy Thomson came to dinner at Cherkley. He was at that time a small Canadian publisher quite unknown in Britain and had come here in the hope that he might buy the ailing *News Chronicle* on the cheap. It was clear that although Beaverbrook was polite to him he did not regard him as a person of substance.

Beaverbrook did not react when Thomson expressed a desire to see the *Daily Express* plant in Fleet Street and so it was I who found myself inviting him to come and see over the office the following evening. The next day I went out and bought a half-bottle of gin and a half-bottle of whisky so that I might be able to entertain him in the little cubicle which was my office. To my chagrin he refused all offer of a drink and plunged straight away into a tour of our machine-room. He was quite goggle-eyed and enthusiastic about our presses and said he had never seen their like before.

In the event Roy did not get the *News Chronicle*. He got what turned out to be a much juicier plum – the *Scotsman*. He did so because when that paper had been founded there was a clause in its constitution stipulating that it could never be sold into English proprietorship. No one all those years back had ever even entertained the possibility of a Canadian wanting to buy it.

So Roy, funded by the Royal Bank of Canada, got the *Scotsman*, which meant that when commercial television came along he got the Scottish franchise – a franchise which, as he said at the time, was a licence to print money. And so it has remained.

I also met Stanley Morison around the Cherkley dinner table. The distinguished typographer of *The Times*, he was in his late sixties and looked rather like an elderly silver-haired eagle with a reddish face and gold-rimmed spectacles.

He had met Beaverbrook while writing the history of *The Times* and the two men had become firm friends. They were the most unlikely pair. Morison was a Jesuit intellectual with an extraordinary hobby. I found him at Waterloo Station one evening with a notebook in his hand. He looked rather discomfited by my asking him what on earth he was doing there. It emerged that he was train-spotting!

Before Beaverbrook's second marriage to Lady Dunn, Morison was in constant attendance at Cherkley. On one night there was a hiatus in the conversation around the table and Morison's high-pitched voice could be heard saying, 'There is no question about it. The porridge in Winchester gaol is the best of any prison in England.'

'How on earth do you know that?' one of the women asked, leaning forward.

'Because I have been a prisoner in almost every gaol in the South of England,' Morison replied delightedly.

And, as it turned out, he had been too. He had been a conscientious objector in the First World War and had gone to prison many times. Unhappily, Lady Dunn disapproved of the friendship and, when she married Lord Beaverbrook, Morison was seen a great deal less at court.

In my boyhood I had looked upon Sir John Simon – a leading member of Neville Chamberlain's pre-war Cabinet – with loathing as one of the men of Munich who had let down the League of Nations and paved the way for Hitler's conquest of Europe. It was therefore with some misgiving that I found myself lunching with him and Lord Beaverbrook at Cherkley. There were only the three of us, and afterwards we sat out on the veranda in the sunshine overlooking the lovely Cherkley Valley without another house anywhere to be seen.

It was a peaceful summer afternoon and it was difficult to avoid liking Sir John in his old age. For he was full of stories against himself. After an election meeting in Dundee he had been carried shoulder-high spontaneously by cheering supporters, only to discover afterwards that his gold watch had been pocketed by one of the men who carried him.

In the early 1930s, he told me, when he was Foreign Secretary and there was an urgent need to repair Britain's friendship with France, it was arranged for the King and Queen to visit Paris. Before the Royal visit, Simon had gone over to mend fences with his French counterpart, Monsieur Barthou.

Barthou was a member of the French Academy and was intensely proud of his membership.

During lunch Barthou said to Simon, 'Sir John, if you were not a politician what would be your greatest ambition, your pinnacle of achievement?'

Simon considered the question and then answered quite truthfully, 'Outside politics my passion is golf and if I were really put to it my ambition would be to become Captain of the Royal and Ancient.'

Barthou looked at him astounded. He obviously thought Simon was joking.

'Come, come, Sir John,' he said. 'Leave golf aside. Apart from golf what would your ambition be?'

Simon thought again and then replied, 'Well, Monsieur Barthou, apart from becoming Captain of the Royal and Ancient I would very much like to become President of the MCC.'

Barthou began to look irritated.

'Leave sport aside,' he said. 'In serious things what would you like to be?'

Simon looked at him and after a pause said, 'Well, Monsieur Barthou. I suppose I would like to be a member of the French Academy.'

Although Beaverbrook's guests glittered, Cherkley Court bore none of the hallmarks of a really rich man, although Beaverbrook was just that. It was not unknown in times of heavy rainfall for a bucket to be placed in the drawing-room to catch the drips from the roof. And the food served at Beaverbrook's table was invariably bland and the vegetables were always puréed. This was because he had once suffered from diverticulitis and so the blandness was presumably on medical advice. At one stage because of his illness, and before my time, he had existed largely on a diet of slops, bread cut into pieces covered with sugar and soaked in hot milk.

Freddy Lonsdale told me how one day during this period he had gone to lunch at Cherkley with Beaverbrook and the only other person at the table was a brand-new male secretary. When the butler served the food, the unfortunate secretary spotted the dish of bread and milk, said 'That looks interesting, I'll have some please' and proceeded to help himself to two-thirds of the dish.

The look on Beaverbrook's face, according to Lonsdale, was quite wonderful to behold. The old man did not say a word. He just got up from the table, lay down on a couch and pulled a blanket over his head.

The servants at Cherkley were a strange bunch. The chef was called Saucisson and was supposed to be French, although many believed that he was German and had as a German travelled with Beaverbrook and Churchill during the war when he should by rights have been interned.

At one stage in the South of France Beaverbrook suspected that Saucisson was cheating him with the housekeeping and persuaded his nurse, Christine, to do the shopping instead. I watched in admiration as he counted up the small change and queried the price of tiny items such as butter and eggs after each shopping expedition. Saucisson was furious at this interference in his affairs and his voice could often be heard, raised in anger, in the kitchen. He was, I imagine, the only person for whom Beaverbrook had respect and, indeed, fear in that household.

There were two butlers, Mr Mead and the long-serving Albert, who always wore a blue pin-striped suit and had a complete contempt for everyone, including Lord Beaverbrook. Albert once told me how, before the war, Beaverbrook had insisted on going to buy a blue serge suit from the Fifty Shilling Tailors and afterwards was caught in it in a heavy shower. His legs were dyed almost permanently blue.

The valet, Knockels, was having it off with the housekeeper, Mabel, and subsequently married her. He was a grand character with his nose slightly in the air and with a disdain for everyone as humble as himself. He was replaced by a valet called Bowes, nicknamed Bosey, a charming little fellow who came in too often smelling too heavily of Lord Beaverbrook's decanter.

Although Mr Mead always wore a black jacket and striped trousers when he served at dinner, none of the other servants apart from Albert had any uniform of any kind and dressed in the most casual of clothes. Sometimes, too, they acted towards guests in the most casual of fashions. For Beaverbrook remained a peasant at heart and was not given to displays of ostentation.

On his birthday Beaverbrook had the agreeable habit of giving a gift to each of his dinner guests. It happened to me only once. My wife had not been invited to that particular dinner but, when I took my seat, I noticed an envelope addressed to her on the table in front of me. I slipped it into my jacket pocket. Beverley Baxter, who was on the opposite side of the table, had a similar envelope addressed to his absent wife. Baxter was less punctilious than me. He slit open the envelope and began to count the fivers. When Pam opened the envelope later that night it contained £100 – to us quite a fortune in those days.

There were many women in the life of Lord Beaverbrook. Jean Norton had been the great love but that was long before my time. Indeed there was a rumour that Beaverbrook's vendetta against Mountbatten had originated in the fact that Mountbatten had once made a pass at Mrs Norton.

When I arrived, the woman temporarily in his life was his young, long-legged Irish nurse, Christine O'Halloran. In her white starched uniform she looked gorgeous. And when she appeared in that uniform at dinner, for she always dined, no matter who the guests were, she looked splendid. But there were occasions when Beaverbrook allowed her to wear her normal clothes, and then it was rather sad to see this girl cheaply dressed and wearing garish jewellery, and yet beautiful under it all, sitting at the same table as immaculately gowned women like Pam Churchill.

Sometimes in the South of France, Beaverbrook would encourage Christine to sing an Irish song at table. The trouble was that she had no voice but she still did as she was told. The old man also encouraged her to go swimming even when the sea was rough at Cap d'Ail, far too rough for him to venture in. She was a good swimmer and Beaverbrook tied a rope around her for safety. He seemed to enjoy it, but on one occasion I saw her coming out of the water cold and shivering, and she clearly did not. Beaverbrook could be sadistic.

The next woman I knew, two years later, was French and I always called her Santa Maria. Her name in fact was Maria-Edmée Escarra. I was told that she had been the mistress of one of the Paris Rothschilds. She herself came from the *haute bourgeoisie*; her father had been President of Crédit Lyonnais.

Santa Maria was a splendid lady with a wonderful figure and a friendly but intensely freckled face. She spoke very little English and on occasion in those early days of courtship I would accompany Lord Beaverbrook and her while Beaverbrook recited poetry to her on his walks through the Cherkley woods.

On Santa Maria's very first night at Cherkley, Beaverbrook invited my wife and me to dinner and as a special treat for his French visitor he arranged for a French film with English subtitles to be shown in the cinema afterwards. Unhappily, it turned out to be a grotesque, cheaply made slapstick comedy featuring the French equivalent of Norman Wisdom. The reaction of Beaverbrook's sophisticated guest was a joy to behold.

Not long afterwards, Beaverbrook invited Pam Churchill to dinner with Santa Maria. Pat Hennessy tells how during the war Pam was encouraged to befriend Roosevelt's special adviser, Averill Harriman, as part of a plan to keep Averill Harriman on the British side. What is for sure is that Pam later married Averill Harriman. But that evening at Cherkley, meeting Santa Maria for the first time, Pam looked regal. She had a scintillating flow of conversation, an enormous supply of society gossip. Beaverbrook had his notepad out and was scribbling away with ideas he would use for the next day's *Evening Standard* Diary from the flow of Pam's conversation.

I sat watching Santa Maria. She was clearly put out and jealous and with her lack of English quite unable to enter the conversation. She was wearing a dress with a jacket top. Suddenly, she took off the jacket and there was a splendid strapless figure for all to see. Beaverbrook stopped listening to Pam Churchill and started looking at Santa Maria.

But Santa Maria's days were numbered. As I was soon to find out when Beaverbrook returned from the South of France and I was called round to see him on his first morning back.

It was a warm, sunny day and we were sitting out of doors next to the Cherkley lily pond. Beaverbrook looked round to make sure no one was in earshot and then said conspiratorially, 'You'll never guess what happened in Cap d'Ail. Raymond has fallen in love with Miss Rosenberg.'

Raymond was Lord Beaverbrook's valet at the time, a good-looking, wavy-haired young man who had never previously given any indication of being a lady's man. Miss Rosenberg was a new secretary. Beaverbrook was clearly very impressed with her ability in having attracted Raymond. It was the end of Santa Maria and the beginning of Miss Rosenberg.

Santa Maria came to an unhappy end. My understanding is that some time after she left Beaverbrook she committed suicide.

Miss Rosenberg, delicious, delectable Jo. She was quite a girl. Bob Edwards, when he was first with the *Sunday Express*, once went to Cap d'Ail unaware of Beaverbrook's relationship with her. At that time, Miss Rosenberg was not sleeping inside the big house but in the keeper's lodge at the gates.

On his second night there, after a good dinner at which Miss Rosenberg was present, Bob insisted on seeing her home, much to Beaverbrook's disgruntlement. But Bob, always the polite chap, kept on insisting that he would accompany Miss Rosenberg to her chamber door – and did, indeed, do so. But when he came back to the big house, he found that everything was locked up and Beaverbrook in a temper had gone to bed.

Bob was damn lucky not to have been sent home to London the next day. It was a lesson he never forgot.

The next and most formidable lady in Beaverbrook's life was Lady Dunn. She was the rich widow of Sir James Dunn, one of Beaverbrook's boyhood friends from Canada, and at first Beaverbrook was only interested in persuading her to spend some of the money she had been left on paintings which she would then donate to the Beaverbrook Art Gallery in Fredericton, New Brunswick.

She and James Dunn had been a remarkable couple. They flitted from one health diet to another. At one stage when they crossed the Atlantic they were on a sea water diet, but rightly they always insisted that the sea water be collected from the front of the *Queen Elizabeth* rather than run the risk of effluent from the water gathering at the back. When I knew her she was sometimes on a steak diet and would eat nothing but a one-pound steak, at other times on a pear diet when she would eat nothing but pears.

Christoforides Dunn had made her money in quite an interesting way. She had been a secretary in the *Evening Standard* typing pool working occasionally for the City Editor, W. S. Alexander, when Sir James Dunn came to town and wanted a temporary secretary. He ended up with her. At that time she was about nineteen and he would have been fifty-three. He was already married to his, I believe, second wife.

In Canada to which they returned, Sir James had a heart attack, whereupon his secretary wrote to his wife in London and said, 'This man needs attention. If you want to look after him I will step out of his life. But if you want me to look after him I suggest you step out of his life.' She married Dunn.

Sir James was Chairman of a company called Algoma Steel and before the war he had poured every cent he had into it but it was still not making a profit. Eventually, facing bankruptcy, he desperately needed a few extra thousand dollars to keep it going. Christoforides never hesitated. She handed over every penny he had ever given her in money and jewels to what seemed to be a hopeless task.

But in the end, thanks to the war, Dunn's enormous vision of Algoma Steel flourished and, when he died at the age of eighty-three, he left his wife something like £24 million, a huge fortune in those days. And, after his death, instead of living it up on the lolly, Lady Dunn sat, dressed in black, in a room in Canada mourning his ashes which she kept in an urn on the mantelpiece.

Chapman Pincher and his wife were invited by Lady Dunn to attend the opening of a James Dunn Medical School in a Canadian university, Dalhousie. When they arrived at their hotel in Dalhousie, they found that each of them had a bedroom with a separate bathroom and a joint sitting-room. It was a pretty palatial affair. When Pincher went to his private bathroom he noticed that there were two great tablets of soap in the bath – a soap called Sweetheart Soap.

That night after the ceremony he found that there was only one tablet of soap. He remarked on the disappearance to his wife who said, 'That's strange. The same thing has happened in my bathroom, too.'

Pincher, being a wonderful reporter, quickly found the answer to the mystery. James Dunn's favourite soap had been Sweetheart Soap. Lady Dunn, in tribute to his memory, had decided that all her guests would have Sweetheart Soap. But Lord Beaverbrook, who had also been invited to the opening, had found two tablets in his bathroom, had enquired why and had thought to himself, 'What a waste of soap since we are all only staying here one night.' So he sent his valet round to collect the spare soap from every guest's bathroom. The valet was instructed to take the soap back to Cherkley.

Lady Dunn was an arrogant, imperious, bird-like character, insufferably ignorant on many subjects, but there was one thing she was good at. She looked after Beaverbrook in these last declining and, I think, probably quite sexless years. She protected him like a ferocious nanny and she tried to treat all of us like wayward children.

On my last visit to Beaverbrook, then very ill in the South of France, Michael Foot was there, too, and after dinner I tried to persuade Michael to come into Monte Carlo with me since we knew that Beaverbrook would be going to bed at nine o'clock – a sad change from earlier days.

Lady Dunn wagged her stern finger. 'You will not go out

tonight,' she said. 'I will not have you coming back here disturbing the peace and disturbing Lord Beaverbrook. Why can't you, too, go to bed?'

In fact Michael, who was suffering from the after-effects of a car crash, did not come with me. So I went out on my own and didn't come back until two o'clock in the morning. I was not going to take orders from Lady Dunn. Nevertheless, when I did get back I took damned good care to take off my shoes and tiptoe up the stairs like a frightened little mouse.

There was one other woman in Beaverbrook's life during my time with him – Jean Campbell, his granddaughter.

She was high-spirited, black-haired girl and a most talented journalist. She later became the wife of Norman Mailer, briefly, and was also made correspondent of the *Evening Standard* in America. Beaverbrook adored her. To the old man, I suppose, she was the apotheosis of all his ideals and also of innocence.

At the time I first met Jean in the South of France with Beaverbrook she was nineteen, vivacious and could twist her grandfather round her little finger. She bounded in one day and told him that she had just met a charming old lady called Mrs Kelly who lived in a nearby villa and was there with her young grandson. Would he please invite Mrs Kelly and the grandson to dinner one evening? The grandson would have to come because Mrs Kelly had no staff and no one with whom she could leave the child.

Beaverbrook agreed, and Mrs Kelly and her grandson, about twelve years old, duly arrived for dinner. Mrs Kelly was a Blackpool landlady and, when I say landlady, I mean a boarding-house landlady. She must have made a comfortable fortune in Blackpool looking after bed-and-breakfast boarders. Enough to educate a son, so she told us, who had become a distinguished doctor. Enough also to buy a villa in Cap d'Ail, a villa which even in those days must have cost quite a bit of money.

Mrs Kelly sat on Beaverbrook's right-hand side at dinner. She clearly was absolutely unimpressed by him. She did not give a damn about politics and knew nothing at all about political figures. I doubt if she had even heard of Lord Beaverbrook.

Certainly she gave no indication of ever having read the *Daily Express*. Beaverbrook was absolutely out of his depth. His scintillating conversation fell on completely deaf ears. The evening dragged on miserably.

After dinner we went into the library, and there, Beaverbrook, clearly bored by it all, fidgeted restively and prepared to announce his need to go to bed. But Jean had put on the radiogram and there was at that time a song of which Beaverbrook was particularly fond. It was called the 'Whiffenpoof' song and it had a melody which went, 'Three black sheep, gentlemen songsters, out on a spree/damned from here to eternity.'

For the time being this was Beaverbrook's song and when it was on the radiogram he settled back to listen to it. As it finished he got up to say goodnight to everyone, but the record player jammed and instead of a new tune coming the 'Whiffenpoof' song came up again and again and again and each time Beaverbrook felt compelled to listen.

Eventually the evening ended with Beaverbrook still there. He escorted Mrs Kelly and her grandson graciously to the door. To Mrs Kelly he said, 'Goodnight, Mrs Kelly.' But to the little grandson he shook his hand warmly and said, 'It was so nice having you.'

But Jean was growing up when I knew her. She was of Beaverbrook blood and of the same inclinations as well as the same talents. She became friendly with Prince Stanislaus Radziwill, who was probably twice her age, a Polish aristocrat already twice married and soon afterwards to become the husband of Jackie Kennedy's sister, Lee.

The old man was appalled. He froze in angry Calvinistic reaction towards the liaison. Radziwill became very unpopular indeed. Jean herself took the agony of separation from her grandfather. They were no longer nearly so close.

But perhaps the worst blow for Beaverbrook came much later, on Christmas Day 1962. Just after midnight on Christmas Day I received a telephone call from New York. It was from Jean.

She was on the point of setting off to fly to England. Could she possibly come and have lunch with me at my home in Surrey?

77

And could I possibly arrange for a car to meet her at the airport? I replied that of course I would. The car met Jean and Jean duly arrived rather late for Christmas dinner with my family.

She was very, very pregnant – by Norman Mailer. And the reason for her flight was that she planned to go and break the news to her grandfather. It must have been a very sad Christmas Day for the old boy.

But then maybe Beaverbrook deserved what happened to him. For he was certainly not too good in his treatment of his grandchildren. His grandson, Johnny Kidd, was very self-conscious about his height as a child. Between the ages of ten and fourteen he grew at a rate of more than three inches a year and by the time he went to Harrow at the age of fourteen he was six foot three.

Every school holiday he tried desperately to see his grandfather. Not simply because he had an enormous affection for the old man – which he had. But for the more practical reason that it usually meant £1 and possibly even £5 being put into his hand at the end of the visit.

During one holiday, he went to Arlington House in London to see Beaverbrook. The butler, Mead, showed him to the sitting-room and said, 'Will you wait in here? His Lordship will be with you in a minute.' Johnny stood there waiting and a few minutes later Beaverbrook entered the room, looked at the youngster and said 'My God!' – a reference to his gangling height.

He then said to the boy, 'What do you plan to do when you leave school?'

Young Johnny was ready for the question and had an answer prepared which he thought might well qualify for £5 rather than £1.

'I am thinking of going into newspapers grandfather,' he replied.

'I've got a better idea,' said Beaverbrook. 'Why don't you join a circus?'

It was a cruel, crucifying remark which left the boy without any words of answer.

In 1953 Beaverbrook appointed me Deputy Editor of the *Evening Standard*.

I served on that newspaper for over a year and found it a happy experience apart from the fact that I was in enormous pain from a stomach ulcer – an ulcer of which happily Beaverbrook knew nothing. For he disapproved of illness and he had a tendency to write off anyone who suffered anything other than the most trivial of illnesses. Sometimes he was right in doing so. At other times he was wrong.

Harold Macmillan, for instance, he wrote off around that period because Macmillan had had a gall-bladder operation. He was quite wrong, of course. Macmillan's gall-bladder operation was carried out successfully, whereas poor Anthony Eden's was not. And whatever went wrong after Eden's operation was to change the whole course of history.

But meanwhile I was arriving at the *Evening Standard* very early in the morning feeling quite ill for a good deal of the time. At one stage I was going through a tin of De Witt's anti-acid powder every day.

Percy Elland, the Editor of the *Evening Standard*, was a great-hearted, plump, rosy-cheeked man with twinkly eyes and a splendid sense of humour. He also had an enormous sense of duty. He once staggered me by discussing quite seriously how he could get to the office in the event of war breaking out and London being atom-bombed. The thought of getting to London at all in such circumstances had never even occurred to me.

At times Percy found the going a little tough. He was not a political editor, and so found himself at a disadvantage with Beaverbrook.

At one stage I returned from holiday on a Monday to find to my horror that the first edition had devoted its front page to racing. I had no time to comment on it before Elland and I were summoned to see Lord Beaverbrook at Arlington House.

When we arrived there we found that Max was already in attendance.

Beaverbrook was hopping mad.

'Who took the decision to put racing on page one of the *Evening Standard*?' he demanded, almost screamed.

He looked at me. 'Do you agree to having racing on page one of the *Evening Standard*?'

I replied that I most certainly did not, which although true was perhaps a shade less than loyal of me.

He glared at Max. 'Do you agree with having racing on page one of the *Evening Standard*?'

Max said he did not agree.

Beaverbrook turned on Elland but Percy gamely held his ground. He argued that the first edition was essentially bought by people wanting to know which horse to back, that sales had been falling off recently, especially in the suburbs, and that this was a calculated and deliberate attempt to regain some early edition sales. His argument was that people who bought the first edition for racing would subsequently buy later editions to see the race results.

Beaverbrook listened to this and his anger evaporated. Grudgingly, he agreed to give the new scheme a trial.

Afterwards Percy and I went down in the lift together and back to the office. On our way to the car Percy looked at me musingly and said: 'Do you know whose idea it was to put racing on the front page? It was Max's.'

This may seem like a story against Max Aitken. It is not. Max was in many ways a wonderful, good-hearted, splendid leader of men. He was himself a man of enormous courage and with a proven record of gallantry. He venerated his father and sometimes was treated roughly by him but he never stopped loving him and respecting him. And he was afraid to confess that it was he who had taken the decision.

Then, one morning in the early summer of 1954, Beaverbrook took me walking again at Cherkley and said, 'In the autumn I will make you Editor of the *Sunday Express*.'

It was a heady prospect to face a summer which was going to end in such enormous triumph. But, of course, it was all very secret. The current Editor of the *Sunday Express*, Harold Keeble, knew nothing about his approaching demise. Nor did anyone else except Beaverbrook and myself.

All summer the pain from my stomach increased.

Although he himself drank only whisky, Beaverbrook insisted that his dinner guests drank champagne.

I have never much cared for champagne. In 1954 it was torture for me even to touch it.

But I dared not tell Beaverbrook.

So I drank the champagne and subsequently suffered after every dinner the most appalling pains and sickness. But Beaverbrook never knew about it and in October at the age of thirty-five I took over at the *Sunday Express*. A few weeks later I keeled over in the office with a massive stomach haemorrhage from a duodenal ulcer.

IV

IN THE SOUTH of France or whenever it was warm Beaverbrook had the habit of sitting out of doors naked except for a large floppy straw hat.

I remember one Sunday afternoon at Cap d'Ail, the Sunday newspapers had just arrived by special dispatch from London. Beaverbrook began to devour the *Sunday Express*, handing me the *Sunday Dispatch*.

At that time there was a multiplicity of Sunday newspapers, all costing two old pennies. There was the *Sunday Times*, the *Empire News*, the *Sunday Graphic*, *Reynold's News*, the *Sunday Pictorial*, the *People*, the *Sunday Dispatch* and, of course, the *Sunday Express*.

But it was the *Sunday Dispatch* that was our main rival and the fight that went on between us we knew was to the death. And the *Sunday Dispatch* was doing rather well – because it was publishing soft-porn serials. The current one, 'Caroline', was the tale of an attractive, nubile aristocratic girl during the French Revolution.

That week the author had excelled himself. He had Caroline in a hay loft being attacked by a lusty French peasant. There was a blow-by-blow account of her struggles, of her clothing being ripped off and finally of the ecstasy which despite herself swept over her.

I said to Beaverbrook, 'This is the worst yet. They really have descended to the depths this week,' and handed over the paper to him.

He began to read. But not for long. Pressing a towel round his middle he said, 'I think I'll take this up to bed and read.'

It was clear that even in his seventies Beaverbrook had not lost the capacity to become sexually excited.

Nor the capacity to keep his nerve. For it was during this period that Randolph Churchill began to attack Lord Rothermere, the owner of the *Sunday Dispatch*, calling him the 'Pornographer Royal' for running salacious serials like 'Caroline'. Rothermere lost his nerve and ordered the editor to clean up the paper. The result was disaster. And a succession of editors.

'The *Dispatch* have appointed a new Editor,' Beaverbrook said to me on the telephone one evening in my cottage at Mickleham. 'He is a young fellow called Wally Hayes. I'm told he is very good. You're going to have to be on your toes.'

I was bloody angry. I retorted, 'Well, if he's better than me there's nothing I can do about it. But if he's no better than the other editors they have had, then he'll go the same God-damned way as the rest of them.'

He did too. He went to the Ford Motor Company where he ran their public relations department and has since had a meteoric career, becoming Vice-Chairman of Ford of Europe Inc.

The next Editor of the *Dispatch* was Herbert Gunn, whom Beaverbrook had fired from the *Evening Standard* for Gunn's largely innocent part in the Strachey–Fuchs affair. I had considerable respect for Gunn's qualities as a news man. But perhaps I had overestimated him. Or he had lost his touch? One story illustrates the point.

On Saturday nights into each Sunday newspaper office come the first editions of its rivals. They are eagerly scanned lest there is a news story which has been missed, though quite often it is an established part of policy, certainly it was on my part, to keep a really good story out of the first edition so that the rivals are not subsequently able to catch up.

On this particular night the *Sunday Dispatch*'s first edition had the front-page headline: Who Is the Mystery Man in the Wills

Divorce? The story under it was a follow-up on a court case which had been absorbing the attention of the British public during the previous week. It involved Edwina Wills, of the great tobacco family. She was fabulously rich, there was a great deal of scandal and there had been a man involved whose name had not been divulged in court.

When I saw that *Sunday Dispatch* headline I thought it could mean only one thing – that Gunn knew the name of the man, was deliberately holding it out of the first edition and would announce it to the world in later editions.

The *Sunday Express* would not be left behind. It became absolutely essential that we get that name ourselves for the third edition. We had less than three hours in which to do it. And by the greatest of flukes we did. The result was that the following morning the *Sunday Dispatch* still came out with the headline about the 'Mystery Man' and the *Sunday Express* headline gave the answer.

It was the end of Gunn. The *Sunday Express* continued to outstrip the *Sunday Dispatch* in every possible way. And in 1961, not long after this, the *Dispatch* finally put up the white flag and was taken over by the *Sunday Express*.

But there were times when I found the job of Editor a tough one.

When I returned from my illness, I was living on sponge cake and consuming large quantities of milk and cocoa every day on a duodenal diet. Christmas time arrived and I was proposing to run a series of articles in the newspaper on 'How to Make a Million' by our City Editor, Edward Westropp.

Westropp's first article arrived on the Thursday morning and, although I realised there was a good deal that still had to be done to it, I had it put into type. At the same time I rang Westropp and told him the changes and alterations and additions which the article would require.

At about 4.30 p.m. I left the office to take my children to the Bertram Mills circus at Olympia. When I arrived home later that night I had an angry Max on the telephone. Where had I been? Did I not realise that the Chairman, E. J. Robertson, had been trying to contact me? Was I unaware that the Chairman did not like the idea of the series of articles we proposed running on Sunday?

He went on and on on this tack. Rather frostily, I told him that I had been given the job of editing the newspaper and if they didn't have faith in my judgement then they ought to get someone else. In my opinion, the articles were good and would be successful.

This incident in a way is symptomatic of the problem facing a new editor. Quite rightly in any newspaper the management are fearful of a new editor because, while it may take many years to build a paper, a new man can very easily destroy it in a very short time.

I was perhaps too young, impatient and hot-headed to realise that at the time. Confidence in an editor comes with success and the more success there is then the less interference with his judgement. At the same time it is absolutely necessary for an editor to stick hard by his opinion. If he becomes a tool of management then he is doomed to disaster. And so is his newspaper.

In the case of the Westropp articles, I wondered how E. J. Robertson ever came to read them since that was not in his province at all. It has only recently occurred to me that John Gordon, a former Editor, had probably been stirring things up a little. At any rate, I emerged from this first encounter reasonably triumphant. And I had also imparted quite firmly the knowledge that I was not prepared to be mucked around in my judgement.

About a year later we published a fine splash story on a Saturday night alleging that Britain's supersonic fighter aeroplane, the Swift, could not break the sound barrier – not unless it was going downhill with a following wind. The story, written by Arthur Brenard, was a sensation. Vickers, who made the aeroplane, were very angry indeed. For some extraordinary reason it also upset Beaverbrook, even though it was true.

I was asked why I had printed the story without consultation. I replied that I saw no need for consultation since I had satisfied myself that the story was correct. A few days later it was suggested to me that from now on the manager of the *Sunday Express* should sit in at my editorial conference.

I recalled the wise advice once given to me by Percy Elland to the effect that an editor should never have a manager sit in at an editorial conference since it meant a conflict of loyalty among the staff. For they never know for sure who is running the show – editor or manager.

So I refused. I refused adamantly. And under pressure I continued to refuse.

There followed the unhappiest months of my editorship. Every issue of the *Sunday Express* was criticised. It was made clear that I was making a poor job of producing the paper. The campaign reached such a pitch that it became obvious that I was being pushed out.

I saw Max Aitken and told him my thoughts. He did not disagree. I went home to Mickleham and told Pam that she must go out that very day and find us a new house of our own which we would certainly need when I left the *Sunday Express*.

The next day I was told that Beaverbrook would see me on Friday morning. I went to see him at Arlington House and we went walking in the park. He proceeded to continue with the criticism of the *Sunday Express* and then he said, 'Why don't you let a manager come and sit at conference?'

I told him why. He seemed unimpressed.

At the end of our walk Beaverbrook made a gesture of conciliation. He thought things would go better on the *Sunday Express*. He still had faith in me. Would I now allow a manager into conference? Again, I shook my head.

But I remained as Editor and I feel in retrospect that all this was a plan merely to exert a degree of control over me to which I was not prepared to submit.

For Beaverbrook exerted the most careful control. While he was in this country he kept close contact with his editors by telephone. In the early morning he would be on the telephone to the Editor of the *Evening Standard*. By lunchtime he had switched to the Editor of the *Daily Express* and by the afternoon he was speaking to the Editor of the *Sunday Express*.

Even when he was out of the country, which I guess for tax purposes was for most of the year, he still read every one of his newspapers every day. He would then dictate a series of messages on his dictaphone to his editors and in London his secretary, George Millar, would transcribe the disc which had been sent by airmail and circulate the various items of praise or criticism.

So even when he was abroad, you knew that every article you published, every news story which you missed was being observed by the proprietor. It gave each editor the impression that Lord Beaverbrook was looking over his shoulder, even though he might be some three or four thousand miles away.

In the post-storm calm which eventually followed our row, Beaverbrook said to me, 'Even after forty years I still don't know what sells the *Sunday Express*. A newspaper which devotes so much of its space to politics should not really sell more than two million copies.'

Even that figure was an exaggeration. The facts of the matter are that no newspaper beamed at an AB socio-economic readership has ever sold more than 1.6 million. There seems to be some sort of sound barrier beyond which a serious newspaper cannot pass.

One of the reasons why the *Sunday Express* had such a large circulation at the time was that all Sunday newspapers sold for two old pence. These were the days before decimalisation. And two old pence are less than one new penny. There was little if any television as a Sunday counter-attraction to reading newspapers. Many families took three or four Sunday newspapers to while away their day. And the newspapers themselves were small in size. The *Sunday Express* was confined to some eight pages when I became its Editor.

Over the years all that changed.

The *Sunday Express*, which had formerly sold at exactly the same price as the *Mirror, People* and *News of the World*, found itself selling at a price considerably higher than its rivals. These were circumstances in which the circulation was inevitably bound to drop. But it still remained astonishingly high and the newspaper remained quite astoundingly financially successful. For we still retained the highest AB readership of any newspaper in the land. While having a spread of Cs and Ds as well.

There were from time to time attempts to make me change the formula. In the 1970s Victor Matthews, who rarely read anything outside the financial pages, was keen that we should have more of them in the *Sunday Express*.

My reply was, 'Of course we can. We can have five City pages just like the *Sunday Telegraph*, providing you are prepared to accept the fact that we will then also have a *Sunday Telegraph* circulation.'

For in fact it was enormously difficult substantially to alter the *Sunday Express* formula.

If I had tried to push it down-market by introducing sex and sensation I would have alienated the up-market readers as well as some of the down-market readers who bought the *Sunday Express* precisely because they wanted a newspaper that was fit to leave lying around the house for their children to read. On the other hand if I had tried to put it up-market, by introducing more City pages for example, I could only have done so at the cost of introducing material into the newspaper which perhaps the majority of our readers uninterested in finance would not read.

From the start, I was utterly determined that the *Sunday Express* should be a newspaper which made people feel better, not worse, on a Sunday. That it should be a newspaper of optimism. I had been brought up in Glasgow where the mournful sound of church bells pealing across grey tenement streets had made Sunday a day of gloom. I wanted to make it a day of cheer. And I introduced country articles which brought a breath of fresh rustic air into the lives of readers who were city-dwellers.

I think in retrospect that I can claim to have been reasonably successful in keeping the balance.

In my early days as Editor I made my first and last contact with that legendary socialist Prime Minister of the immediate post-war years, Clement Attlee. His decisiveness in Cabinet was said to have been without equal. I wanted a leader-page article for the *Sunday Express* and it occurred to me that Mr Attlee, by this time Lord Attlee, would be the perfect man to write it.

He was at that time living in a house called Cherry Tree Cottage. I rang him. He answered the telephone himself and I explained the purpose of my call. He listened attentively as I outlined the argument I wished him to pursue. Occasionally he interrupted with a 'Yes' in a very clipped tone.

At the end of my conversation, in which I outlined the entire argument, he said quite simply, 'How many words?'

'Nine hundred,' I replied.

'How much?' he asked.

'One hundred pounds.'

'I am coming up to the Oxford & Cambridge Club tomorrow,' he said. 'I will have the article finished by that time. Could you send a messenger to collect it at 12.45?'

I put down the telephone and told myself what a wonderful Prime Minister he must have been with this enormous clipped power of decision. No wonder he had been so able to control a Cabinet.

At 12.45 p.m. on the Friday, my messenger went to the Oxford & Cambridge Club and picked up the article. It bore not the slightest relationship to the subject we had discussed. It was a long rambling account of Attlee's early days in the East End. We sent him his cheque. But there was only one place to put the article. The dustbin.

My respect for Attlee evaporated.

But not my respect for Winston Churchill. The great ambition of every young newspaperman in the 1950s was to meet him. It was certainly mine. And one evening Beaverbrook asked me to look in at Cherkley on my way home.

He was in his library and told me that he would be leaving in a few minutes' time as he was going to Chartwell to dine with Churchill. He had so little else to say to me that I wondered if that indeed were the reason he had invited me to look in – just so that he could name-drop about going to Chartwell.

His butler Mead appeared. 'The car's at the door, Sir,' he said, helping Beaverbrook on with his overcoat.

Just as they were leaving, Beaverbrook shouted 'Clark' and out of one of the other rooms scuttled Douglas Clark, who by this time had moved from the *Sunday Express* and was parliamentary lobby correspondent of the *Daily Express*.

'Come on Clark,' said Beaverbrook. 'We'll be late.'

Douglas Clark flashed me a friendly smile and disappeared

into the night with Beaverbrook. I felt deeply envious at the thought that Douglas was going to be meeting Churchill and having dinner with him – something that had always been my dream.

But I had forgotten my envy by the next time I saw Douglas. 'How did it go?' I asked. 'Tell me, what is he like?'

Douglas Clark grinned ruefully and told me that on the way to Chartwell on a dark night and in a country road Beaverbrook had suddenly said to the driver, 'Stop at the bus stop. Mr Clark is leaving us here.' He turned to Douglas. 'You can find your own way home from here, can't you, Mr Clark?'

So Douglas came no nearer to meeting Churchill than I did.

Some years later, in 1962, I came near to meeting him again. Lord Rothermere was giving a party in a house by St James's Park and the guests of honour were Winston Churchill, then a very old man, Harold Macmillan and Lord Beaverbrook. The three of them sat together on a settee and the other guests filed past and genuflected, almost literally, in front of them.

I was milling around the bar when I noticed a quite ravishing woman who could not have been much more than thirty-eight or thirty-nine. We talked about Lord Beaverbrook. 'I had him once during the war,' she said. I had not the slightest doubt that she was telling the truth. Yet during the war she must have been in her teens while Beaverbrook was in his late sixties.

Beaverbrook once told me how at the time of Dunkirk, Churchill had called the Chiefs of Staff one by one into his study at 10 Downing Street and, with Beaverbrook sitting beside him, asked each of them the same question.

'Can Britain survive?'

And each single one of them gave the same answer.

'No. We have now no chance of avoiding defeat.'

Which raises the question: If the Germans had made a successful landing in England would Churchill himself have remained to fight them on the beaches and in the streets or would he have lit off for America to form a government and continue the war from there?

I suspect that he would have gone to America. But so what? It seems to me that it would have been just as honourable for

Churchill to go to America as it was for de Gaulle to come to England. Certainly George Malcolm Thomson, who was then Beaverbrook's secretary, swore to me when we were both writing leaders on the *Daily Express* that one weekend in 1940 all of them, including himself, had their bags packed for the transatlantic crossing.

There is another question. How loyal was Beaverbrook to Churchill? Did he ever want to become prime minister himself? In my own mind there is but one answer to those questions. He was loyal, but he also wanted to become prime minister and he thought at one stage that there was a good chance that he might. And that, according to Pat Hennessy, was the basic reason for Beaverbrook's resignation from the wartime government and his outspoken advocacy of the Second Front. Beaverbrook certainly always openly lamented his decision to have accepted a peerage comparatively early in life.

Sir Jock Colville had been secretary successively to Chamberlain, Attlee and Churchill, and to Princess Elizabeth, and was again by Churchill's side after the Tory victory in 1951. I met him at Beaverbrook's dinner table and we became friends and frequent luncheon companions.

At one stage, we formed a lunch club which we called the Hedgers and Ditchers. The club's membership was exceedingly limited. Apart from Jock and myself it consisted of Roy Jenkins, Mark Bonham-Carter, Edgar Lustgarten, Quintin Hogg, Walter Monckton and Ian Gilmour. We met once a month in the Braganza restaurant in Soho where we ate well at a modest price. I still have a letter from Quintin Hogg in which he told me he was enclosing a cheque for two pounds five shillings and one penny in payment of his share of the previous month's bill.

The club did not last long but my association with Colville did. And he told me, years later, an eerie story about Churchill. At the time Churchill was living in a house in Hyde Park Gate. One January morning he was standing at the window of his study looking out at the rain-swept park while Jock was busy sorting out the papers on his desk.

Suddenly Churchill broke the silence. 'Do you know, Jock, that my father died this day?'

Colville muttered something non-committal, sensing that Churchill was thinking aloud rather than talking to him. It was Churchill's next remark which shook him.

'I will die this day too,' he said. And then after a moment's silence he added, 'If only he had lived I think I would have got on terms with him.'

And so bizarrely it came to pass. Lord Randolph Churchill had died on 24 January 1895. Winston died on 24 January 1965.

During the last year of Winston's prime ministership his mind was no longer what it had been. He had suffered a series of strokes, the first of which occurred while staying with Beaverbrook at Cap d'Ail and which had been kept secret from the public. During this period Rab Butler used to say that the effective government of the country was in the hands of two young men, Winston's Principal Private Secretary, who was Jock Colville, and his Parliamentary Private Secretary, who was his own son-in-law, Christopher Soames.

If that were indeed so, then the country would not have been all that badly served. Both were men of exceptional talent.

Christopher was to become and remain a good friend throughout the years. He was a joyous companion always full of fun and fizz but with a sharp first-class brain and an acute awareness of what ordinary people were thinking – a quality not too often found in Tory MPs. He told me how at the start of his political career he used to get physically sick before every big public meeting he had to address. He confessed his failing to his father-in-law and was staggered to be told in reply, 'Don't worry, my boy. It's exactly the same with me.'

I first met Bob Edwards on the night Churchill resigned as Prime Minister. We were in the middle of a newspaper strike and so a bunch of us were invited to discuss the resignation on BBC radio after the nine o'clock news.

I liked Bob very much. He was then Editor of *Tribune*, which was very much in the control of Michael Foot. In fact I so liked Bob that I decided I ought to take him on to the *Sunday Express* and told Beaverbrook of my intention.

Beaverbrook was at first agreeable, but then one Saturday

night he telephoned me at the Savoy and said that he had changed his mind, that Michael Foot had pleaded with him not to interfere with the editorship of *Tribune* and he felt that in these circumstances we should lay off Bob Edwards.

I felt a little aggrieved about this since I felt it was very unfair on Bob. I need not have worried. Shortly afterwards Beaverbrook signed Bob Edwards himself and put him on to the *Evening Standard*, where he used him to write pro-Tory articles under a pseudonym. No doubt the old man himself felt it was a little droll to have the former Editor of the socialist *Tribune* writing Tory articles under the name of Lord Richard Strong.

After a year on the *Evening Standard*, Bob came to join me on the *Sunday Express* as Deputy Editor. One Friday evening in a television show Randolph Churchill made a vicious attack on Bob and described him as a paid hack.

I had not seen the programme but the next morning Beaverbrook rang me and said that he had seen it, that he thought it was a terrible attack and that I ought to try and 'steam' Bob up about it. Bob really, suggested Beaverbrook, ought to take legal action. Was it not terrible that Churchill, who had himself won a legal action after being called a hack, should be calling Bob Edwards the same thing?

It was clear to me that Beaverbrook must be in the midst of one of his recurrent huffs with Randolph. Nevertheless I did as I was told and found that Bob had not seen the programme either. But he very quickly did become steamed up. The office lawyer also helped in the process and within no time at all Bob had taken out a libel writ against Randolph Churchill.

So far so good. It seemed certain that he would win his case. Time passed and one Thursday morning I was invited to go walking with Beaverbrook on Hampstead Heath. We tramped about the Heath and finally Beaverbrook came to the point. 'I think,' he said, 'that this boy Edwards is making a great mistake in his libel action against Churchill. Journalists shouldn't go to law. I think he is very ill advised. I suggest you try and persuade him to drop the case.'

I realised what had happened. Either there had been a *rapprochement* between Randolph and Beaverbrook or else

Randolph was making threatening gestures in other directions.

At any rate I wanted no part in it. I explained to Beaverbrook in mounting anger that on his own express instructions I had urged Bob to take legal action in the first place. It would be quite impossible at this stage for me now to try and persuade him to drop the action. We parted on rather cool terms and I rushed back to the office, arriving there just as Bob was leaving for lunch.

Briefly I explained to him what had happened and said, 'The old so-and-so is trying to get you to drop this action. Let's talk about it after lunch.'

But after lunch Bob did not return to the office, and at half-past three I got a call from Beaverbrook. 'Can you imagine what has happened? That crazy fellow Edwards has resigned. He has written me the most extraordinary letter in which he has more or less told me to go and get stuffed.'

The result was a triumph for Bob Edwards. He was persuaded to withdraw his resignation and Randolph Churchill settled out of court. It also meant that Bob had gained the respect of Beaverbrook. The old man now knew that he could go just so far with him, but no farther.

While Bob was still my deputy he was, of course, in charge of the newspaper while I was on holiday. On one such occasion I arrived back from a break and Bob told me that he had been asked by Lord Beaverbrook to publish an article by a distinguished Australian who had been the Australian High Commissioner in London and whose name is so distinguished that I have completely forgotten it.

Bob, who was now himself going on holiday, left the article over for me. I read it and was appalled. It was dreadful. The next weekend was a Bank Holiday and it never occurred to me to use such a dreadful article on a Bank Holiday. I simply put it on one side and forgot about it.

On the following Tuesday morning Max Aitken asked me to come and see him.

'What,' he asked me, 'ever happened to that article which Lord Beaverbrook wanted to have printed?'

I replied that it was such a dull article that it would have been quite impossible to have used it in the *Sunday Express*, especially on a Bank Holiday Sunday.

Max looked at me ruefully and then he said, 'You ought to have been with me on Sunday. It was a fantastic experience. There we were at Cherkley with my father turning over page after page looking for this article. Finally he arrived at the last sports page and he looked at me and said, "But there is no article in here. What has happened to it?" '

And as Max told me the story he himself dissolved in laughter at the recollection of his angry father's face.

One Christmas Eve, Bob was delighted to receive a telephone call from Lord Beaverbrook inviting him to come and bring his wife to dinner.

On his way down to Leatherhead Bob suddenly realised that he should take a Christmas present to Lady Dunn who was then Lord Beaverbrook's house guest. But all the shops were closed. He managed to find one florist in the suburbs of London which was still open and dashed in and bought a huge armful of the most expensive flowers they had. Those he duly presented to Lady Dunn.

Lady Dunn disappeared and returned soon afterwards to hand Bob a little present in return. It was a cigarette lighter in a beautiful Asprey's box.

Bob was enchanted with it. There was only problem. It didn't work. So Bob took it into Asprey's and asked an assistant whether it could be put into working condition. The assistant took the lighter away and shortly afterwards returned with it working perfectly.

Bob accepted the lighter and said, 'Thank you very much. But tell me, isn't it slightly odd that a great firm like Asprey's should provide a defective lighter to one of your most important customers.'

The assistant looked startled. 'Which customer, Sir?'

'Lady Dunn,' said Bob.

'But Sir,' the assistant replied in a rather diffident voice, 'this lighter was not bought here. We would never let a lighter go out in that condition. I think you will find, Sir, that it had already been used.'

But if Bob's career went up like a rocket, from time to time it came down like a rocket too.

From Deputy Editor of the *Sunday Express* he went to be Editor of the *Daily Express*. There was one great, insuperable snag, however. For while Bob adored Beaverbrook, he was at heart still a Labour supporter and the leader column of the *Daily Express* and some of the leader-page articles began to show less than white-hot enthusiasm for the Tory cause. In the end he got the sack. But when he failed quickly to get another job it was Beaverbrook who came to his rescue and to the astonishment of everyone sent him to Glasgow as Editor of the *Evening Citizen*. There was even greater astonishment when one year later he was restored again as Editor of the *Daily Express*. In the whole history of Fleet Street there had never been anything like it.

Bob's own view of the matter was that his original sacking had been because of pressure from Max Aitken, that Max didn't like him, that Max resented his closeness to Beaverbrook and was maybe even jealous of him. He was fortified in that view when Max sacked him again shortly after Beaverbrook's death. But he was quite wrong. The only reason he was sacked was that he was not the right man to edit a Tory newspaper. Although, as his subsequent distinguished career with the *People* and the *Sunday Mirror* showed, he was the brilliant editor of a socialist one.

It was not until many years later when I read his memoirs, *Goodbye Fleet Street*, that I realised where Bob Edwards had gone wrong.

Because he had never known his own father, a fact of which I was at the time quite unaware, he looked upon Beaverbrook as a father figure. I think he also deceived himself into thinking that, in return, Beaverbrook looked upon him as a son. He was wrong. Beaverbrook loved only one man like a son and that was his son, Max. He might often have spoken disparagingly about Max, and he might have treated him like an office boy, but he still adored him. And for Bob to imagine he was in any way ever going to supplant Max was crazy.

John Gordon, who had the title of Editor-in-Chief and was a predecessor of mine as the Editor of the *Sunday Express*, was one of the greatest journalists of his time. He had an enormous capacity for sensing what ordinary people were thinking. He himself came from a humble background in Dundee. He remained throughout his life a Scots Presbyterian but it was extraordinarily difficult to like him. He had a huge conceit of himself and an absolute unwillingness ever to admit to having been wrong. Once when in his column he had made a dreadful error and was forced the following week to apologise, he put all the blame on 'my trusted researcher'.

My early days with Gordon were difficult. I suppose in part that was because I disliked the idea of his having even the honorary title of Editor-in-Chief. But none the less he was a very great journalist even if he was inclined on occasions to be a little on the mean side.

Hugh Cudlipp during his time on the *Sunday Express* told how on one occasion Gordon said to him, 'Are you doing anything on Sunday, Hugh?' Cudlipp thought to himself, 'My God, this is it. He is going to invite me to his home, perhaps with my wife, for lunch or for dinner.'

'No, nothing at all,' he said eagerly.

'Good,' said John Gordon. 'In that case can I suggest you drive past my house in Addiscombe? There is a wonderful display of daffodils.'

On another occasion Logan Gourlay, who was then the show business writer for the *Sunday Express* and was quite new to the job, received a present of a magnificent Ronson table cigarette lighter. He was unsure whether or not he should accept the gift and went in to see John Gordon.

'What do you suggest I do with this, Sir?' he asked. 'Should I send it back?'

'No, don't send it back,' said Gordon. 'Just leave it with me. There is no chance of my being corrupted.'

The only difficulty I have in swallowing this story entirely is that it was a bit out of character for Logan Gourlay to have refused a gift of this kind even during his first few weeks on the *Sunday Express*.

Logan Gourlay was working one Friday night on the *Sunday Express*, and because it was Friday night he was utterly alone in the office. Suddenly a telephone began to ring. No one answered it, naturally enough, because there was no one at the extension. Then another telephone rang. Then another and another until finally Gourlay picked up one of them and a voice at the other end said, 'Is that the *Sunday Express*? Hold on, Mr Churchill wants to speak to you.'

And before Gourlay knew what was happening on to the telephone came Winston Churchill, then Leader of the Opposition in the days before his own return to power in 1951.

'What's the news tonight?' demanded Churchill.

Gourlay looked desperately around at the empty desks and said, 'I don't really know, Sir.'

'What do you mean, don't know?' demanded Churchill.

'Well, it's only Friday night, Sir,' said Gourlay. 'We don't come out until tomorrow night.'

'Good God,' said Churchill, 'I've got the wrong day.'

As far as Gordon is concerned, my only experience of his meanness was when he telephoned me one day and said, 'Do you use safety razor blades?'

I replied that I did.

'Good,' said Gordon, 'I don't use them myself and someone has sent me a gross of them. I'll let you have a packet.'

And so he did. One single packet of safety razor blades. Heaven knows what he did with the remaining 143.

But by the time John Gordon had reached the grand old age of eighty he was quite reconciled to me and I to him, although we never came close to any form of friendship and I certainly never admired him in the way I admired Beaverbrook.

On his eightieth birthday we arranged a magnificent dinner for him in the banqueting room in Whitehall. Max was going to make the main speech and a second speech had to be made. Privately I suppose I had been hoping that it might be me who was asked to make it. Instead Max decided to ask Peter Rawlinson, who had been our office lawyer and who was then Attorney-General. In the event Rawlinson was unable to appear and at the last moment Max asked Sir Arthur Bryant, the eminent historian who was on a retainer from the *Sunday Express*, to make the speech.

It had been arranged that a present was going to be given to John Gordon – a Rolls-Royce which was sitting outside awaiting the end of the dinner.

Arthur Bryant, in this crowded and distinguished gathering, got up to make his speech and unhappily he got just one thing wrong. Instead of alluding to John Gordon throughout the speech he, perhaps because he hardly knew John Gordon, and perhaps also because he had not had time to prepare a speech, referred throughout to 'John Junor'.

As he sat down Max got up and said, 'Well you made a right balls of that one, didn't you?'

My reaction was that if Bryant had kept on speaking a few more minutes it might have been me and not John Gordon who got the Rolls-Royce.

Manny Shinwell told me how during the 1947 fuel crisis, when he was Minister of Fuel and there was a tremendous shortage of coal and anthracite, he received an anonymous letter which alleged that John Gordon, then Editor of the *Sunday Express* and an outspoken opponent of the socialist government, was buying great loads of anthracite illegally and off the ration. It could have meant a charge against John Gordon in court and the letter was very well documented.

Shinwell decided on a move which he thought might do him no harm from a public relations point of view. He wrote to John Gordon, told him what the anonymous letter writer had said and further told him that he, Shinwell, intended taking no action of any kind.

John Gordon wrote back saying how pleased he was at what Shinwell had done and adding that he thought he knew who had written the anonymous letter – someone with a grudge.

The very next Sunday John Gordon's column came out in the *Sunday Express* with a most devastating attack on Manny Shinwell. Which goes, I suppose, to show that you cannot buy a hard-hitting journalist.

And never was that more true than of Edward Westropp, our brilliant City Editor. When he died Ted left only pennies. That was because of his absolute honesty and his utter refusal ever to speculate or to make money out of the shares which he tipped.

He once told me how Lord Fraser, the father of the late Sir Hugh Fraser, had arranged a meeting with him, a meeting in which he presumably hoped to influence Westropp. Fraser arriving carrying a suitcase full of pound notes. Westropp laughed at the pound notes but he liked Fraser, as indeed I did too. There was always in the *Sunday Express* a friendly word for Lord Fraser. But there was never any question of bribing Ted Westropp.

Ted alas died before his time in a car crash in 1962 on the Kingston Bypass. He was dragged from his wrecked car saying, 'I'm not too bad, not too bad at all.' It was a severe blow, for his column was avidly read by investors everywhere. And nor was it the only blow which affected the *Sunday Express* enormously during my early years there. A second major blow was when we lost perhaps the most fantastic, exciting man who ever worked for me – Bob Pitman.

His story began when he submitted an article on the Liberal Party to the *Sunday Express*. Our Features Editor of the time, Gordon Robinson, liked it and sent it through to me. I was captivated by it and suggested to Robinson that he invite Pitman to submit another article. The second article was as good as the first.

I asked Pitman to come in and see me. He was then a schoolmaster earning, he told me, a salary of £675 a year. He had a wife and two children and was an Oxford graduate. His wife Pat he had married while he was still at university. I offered him a job on the paper at £20 a week. Without a flicker of hesitation he accepted.

Thus began the most scintillating career.

Everything Bob Pitman touched turned to gold. He began to write book reviews and he wrote them in a fashion which entranced and infuriated the rest of Fleet Street. Within weeks of his arrival Bob had captured the attention of Beaverbrook and indeed of everyone else in the country. Soon he was appearing on television programmes. Soon he was writing articles of all descriptions. He joined me as a rabid left-winger. He was against the H-bomb. He was against capitalistic society. But my goodness how he mellowed under the influence of the good company on the *Sunday Express* and the ever-increasing amount of money he earned.

There was a stage in Bob's meteoric career when we had a slight crisis. When he wrote for the leader page, and elsewhere in the paper already had a book review under his own name, he used the pseudonym of Percy Howard. Once when I was away on holiday he wrote a leader-page article under this name and Beaverbook tried to persuade him to put his own name on the article. But the article was of a right-wing nature and at that time Bob was still left-wing, so he refused. I was afterwards warned with great solemnity by Max Aitken, 'Watch it. We understand that Pitman is a communist.'

But Pitman was very far from being a communist. He was simply a great, wonderful extrovert with huge energy who chased every party and every girl within sight.

He would do the most outlandish things. He would suddenly decide at half-past eleven at night that he wanted to visit a friend and he would take to that friend's house whoever he had with him at that moment. On one occasion he arrived at the house of Douglas Clark, my successor as Cross-Bencher and then living in Kew, with a handful of friends on the stroke of midnight. Douglas, who was himself amazingly generous and hospitable, was in bed at the time but quickly he got up and dressed and came down to join the Pitman party.

Bob as he grew older became more and more right-wing. He embraced the anti-Common Market cause with enormous eagerness. He also embraced the imperialist cause. He began to write a column for the *Daily Express* as well as his book reviews for the *Sunday Express* and very soon he was earning about £10,000 a year – about £100,000 at today's values. Yet he was generous to a degree and he was also a real family man in the sense that he adored all his relatives and tried to help them in every possible way. He would seek jobs for his brother, for all his relatives. His father was half blind and his mother, a wonderful little woman, was a strong socialist.

Then came the dreadful news. Bob had always been an enormous hypochondriac. For example, one night in bed he discovered his breastbone for the first time with his fingers and wondered whether it might be some mysterious tumour he had developed. But finally it was not a question of hypochondria. Bob had leukaemia. He went to Bart's and it seemed certain he would die. Then he had a remission but the remission was not to last for long.

Bob knew clearly that he was dying and thereupon he not only went further to the right, he also from having been an agnostic started to embrace religion. It was announced that he had become a convert to the Church of England. It was further announced to our combined stupefaction that he wanted two arch-sinners, Bob Edwards and myself, to be the sponsors at his baptism.

A date was fixed. The baptism was to take place in his hospital bed. I looked forward to the business with complete dread. I hated hospitals and I hated the idea of seeing a dying man.

But I steeled myself for the ordeal. That day I was lunching with Sir Edward Lewis at the Escargot. Half-way through lunch my secretary telephoned me to say that my presence in the hospital would not be necessary. Bob Pitman was dead. He had died sitting up in bed feverishly clutching the robes of the priest who was baptising him.

What of the ethical questions which any journalist, or indeed editor, has to ponder? What for example is intrusion? Should a newspaper publish a story even if someone is hurt as a result? There are many people who cry out that the answer to that second question should be 'No'.

But of course newspapers cannot work without accidentally hurting people. Every news story which is published means hurt for someone. When a murder trial is publicised – and it has to be publicised if justice is to be done and really seen to be done – then not only the murderer suffers but so do the innocent. His family, his wife, his children, his mother, his brothers – all share in the odium. And yet there are few who would wish criminal trials to be held in privacy. If that were to happen then justice would come to an end.

There are two stories that come to my mind to illustrate the question of privacy and intrusion by newspapers. In the *Sunday*

Express Town Talk column one day we had the chance of publishing an extraordinary and vivid human tale. A very well-known man had died and his widow – or at least the world thought she was his widow – clearly wanted to unburden herself to our reporter.

And to our reporter she confessed that she had never been married at all to the dead man, that he had had a previous wife who had refused to divorce him and that for many years she and the dead man had lived in sin and had brought up a family. She spoke movingly of the faults in the divorce laws that permitted this to happen. She spoke lovingly and with enormous affection of her late lover.

It was by any standards a most moving human story. Yet I elected not to publish it. And why did I do so? Because I learned that she and the dead man had two daughters still at school. I did not see that it was my business – even if their mother were willing to speak freely – to subject them to the pain and humiliation of opening their *Sunday Express* at boarding school on a Sunday morning and see written there for all the world to know that they were bastards.

But there are cases where it is impossible to avoid hurt. Like the bank robber or the clerk who defrauds his employer – all their trials bring damage to the innocent.

And sometimes damage is done inadvertently. I remember a year later taking part in a television programme on the subject of intrusion by newspapers. The person opposing me in the programme was Lord Mancroft. We argued sensibly and reasonably for the duration of the programme and afterwards we repaired to the BBC bar to have a drink.

That morning in the Hickey column of the *Daily Express* there had appeared a story about the impending marriage of Lord Mancroft's stepdaughter. It related that she was going to marry a Roman Catholic and they had decided that the marriage should be in a Roman Catholic church. An absolutely harmless story, which was written without malice or with any hurtful intent.

But suddenly Mancroft rounded on me and said, 'I couldn't say it on a programme, but that is what I mean by intrusion. Do you realise the harm that story did?'

I replied that I could not see that it had done any possible harm.

He looked at me again. 'My old mother suffered enough when I, a Jew, married outside my religion.' he said. 'How do you think she felt this morning when she read that my stepdaughter was going to marry in a Roman Catholic church?'

I had no answer. But is there an answer?

It was in retrospect Beaverbrook's extraordinary quickness of mind and instinct for news that saved me from disaster during my early years of editorship. For one Saturday morning I received a phone call from a very excited Manchester Editor, Howard Bygrave. He had in his hand the picture scoop of all picture scoops – a picture of the Loch Ness monster.

He explained the circumstances in which he had obtained it. Two Manchester youths had been on a camping holiday in Scotland and on their last night had pitched their tent beside the loch. Early in the morning one of them rose to relieve himself and heard a noise over the water. He roused his companion and the two of them, one with a camera around his neck, peered into the dawn mist. Suddenly, less than fifty feet from the shore, they saw it. Click went the camera and whatever they had seen disappeared as suddenly as it had appeared.

Shaking with fear as well as excitement they had packed their belongings, mounted their motorbikes and headed for home. On arrival in Manchester they went straight to the *Sunday Express* office, stammered out their story and handed over their camera, the film still inside it. When the film was developed, one picture showed a long-necked creature peering out of the mist straight at the lens.

Bygrave pointed out that since our own darkroom had developed the film there could have been no tampering with the negative. The picture just had to be genuine. The youths were also transparently genuine, decent youngsters from middle-class families. The picture was sent by wire to London. And it really was a terrific shot. We prepared to run it huge on page one. Then, around 5 p.m., Beaverbrook made his usual Saturday night phone call.

'What's the news?' he asked. I told him of our enormous

picture scoop which would be a sensational exclusive the following morning. His reaction was one of utter alarm.

'Don't print it,' he beseeched. Patiently I explained the circumstances in which the picture had been taken and how there was no possibility the negative had been interfered with.

'I don't care,' he said. 'Don't print it.'

'But why not?' I pleaded.

'Because,' he said, 'there is no such thing as the Loch Ness monster and although I don't know how they did it, the picture just has to be a fake.'

Nor did he want to know when I tried to tell him of a friend of mine who years ago had actually seen the monster. So despondently I killed the story and the picture even though I knew it would have caused the *Sunday Express* to sell thousands of extra copies the following day. And my God how glad I later was that I had. The youths turned out to be university students taking part in a rag week. And of course the negative had not been tampered with. There had been a monster in the loch all right. A blown-up rubber one.

But Beaverbrook was unable or unwilling to save me not long afterwards. It was at the time of Suez when I ran into personal trouble. Big trouble.

Suez had started off with great expectations. Quintin Hogg was First Lord of the Admiralty and Quintin and I by this time were at the beginning of a close friendship. The day on which the announcement was to be made as to whether or not we would take action on the Suez Canal, Quintin and I lunched at the Caprice. During lunch we talked excitedly about what might happen when the Prime Minister, Anthony Eden, made his statement in the House of Commons. Both of us eagerly hoped for British intervention. The lunch ended with Quintin saying, 'I hope to God he speaks for England.'

Eden spoke for England all right. But within weeks the Suez operation was in ruins and so was Eden's health. The Suez Canal was closed and shortly afterwards as a consequence petrol rationing was introduced – unprecedented in peacetime.

There came into my hands a circular which had been sent round to all political parties which made it quite clear that although tradesmen would suffer and ordinary motorists be severely restricted, there were to be very lavish petrol rations for the political parties. On 16 December 1956, I therefore published a leader in the *Sunday Express* under the provocative heading *Privilege* which attacked politicians for treating themselves infinitely more generously than they were treating members of the public.

Here is what I said:

PRIVILEGE

Tomorrow a time of hardship starts for everyone. For everyone? Include the politicians out of that.

Petrol rationing will pass them by. They are to get prodigious supplementary allowances.

Isn't it fantastic?

The small baker, unable to carry out his rounds, may be pushed out of business. The one-man taxi company may founder. The parent who lives in the country may plead in vain for petrol to drive the kids to school.

But everywhere the tanks of the politicians will be brimming over.

What are MPs doing about this monstrous injustice? Are they clamouring for Fuel Minister Mr Aubrey Jones to treat politicians like the rest of the community?

If it were a question of company directors getting special preference you may be sure that the howls in Westminster would soon be heard from John o'Groats to Ebbw Vale.

But now there is not a squeak of protest.

If politicians are more interested in privileges for themselves than in fair shares for all, let it swiftly be made plain to them that the public do not propose to tolerate it.

And let Mr Aubrey Jones know that, if he is so incapable of judging public feeling, he is not fit to hold political office for a moment longer.

The leader caused Parliament to go bananas. Captain Taylor, the MP for Eastbourne, asked the Speaker if this was not a *prima facie* breach of privilege.

The Speaker ruled that it was and I found myself summoned before the Committee of Privileges in the House of Commons. I was not allowed any legal representation. I was not given any advice of any kind, even as to whether I would be allowed to state a case. I simply sat down and was interrogated by the entire committee. At the head of the table sat Rab Butler. Around him were the various members of the committee and as I looked at them all I realised that I had attacked every single one of them during my period as Cross-Bencher.

It seemed to me that they were out to humiliate me. And that being so, I refused to be humiliated. I answered their questions stoutly and without any subservience. But always politely. Yet incredibly when the committee announced their verdict they included a phrase that suggested my demeanour had been unsatisfactory.

The result was that I became the last journalist of this century to be summoned before the Bar of the House of Commons.

In fact I soon had some indication that behind the scenes Rab Butler was doing his best for me.

On 12 January, 1957, I received the following memo from a *Sunday Express* reporter, Jack Smeaton, who had been interviewing Butler on another subject:

Mr Butler told me this morning he was 'sorry about the run-in we had with your paper over the privilege business'. He said he had tried to help you out during the committee hearing, 'But Mr Junor seems to be a very proud man.' He went on to say that he did not personally blame you for your attitude as he felt you were 'honest and sincere in your feelings over the matter'. He asked me to pass this on and said there was no need to worry. 'Privilege questions are always difficult,' he said. 'But as long as both sides keep calm they should turn out all right.' Here he mentioned that he had 'unfortunately' missed the committee meeting which had taken the decision regarding the complaint owing to a crisis in the House. I took the inference that had he been there the decision might have been lighter.

He asked me to tell you that it might be worth considering sending a note expressing regret (not apology) even at this late hour. But whether he does or not, 'tell Mr Junor that I admire his honesty and will do my best to dampen any fires when the matter comes up again. I will definitely not bring bellows to bear on the flames.'

Mr Butler said that this talk was quite off the record. 'I should not talk about it at all,' he said, 'as the matter is to some extent *sub judice* for one thing and because of my position. But I would like Mr Junor to know my views.'

But whatever Rab might have been doing for me behind the scenes I was still summoned. Hansard for 23 January 1957 records that the Secretary of State for the Home Department and Lord Privy Seal stood up in the House of Commons and said, 'I beg to move . . . that Mr John Junor do attend this House tomorrow at a quarter-past three o'clock.'

The night before my appearance I received two telephone calls at my home. The first was from Dick Crossman who had supported me during the debate. He urged me to use my time at the Bar of the House to speak out in favour of the newspapers, in favour of freedom of the press and to tell the House of Commons to go to hell.

The second telephone call was from Manny Shinwell and dear Manny wanted me to placate the House of Commons and say I was sorry.

In the event I accepted the advice of both of them. I had made up my mind that while I would apologise for having upset the House I would still insist that what I had written was fair and inescapable comment on a matter of vital public interest. But while I was prepared to speak out loud and clear and in complete defiance, alas there was not a whisper of support from Lord Beaverbrook. I suspect he felt that if I refused to apologise then he himself might be called before the Bar. And whatever else he may have been, the old boy was no hero.

I had lunch in the Escargot with Hugh Dundas before the

hearing, and afterwards we walked to the House of Commons. For what happened thereafter I give here an account which was written at the time:

I arrived at St Stephen's entrance at the House of Commons at 2.45 p.m. A police lieutenant stepped out, shook hands with me and told me that I was technically in his custody and that his duty was to take me to the Assistant Serjeant-at-Arms – a Commander Swanston. He was a pink-faced little fellow, dressed in black tights and obviously very excited at what was, for him, a welcome change in the drab routine of the Commons. He fussed around me and asked if there was anything he could do for me.

Would I, for instance, like a cup of tea? A cigarette? Would I also like to know what the procedure would be?

He was about to start explaining it to me when the Deputy Serjeant-at-Arms arrived on the scene – a Colonel Thorne. He was a tall, slim and even more imposing figure with a little moustache. He too was dressed in black tights and had a long silver sword. He too was clearly excited at the unusual occurrence of preparing an offender to be taken to the Bar.

The task of actually escorting me belonged to the Serjeant-at-Arms himself, Major-General I. T. P. Hughes.

Colonel Thorne promptly and summarily ordered the Assistant Serjeant-at-Arms out of the room and proceeded with great and undisguised pleasure to explain the procedure to me.

He offered to rehearse the steps and bows with me. He warned me not once but twice that after retreating backwards from the Speaker once I had completed my statement, I should be careful in my right about turn, since the Serjeant-at-Arms would also be making a right about turn at the same time and in view of the fact that he had a mace in his hand, I would be well advised to steer clear of him to allow him room for manoeuvre.

At 3.25 p.m. I was taken to the little inner lobby which leads directly into the House. I sat there and could see the crowded House through the glass section of the door. Various Members who tried to enter the House through the main doors were told by the attendants to use the side doors, 'since the Bar had to be kept clear'.

Several of them looked at me inquisitively and I heard one say: 'Oh yes, we have to keep the Bar clear for the prisoner.'

At this moment Sir Beverley Baxter approached me, beaming and benevolent.

He put his arm round my shoulder and said, 'Johnny my boy, did you see that I was on your side yesterday?'

Remembering the utter ineffectiveness of his speech, and the fact that he had described the *Sunday Express* leader as 'disgraceful', I put my arm round his shoulder and replied: 'Yes, Bax, and I wish to God you had been on the other side. Then I might not be here today.'

Questions ended very late and there was a false alarm that a Division would be held so I was rushed out of the lobby into a little waiting-room. Shortly afterwards – the Division not having taken place – I was hustled back to the lobby where the Serjeant-at-Arms met me with the mace. I then walked into the House with him. It was crammed to capacity. The only feeling I had was that no matter what happened I would show no trace of nervousness. Nor in any circumstances would I appear abject. I had always dreamed of making a maiden speech in the Commons. But I had never envisaged circumstances such as these.

I took a deep breath, pulled my shoulders back and said:

'I wish to express my sincere and unreserved apologies for any imputation or reflection which I may have caused upon the honour and integrity of members of this House of Commons in the article which I published in the *Sunday Express* on December 16th.

'At no time did I intend to be discourteous to Parliament. My only aim was to focus attention on what I considered to be an injustice in the allocation of petrol – namely the allowance given to political parties in the constituencies.

'In my judgement these allowances were a proper and

indeed an inescapable subject for comment in a free press. That was a view which I held then and hold now. But I do regret deeply and sincerely that the manner in which I expressed myself should have been such as to have been a contempt of this House.

'I have nothing more to say, Sir. I now leave myself in the hands of this House.'

The statement was heard in absolute silence.

The more percipient observed that although I appeared to be making an apology, the apology had a very hard centre.

After I had made my statement and had withdrawn from the House, I was taken back to the Serjeant-at-Arms' office where I was asked if there was anything I wanted.

Expecting a longish stay there, I replied, 'Yes, I would like a pot of tea, three rounds of toast and some cakes.'

The Assistant Serjeant-at-Arms telephoned the order through to the canteen, making it clear that this would go on an account which was specially reserved for 'visitors' such as me.

The next thing that happened was that suddenly the ticker-tape announced the whole business was over. So I left without my tea or my toast.

The next day I had a marvellous press. The *Yorkshire Post* was kind enough to say: 'He made a favourable impression in all quarters of the House and not least among his colleagues in the Press Gallery. The House agreed at the end that its dignity had been maintained and sustained. Mr Junor withdrew without any loss of his and indeed seemed to have gained in stature.'

I also received a friendly letter from Dick Crossman.

I congratulate you on a demeanour unsurpassed since Charles First stood in the Great Hall. Even the serried ranks of Socialist Tuscany could scarce forbear to cheer Horatius.

Yours ever,
Dick Crossman

It was a friendlier tribute than that which I received from my beloved son Roderick, then aged twelve, when I returned home that night after my appearance at the Bar. He had been watching the news on TV and was in tears when I entered my home. 'You gave in Daddy,' he said. 'Why did you give in?'

The fall of Eden after Suez meant, of course, the rise of Harold Macmillan. It appeared to me a good idea that a quick and brief life of our new Prime Minister should appear in the *Sunday Express*.

But who could write it? It had to be a staff writer if it were going to be written quickly. The man on the staff who could write most quickly and stylishly was Robert Glenton. But Glenton was our motoring correspondent and at that time knew little or nothing about politics. None the less I decided to use Glenton. I expected him to do a job simply from cuttings.

But I had not counted on Bobby Glenton's initiative. He wrote to the Prime Minister and asked whether the Prime Minister would see him. To my absolute astonishment the reply came that the Prime Minister would certainly see Mr Glenton.

Mr Glenton thereupon saw the Prime Minister on at least two occasions. One one of these occasions, both of them sitting with a large whisky and reminding themselves that Britain was in a state of crisis, Glenton said to Macmillan, 'Prime Minister, I have been forced to gain most of my material from reading the cuttings in our library. I have come across a story which I am sure is apocryphal. The story says that during the First World War when you were an officer in the Grenadier Guards you were wounded and you lay in the shell hole reading Aeschylus with another soldier, a private, and that when the stretcher-bearers came to take you away you said, "Don't take me. Take that private. He is more badly hurt than I am."'

Macmillan looked at Glenton indignantly and said, 'It's absolutely true. Absolutely true.'

In fact Lord Beaverbrook firmly believed that Macmillan, whom basically he liked, was a great poseur.

Beaverbrook was convinced that after the First World War Harold Macmillan had quite fraudulently claimed to have won the Military Cross. He persuaded me to look up the back-cuttings in our library and sure enough I discovered that when Captain Harold Macmillan had stood for Parliament for Stockton-on-Tees a pamphlet had been issued which quite wrongly ascribed to Macmillan the possession of a Military Cross – an MC which he had never won in battle or anywhere else.

It was suggested at the time that the mistake had been made by an over-zealous agent and that indeed is probably so. Nevertheless it is a matter of public record that when Macmillan did become Prime Minister, *The Times* announcing his appointment described him as The Rt Hon. Harold Macmillan MC.

The fact of the matter is that Macmillan to the day he died was as phoney as a five-bob note. From the moment he was expelled from Eton for homosexualism until the day he died he kept up a façade. And I do not expect anyone will ever know what the real man behind the façade was actually like.

In 1958 Macmillan had a Cabinet crisis. Peter Thorneycroft, Enoch Powell and Nigel Birch all resigned from the government on the grounds that Macmillan was pursuing an inflationary policy. Macmillan dismissed it all as 'a little local difficulty'.

Right in the midst of this crisis Pam and I attended a lunch at Downing Street. I rejoiced at my good fortune. For I was excited at the prospect of being able to discuss with the Prime Minister the present political turmoil.

Alas it was not to be. There were perhaps fourteen people at lunch. Macmillan was at one end of the table and I was at the other. On my right-hand side I had Lady Dorothy Macmillan who spent the entire lunch discussing fruit trees and orchards. At the other end of the table Macmillan had Pam on his left-hand side. I should explain at this stage that Pam in our garden at Mickleham had recently shot a hawk with a .22 rifle. All during lunch she was engaged in the most animated conversation with the Prime Minister. I, of course, at the other end of the table heard not a single word.

When we emerged afterwards into Downing Street I said to her with excitement, 'What did you talk about? I noticed you were having the most stimulating conversation. What did he say about Thorneycroft or Enoch Powell or Nigel Birch?'

Pam looked at me in astonishment. 'We didn't talk about those things. I was telling him about the hawk I shot. And do you know what he said? He said, "Amazing birds hawks, aren't they?" '

Harold Wilson was a great admirer of Macmillan's.

Years later, when the leadership of the Labour Party became vacant and Harold Wilson was contesting it with George Brown, Wilson told me: 'If I become leader I am going to do with the Labour Party what Macmillan did with the Tory Party after Suez. He led them clean away from the Suez disaster while holding up banners all the time proclaiming "We were right about Suez". I will do the same with the Labour Party on nationalisation.'

But if Harold Macmillan was in many ways an old phoney, he did have style. I still chuckle when I remember the story Tony Barber told me about him.

At the time Barber was Economic Secretary to the Treasury and was visiting New York. It was the day when Khrushchev took off his shoe and beat it on the United Nations' table. Young Barber, then a complete unknown, was summoned to the Waldorf Astoria where Macmillan, then Prime Minister, was in conclave with Lord Home, his Foreign Secretary.

It was a hot, sultry, sticky day. Barber found in the street that his clothes were sticking to him, but mercifully inside the Waldorf Astoria all was air-conditioned. He went up in the lift to the room in which the Prime Minister and Alec Douglas-Home were sitting, and when he opened the door it was an inferno of heat.

The Prime Minister and the Foreign Secretary were sitting on the settee, both with their jackets off. Macmillan had his flies unbuttoned to try to get cooling air around them and the windows were open, thus making the air-conditioning an absolute nonsense.

Harold Macmillan looked up and said, 'Come in, dear boy. Isn't this heat terrible?'

And Peter Carrington has a good story about Macmillan in Australia. It happened many years ago when Carrington, then a young man, was High Commissioner in Australia and Macmillan was paying a visit there as Prime Minister of Great Britain.

Macmillan was due to attend a civic reception, a late-evening reception, in Melbourne and beforehand Macmillan and Robert Menzies, the Prime Minister of Australia, went to dine at the Melbourne Club. Macmillan had a fair amount to drink, was obviously enjoying the company and was now sipping port with considerable gusto. Carrington approached him rather timidly and said, 'Sir, I'm afraid it is time for us to go to the reception.' Macmillan looked at him and said, 'Go away'.

Ten minutes and two glasses of port later Carrington again approached Macmillan and said, 'Sir, I'm terribly sorry but really, now we have to go.' Macmillan again looked at him and said, 'Go away'.

Carrington then approached Robert Menzies, explained the situation to him and suggested that he might try to persuade the Prime Minister to leave. Menzies tried but to no avail, and in fact Menzies himself then left for the reception. Finally Carrington, in despair, came to Macmillan and said, 'Really Sir, Mr Menzies has now gone and we will be in great trouble if you don't turn up. They will take it as an insult to their civic dignity.'

Macmillan looked at him warily and then said, 'All right, then. But if I'd been Churchill you wouldn't have done this to me.'

In 1961 I became friendly with the First Secretary at the Soviet Embassy. His name was Eugene Beliakov and it was Bob Pitman who introduced us. Beliakov was a delightful companion. We lunched together often. He and his wife came several times to dine with us at our home in Surrey. And when Ulanova came with the Bolshoi Ballet to London, he not only took my wife and myself to the first night. He even arranged for me to go back stage at the end of the show.

We only once discussed politics. And that was during the deepening of the East–West crisis about the future of Berlin in the summer of 1961 – a crisis which came to a head that August with the building of the Berlin Wall.

We had met for lunch at the Escargot Bienvenu in Greek Street.

'All this talk of war is nonsense,' he said to me. I heartily agreed and expressed my own belief that by this time the following year we would even have forgotten what the crisis was all about.

It was only half-way through the lunch that I suddenly realised the reason Beliakov was optimistic was that he was convinced that the West would give in to Soviet demands and yield West Berlin, whereas my optimism was based on the fact that Khrushchev could not possibly be mad enough to precipitate a war.

Clearly Beliakov had been thinking exactly the opposite. The lunch ended less in laughter than in thoughtful silence.

A few weeks later I received a telephone call from the man in charge of the D-notice system which was designed to prevent newspapers publishing secret defence information. 'A man from MI5 would like to have a few moments of your time, Mr Junor. Would it be convenient if he were to come to see you this afternoon?'

I agreed. The man from MI5 had a snap-brim hat, a military moustache and a silk cravat around his neck.

He quickly got down to business. He understood that I had a friendship with a Soviet First Secretary called Beliakov. They had reason to believe that Mr Beliakov was a low-grade KGB man. It was known to Security that I lunched with many Cabinet ministers and they were worried lest Beliakov had been getting information from me. They also said they were aware that Beliakov had attended dinner parties at my house thirty miles from London and in order to do so he must have had clearance from the very top in the Soviet Embassy.

I retorted that Beliakov had never received any information from me that would not have been available to every reader of the *Sunday Express*. And that was nothing more than the truth.

I did not believe then, nor do I believe now, that Beliakov was anything more than a warm, convivial Russian.

But the conversation gave me an insight into the sort of surveillance that was being maintained. Shortly afterwards Beliakov's tour of duty in this country ended and he returned to Russia.

I have heard nothing of him or from him since.

One of the most famous criminal trials of my early editorship was that of Dr John Bodkin Adams, the Eastbourne doctor who was accused of killing off his elderly female patients, each of whom left money in her ample will to Dr Bodkin Adams.

For me it was a story in three parts. The trial aroused enormous public interest and I decided to visit the Old Bailey to see an hour or two of the proceedings. By good luck I happened to be there on the day when Mr Geoffrey Lawrence, Bodkin Adams' counsel, began one of the most famous cross-examinations of our time.

In the witness box was a nurse who seemed, as she no doubt was, the soul of honour and honesty. She had testified on oath that on a night in question some years previously she had been in a nursing home where one of Bodkin Adams' patients lay desperately ill. She said that Bodkin Adams had asked to be left alone with the patient and had given the patient a drug in excess of normal requirements.

Mr Lawrence rose to cross-examine her. By fluke the day and night books of the nursing home in question had been discovered – unknown to the prosecution. Lawrence was therefore able to compare what she had said on oath with what had actually been recorded by her so many years previously. And what she had written then was at complete variance with what she had been saying during the trial.

The witness was absolutely demolished. Instead of being the soul of honour and integrity she suddenly began to look like a mean, spiteful spinster, eager to wound the doctor.

I was sitting behind Bodkin Adams and I noticed that he twiddled his thumbs in a rotary movement and never stopped turning them during the whole of the proceedings.

The second part of the story was in Lech in Austria. I had broken my ankle while skiing and on the first night after the accident there was a knock on my door and in came a fellow guest at the hotel. He was an English doctor called Corbett Ashby. He asked if I would like some pills to assuage my pain.

In fact I had no pain but the two of us sat – or rather I lay and he sat by my bed – and we demolished a bottle of red wine. It turned out that he had been the expert medical witness in the Crown's case against Dr Bodkin Adams and he told me a fascinating story.

He had been told at Eastbourne of a case in which an elderly lady, a patient of Dr Bodkin Adams, had been seriously ill. She was attended by a companion. One day in mid-winter, Bodkin Adams turned up, said to her companion 'don't bother to show me up to the bedroom – I know my way' and went upstairs.

After some time the companion, becoming a little anxious and perhaps a little suspicious, crept upstairs and opened the door. There was Bodkin Adams sitting dressed in his overcoat. Outside the snow lay deep on the ground. Bodkin Adams had drawn back the blankets over the patient and had opened the window wide.

According to Corbett Ashby the old lady died, but so, alas, did her companion and so it was impossible to bring this evidence to court.

I suspect, though, that the story is purely apocryphal.

For now comes the third part of my story.

I had been for the last time in the South of France with Beaverbrook when he was near the end of his life. I went to Nice Airport to catch an Air France plane back to London and, being one of the first on board, gained a window seat. On to the plane came a collection of gorgeous French models all heading for a fashion show in London. I hoped earnestly that one of them might come and sit next to me. But alas there came and sat beside me a fat old man with a pork-pie hat and a tweed suit.

He was carrying a sporting gun in a leather case.

He sat down beside me and began to make conversation – conversation which I wished very much to resist since I had hoped to read on the way back to London. He began to tell me how he had been in Monte Carlo representing England in an international clay-pigeon shooting competition – hence the gun.

While we were still on the ground I suddenly became aware that his face was familiar. I tried to read the name on the label of his gun case. I saw it was 'Adams'. Intrigued, I had to know the answer to the question in my mind. Before the plane left the ground, I turned to him and said, 'Are you Dr Bodkin Adams?'

He smiled happily. 'I can't disguise my face, can I?'

We were travelling economy class and for the rest of the trip it became a most fascinating conversation. He told me how the police had tried to so lower his morale as to reduce him to a hulk. They had taken away his braces, the implication being that he might try to commit suicide. The officer in charge of the case had been Superintendent Hannam and the main evidence on the part of the prosecution was the fact that Bodkin Adams, when he had been warned of the fact that he was being arrested, had said to Hannam: 'How did you find out? But it wasn't really murder. I was only helping them on their way.'

I have no doubt whatsoever – nor indeed had the jury – that Bodkin Adams never said those words.

On that journey back to London Bodkin Adams told me how, far from over-prescribing drugs, he had tried desperately to under-prescribe them. When a patient asked for sleeping pills he would put two or three genuine sleeping pills into a bottle in which the majority of the pills were just sugar-coated nothings. His belief was that, psychologically, if a patient took a sleeping pill he would fall asleep if he really believed that it contained a drug.

I arrived in London convinced that Bodkin Adams was completely and absolutely innocent and I looked forward to continuing my chat with him in the airport lounge while we were awaiting Customs clearance.

But it was not to be. The moment we left the plane and I headed for the economy-class bus, Bodkin Adams was off like a light to the first-class bus. And when I saw him in the Customs hall he was shepherding two dear old ladies who had been travelling first class and who clearly had been with him in Monte Carlo.

Dr John Bodkin Adams may well have been a lady-killer in one sense but not in the literal sense.

In 1962, a year or two earlier, I had also been in the South of France. Beaverbrook had sent me on a mission – the end purpose of which was to increase the circulation of the *Sunday Express*. In the South of France he had become friendly with Somerset Maugham and Alan Searle.

Graham Sutherland had painted a famous portrait of Somerset Maugham. Then he had painted Beaverbrook. The two portraits drew the two old men together, although of course Maugham was quite a bit older than Beaverbrook.

Beaverbrook knew that Maugham had in his possession an autobiography which Maugham had written some years previously – a bitchy, devastating autobiography in which he revealed his suspicion that he, Maugham, had been tricked into marriage by his wife, Syrie. He regarded her as a scheming woman and believed that the child of the marriage, now Lady Hope, was not his at all but a bastard whom he had been induced into believing he had fathered. From a literary point of view the property was sensational. Beaverbrook wanted to get it for the *Sunday Express*.

He brought me into the plan and it was arranged that I would go to the South of France for a few days and try to persuade Somerset Maugham to sell us the manuscript. I duly arrived in Monte Carlo where I made my headquarters in the Hotel de Paris and then went to see Maugham.

I had already read all his published short stories and I thought and still think that Maugham was the best writer of this century. I was aware that in all his works good never triumphed and there was no such thing as virtue, decency or honesty. Just hardness and cynicism and realism.

But when I arrived at the Villa Mauresque Maugham was far from what I expected. The villa itself was a palatial place. The furniture was exquisite and so were the paintings. When we sat down to dinner – Searle, his secretary and of course his lover, Maugham and myself – there was a manservant behind each of our chairs and we ate richly and off gold plate.

But Maugham was intensely modest. He was old and frail and had utterly lost confidence in himself if ever he had had any confidence.

He kept saying to me, 'I don't know why you are interested in my work. Now if I were Simenon I would understand. Now there is a wonderful writer.'

And it was quite clear that Maugham meant what he said. For over the two or three days that I was there a pathetic picture emerged.

At the foot of his bed he kept a painting of his mother. He

told me how her face (she had died at an early age) was the first thing he saw every morning when he awakened and how often even now in his eighties he wept at the sight of this lady who had died so early in his life.

Searle, who looked much younger than his age, fussed around Maugham with a tolerant arrogance and ate rich chocolates and rich sweets and drank rich wine. I was terrified at one stage that Searle had taken a fancy to me. He offered to show me his bedroom and I retired in some dismay.

Maugham told me about his friendship with Churchill and how sad it was to see Churchill in his dotage. He told me how recently he and Searle had gone to Chartwell to dinner and that when the sweet course came up – a rice pudding – Winston had said rather plaintively, 'Clemmy, do you think I could have a second helping?' And Clemmy had answered sourly, 'Winston, please do remember the servants have to eat.'

In the end my negotiations were successful. We bought *Looking Back*, which was the name of the Maugham memoirs, for £35,000. They created an enormous stir, though many abusive attacks were made on Maugham for having published the story – especially since he seemed by so doing to be illegitimising his own daughter. And although the serialised memoirs in the *Sunday Express* were meant to be the precursor of a book, the book never appeared. Maugham lost heart and retired into his shell.

But Lord Beaverbrook never lost his self-confidence nor his quickness of mind. I shall never forget a visit, when Beaverbrook was quite old, to his farm in Somerset, Cricket Malherbie.

I had just been introduced to his farm manager, a likeable and talented New Zealander called Sandy Copland, and we were wandering around the steading on our own. While doing so we came across a great Ayrshire bull in a penned enclosure. The bars of the pen were round and thick and looked as if they were made of aluminium. Beaverbrook explained to me that the bull was a champion and worth a fortune. I was hardly listening. I was looking at that bull and that bull was looking straight back at me. Not at Beaverbrook but at me. And it was clear it didn't like what it saw. It began to paw the ground and then suddenly it lowered its head and charged the bars of its pen. To my horror they began to bend. I was not going to wait around and prove myself a hero. I scarpered in the direction of the old man's Rolls which was parked about a hundred yards away.

It was then I realised that Lord Beaverbrook was already two yards ahead of me and accelerating fast.

V

1963 BECAME FOR me a year of great personal crisis.

I had been growing steadily more disenchanted with Harold Macmillan's style of government. I had begun by supporting Macmillan. I had watched with admiration the way in which he had handled the restoration of Tory popularity after the Suez débâcle. But the longer he stayed in office, the longer Lord Acton's old maxim of absolute power corrupting absolutely became more and more evident.

The Profumo affair and Macmillan's handling of it I had watched with horror. Then came the Vassall spy case and what seemed to me the quite unnecessary persecution of newspapers and newspapermen, with two reporters, including Brendan Mulholland whom later I took on to the *Sunday Express*, being sent to jail.

I realised that an election could not be far off and that the *Sunday Express* would be required to support Macmillan. For, while Beaverbrook was always independent in between elections, there was no doubt in my mind that when the issue came to the test of a general election then all our newspapers would rally behind the Tory Party.

This I found a most unpalatable prospect.

There were other reasons, too, why I was feeling irritated and frustrated. I had learned from Bob Pitman that Beaverbrook was aiming to have him as a replacement for John Gordon if and when John Gordon ceased to write his column in the *Sunday Express*. Ironically, of course, in the event John Gordon outlived Bob Pitman by a good many years. But I felt a little piqued that Beaverbrook should be planning the affairs of the newspaper of which I was Editor without even bothering to consult me.

But Macmillan was the prime issue. I felt I had to make my position clear and this I did to Max Aitken. He listened and then, of course, consulted with Beaverbrook. The result of all this – and I am cutting a long story short – was that it became quickly evident that either I supported Macmillan or the *Sunday Express* had to find a new Editor.

I had no option but to resign.

I suppose in my heart I felt that my resignation might not be accepted. But it was. It was a Friday afternoon and, after taking the Friday afternoon conference, I had for me the sad duty of telling my colleagues on the *Sunday Express* that I would no longer be their Editor.

I was perhaps a little precipitate. It was quite clear that there was no one immediately capable of replacing me. And in my letter of resignation I had said that I would bind myself to the terms of my contract and would give a year's notice.

Max called me down to see him and told me that they would like me to work out six months of my contractual period and that during that six months I would train an editor-elect. I would then be paid the remainder of my contract money. The man whom I had nominated was Arthur Brittenden, later Editor of the *Daily Mail* and Associate Editor of the *Sun*.

It was further agreed that during the six months which I would serve in training Brittenden I would not be restricted in any way, that I would continue to do my best to promote the welfare of the *Sunday Express* and that in turn my authority would not be eroded with my own staff. Nor would I be humiliated, as could so easily happen, by restrictions being brought in against me.

Two Saturday nights later I was suddenly aware that our office lawyer, who on a Saturday night sat behind the Editor in a chair in order to read the proofs and give legal advice, was disappearing from time to time with the proofs and pages.

I challenged him as to where he was going. He looked very embarrassed and then confessed that he was taking them up to a room on the third floor where Edward Pickering, the former Editor of the *Daily Express*, was sitting reading the proofs of the next day's *Sunday Express*.

I did two things. First I went up to the third floor and asked what it was all about. Pickering looked enormously embarrassed and finally admitted that he had been asked to read the *Sunday Express* proofs by Lord Beaverbrook, just to make sure that nothing was going into the newspaper of which Lord Beaverbrook would disapprove.

I then came back to my own desk and rang Tom Blackburn, later Sir Thomas Blackburn, who had succeeded E. J. Robertson as Chairman of Beaverbrook Newspapers.

I told him that I had entered into an agreement with goodwill for six months in return for certain guarantees. These guarantees, it now seemed to me, were being entirely vitiated. I demanded that Pickering be told immediately to leave the building, or else, I said, I would play the dirty game too. I would leave the building and I would take with me to wherever I went the cream of the *Sunday Express* staff, who I was quite sure would follow me.

Within fifteen minutes Pickering had left the building.

Things from then began to go much better for the remainder of my six months, but there was a lack of offers of future employment coming in to me. I had hoped, I admit, that some other newspaper might be interested in getting me. The only offer I had was from Bagenal Harvey and the *Panorama* team of the BBC, at that time led by Paul Fox. The proposition was that I should appear in *Panorama* in the same sort of role as Robin Day took for so many years.

I suggested that perhaps it would be a good idea if I were to do a dummy run as a *Panorama* interviewer. I was given freedom to choose the person whom I would interview and the BBC in turn would provide cameras and a studio so that they could see how I performed – and I, in turn, could find out whether I liked the idea of interviewing.

'Who would you like to do the dummy run with?' Fox asked me.

I replied with the first name that came to my mind – Quintin Hogg, now Lord Hailsham. I could see Paul Fox's eyebrow lift a little and I realised that he thought it highly unlikely that a member of Macmillan's government would be willing to give up time for a dummy run on a television programme.

This gave me a slight twinge of doubt myself. It was quite true that I was on very friendly terms with Quintin. But then my terms of friendship had been as a powerful Editor. Now I was an Editor with steadily diminishing power. Would he be prepared to give up time from his Cabinet job to take part in an exercise designed only to help me?

I suddenly remembered an incident from my past with Bernard Braden. I had long admired him as a great performer on radio with *Breakfast with Braden* and with *Bedtime with Braden*. And one of the first things I did on the *Sunday Express* was to ask my show business correspondent, Derek Monsey, to arrange a lunch for me with him.

As it turned out there was a mix-up in dates and Braden arrived at the Caprice restaurant on the wrong day. He sat there in the bar waiting for me and it was not until nearly two o'clock that he suddenly realised on enquiry that I had not even booked a table for that day.

The matter was put right by my telephoning him and eventually we did lunch. And he told me something which has always remained in my mind. He was going through a bad spell at the time. There was no radio work for him and precious little television work. 'You know, there is such a thing as the arrogance of success,' he said to me. 'When you are at the top of the pile as a stage performer you gain this arrogance of success. You are sure you are going well, and as a result you do go well. All your jokes come off. Your timing is perfect and the audience roars with laughter. But then suddenly there is catastrophe. You are no longer in demand. And you begin to lose the arrogance of success. You begin to ask yourself, "Was I ever any good? Or was it just luck?" That was why when you did not turn up to lunch, I thought it was because

I was now so unimportant that you were quite prepared to ignore or forget our date.'

That was how I now felt in relation to Quintin. I began to wonder whether it might not be forward and presumptuous of me to ask him to spare the time to take part in the *Panorama* programme.

As it happened, before my next meeting with Quintin I had a lunch date with Harold Wilson. During this lunch I put the proposition to him: would he be prepared to take part in this dummy television programme? Wilson's reply was something for which I will always be grateful. He was then Leader of the Opposition. He was a man almost certainly destined to be the next prime minister. And without a quiver of hesitation he said, 'Of course I will.' And he did, too.

When later I telephoned Paul Fox and said 'Do you mind if instead of having Quintin I have someone else for my dummy run?' I could almost feel him thinking at the other end of the telephone, 'Ha, so he's failed to get Quintin.' And then I said, 'Could I have Harold Wilson instead?' It did my morale a great deal of good.

At the same time I wrote to Lord Rothermere asking for a job and he invited me to have tea with him at Warwick House. It was an extraordinary occasion.

We discussed the Tory leadership and he told me that he knew for a certainty that Reginald Maudling had no desire to be prime minister in place of Macmillan. This I knew to be absolutely untrue. I knew from my own contacts with Maudling how desperately he wanted the prime ministership. But so ignorant and so arrogant and so unaware of what was happening in politics was Rothermere that he refused to believe anything other than what he thought he knew. And alas he knew almost nothing. I left him without his having made any definite offer and I never heard another thing from him.

In fact the first real offer I had came from Beaverbrook himself. With two months of my contractual period remaining he invited me down to Cherkley and suggested that once I left the *Sunday Express* I might continue to write a column for it. I told him I would consider the matter. For while I knew that

Beaverbrook was very angry indeed about my resignation I knew also that he was quite prepared to convince himself, perhaps correctly, that I was no longer of any importance.

The days ticked past, Arthur Brittenden reasonably supposing that he would be the next Editor of the *Sunday Express*. But then two things happened.

Just two or three weeks before my six months were up, Brittenden was told by Max Aitken that he would not, in fact, be the next Editor. The editorship would go to Derek Marks, then Deputy Editor of the *Evening Standard*. Brittenden was affronted and so, indeed, was I. But there was nothing that could be done about it.

And then, as I was shaving in my bathroom one morning and listening to the news on the radio, I heard the announcement which made my razor stand still. Macmillan was going into hospital for a prostate operation. I realised immediately that this must mean his resignation as Prime Minister.

Within hours I was called in to see Max. It was pointed out to me that this might change everything.

The same afternoon Max telephoned me from Cherkley. He wanted to know whether I was now prepared to reconsider my decision to resign. Would I be prepared to stay as Editor of the *Sunday Express*? I replied that, providing they kept their part in the bargain, I would. For in resigning with six months of my contract still to run it meant that a tax-free lump sum would have to be paid to me from the residue of my contract.

And so it happened. The next day Derek Marks was called in to see Max Aitken and the situation was explained to him. He was told that he would not be becoming Editor. Derek's reaction was absolutely typical and admirable. He simply said, 'Oh fuck it.'

There was one interesting by-product of my continuing as Editor in 1963. I resumed my dinners with Beaverbrook. Often I dined with him twice a week. But now there were no more great dinner parties – just Beaverbrook, his new wife, the ex Lady Dunn, and myself. For – and I had been quite unaware of this at the time I resigned – Beaverbrook was desperately ill from cancer of the prostate.

And whereas in the past he had insisted on my drinking champagne, which I did not like, he no longer insisted on that. Instead he provided me with claret – a whole bottle of Château Latour 1953, to myself. Dining twice a week and using two bottles of Château Latour a week, it must have become evident to him that he was going to run out of Latour '53. But he did keep on the Latour until the very end, or almost the very end, when he gave me a case of the '53 for Christmas and thereafter offered me more ordinary clarets.

Beaverbrook clearly was in enormous and increasing pain. He was having deep X-ray treatment and he could only walk with extreme difficulty. But he was proud of his marriage to Lady Dunn. One night at Arlington House he said to me after she had left the dinner table, 'Isn't it fantastic that an old man of my age can get a girl like her?' And it was quite clear that what pleased him was the fact that she could not possibly be after his money since she had so much of her own. Her husband had left her something like £24 million.

Macmillan's illness now meant of course that Rab Butler was odds on to become prime minister, just as he had been odds on previously when Eden had resigned. In fact there were three contenders for the crown, or at least so everyone thought. Apart from Rab there was Reggie Maudling who at that time I did not know as well as I was to know him later. And there was Quintin Hogg, whom I knew best of all and regarded as a personal friend.

But I decided to support Rab rather than Quintin. This was because I thought it only fair that Rab should get the job and also because Quintin had been quite outrageous in his support for Macmillan. He had gone on TV and lost his temper defending the government over the Vassall case. In addition he had said things about newspapermen which I did not like.

I had first got to know Rab Butler seven years earlier when I was called before the Committee of Privileges of the House of Commons. From that time he and I became friends. We often lunched together and invariably Rab would arrive twenty to twenty-five minutes late. Invariably too he would have in attendance an armed detective – even after he left the Home Office where he had been entitled to one.

Rab was an enormously humane person. On the occasion when he lost the prime ministership to Macmillan in 1957 after it seemed he was certain to win, Derek Marks, then political correspondent of the *Daily Express*, spent the whole evening in Smith Square outside Rab's house waiting for him to come back and hoping to find from Rab personally the result of the leadership contest.

It had gone midnight and Derek decided there was no point in waiting any further. He and the photographer walked disconsolately away. They had gone perhaps 150 yards when suddenly the headlights of a car appeared and stopped outside the Butler house. They turned and pounded back. Derek must have weighed all of eighteen stone and he was puffed and panting by the time he arrived on the doorstep, as Rab was putting the key in the door.

Rab just fifteen minutes earlier had learned that he was not to be prime minister. He had every reason to be angry and frustrated. Instead he looked at Marks, smiled and said, 'What are you doing here at this time of night, Marks? You'll catch your death of cold. Come in and have a drink.'

At lunch Rab could be enormously indiscreet. He told me, for instance, that the government was quite willing to let Prince Philip see the State Papers, but that the Queen wished otherwise. Rab thought that this was curious, and I must say so did I. I still do. For my understanding is that the position has never changed.

He also told me that the Cabinet had very good information as to what was happening in the Jack Kennedy court at Washington. The information came from Lady Adele Cavendish, perhaps better known as the sister of Fred Astaire the dancer. She had married into the Cavendish family and so was related to Macmillan. Kennedy suffered from migraine and claimed the only relief he could get was by sleeping with a different girl each night. It had even come to the stage more or less of girls climbing the White House walls.

Harold Wilson was one person who thought that Rab would

get Macmillan's job. His office in the Commons was close to Rab's and he told me how he listened to the Tory footsteps padding along the corridor. There were, said Wilson, lots of footsteps outside Rab's door. So he thought Rab was home and dry. And I at any rate thought that out of Rab, Reggie and Quintin, Rab was the best bet.

And Quintin made a disastrous mistake at the Blackpool Tory Conference which began on 9 October by running a presidential type of campaign in which he renounced his peerage and paraded his wife and baby Kate around. Rab made a bad speech on the twelfth, the final day of the Conference. So did Reggie Maudling. Suddenly the way opened for a fourth man, Alec Douglas-Home. And it was Alec Douglas-Home who, on 10 October, now read out to the Conference the letter which Macmillan had sent to the Queen the previous day and in which he alluded to the 'necessity' of his resignation – but without actually tendering that resignation.

The following few days were among the most politically exciting of my life.

On Sunday 13 October, the day after the Conference ended, I telephoned Rab Butler on his return from Blackpool. He was not exactly full of optimism and clearly thought that everything depended on what Home would do. I pointed out to him that Home's state of health, his personal inclinations, and above all, his speech as Conference Chairman indicated that he did not want the job. Rab agreed but not very whole-heartedly.

Two days later, on Tuesday, I received advance news of the *Daily Express* poll of public opinion which produced the exciting result that Rab was clear ahead of the field with 39.5 per cent of the voters, Quintin second with 21 per cent and Home nowhere. The poll also showed that in the week since Macmillan's resignation there had been a terrific swing to the Tories and that the gap between them and Labour was only 2.5 per cent.

I immediately rang Rab with the news. He was obviously pleased and wanted to know whether the poll would be published the next day. I asked him whether he thought it would be in time to help him. Was there, I put it bluntly, still a chance that he could make it? He said there was and that it was not too late.

But on Wednesday there came unhappy news. I had been trying to get Rab all afternoon but without success. For throughout the whole affair Rab made no attempt to influence or to square the newspapers. All the other candidates for the leadership were practically queueing up to speak on the telephone to any political correspondent who would listen, whereas Rab, normally very friendly with the press, was being scrupulously correct.

Before going home that night I learned the reason why Rab was being so aloof. Earlier in the day I had asked Susan Barnes (later Mrs Anthony Crosland) to try to get an interview with Mrs Butler in case she turned out to be the next prime minister's wife. At 6 p.m., Susan told me that she had a message for me from Mrs Butler. 'Tell Mr Junor,' Mrs Butler had said, 'that his hopes for my husband are not going to be realised. He has been so kind but it is all useless. I feel so sorry. It is so beastly for my husband.' It seemed to me that clearly Mrs Butler would not have broken down in this way unless she was absolutely convinced that the fight was lost.

The next morning's papers were all over the place with their predictions but there was hardly a mention of Home. It seemed to be still a battle of Butler, Hailsham and Maudling. In the afternoon I again tried to contact Rab but failed. The Butlers were taking no calls. Convinced by now that things had gone seriously wrong, I deliberated on what to do next and finally decided to ring Hugh Fraser. His news was startling. He told me that the buzz was that Home was to be prime minister and that an announcement was to be made at midnight.

I pondered a while, and decided to ring Quintin Hogg – a little reluctantly because although he was an old friend he must have been aware that we had not been supporting him and in fact I had made no earlier attempt to get in touch with him. Quintin was explosive on the telephone. He couldn't completely confirm my news but he was pretty certain it was true, although no one had bothered to put him officially in the picture. He talked angrily of the Tory Party committing political suicide and swore that he would never agree to serve under Home.

I suggested to him that it was all Macmillan's doing – as indeed it clearly was – but at this stage Quintin was convinced that Macmillan supported him. In fact all that Macmillan had done was to push Quintin just sufficiently hard to create an apparent impasse and then triumphantly pull out of his own hat a compromise – the man he had really wanted all along.

Tony Lambton then came on the telephone from Wooler in Northumberland wanting to know what news there was. It was by now past nine o'clock at night. He was astounded at the Home news and found it impossible to believe. He rang off and did some checking on his own – with Maudling, I presume, whose campaign he was running – and then came back to me with confirmation of my own story.

So we set to work between us on our own 'Stop Home' campaign.

On my suggestion Lambton telephoned the Queen's Private Secretaries, Michael Adeane and Sir Edward Ford, and Lord Plunket, her Equerry, so that the Queen could be warned of the constitutional dangers of asking Home to form a government at a time when the Cabinet had never been consulted as to whether Home was acceptable – as it had not been.

The next call was from Molly Butler. This must have been getting on for 11 p.m. Did I know of the latest development? Did I know that Rab had only been told about Home that evening at 7 p.m.? Rab then came on to the phone himself. He sounded indignant. The cock clearly at last was going to fight. I told him that I had been in touch with Quintin and that in my view Quintin was prepared to accept Butler rather than serve under Home.

I then rang Quintin and put it to him straight. Would he telephone Rab right away and pledge himself? To my delight he said that he would. But he also said in a very plaintive voice, 'Do you realise that you are making Rab prime minister?' And during the conversation one fact clearly emerged – he was worried about money. He kept saying he would have to sell his house if he lost ministerial office. I gave him a categoric assurance that he could make as much writing for the *Sunday Express* as he was getting from the government.

The following morning, Friday 18 October, the *Express* and the *Mail* had the story of the Cabinet's midnight revolt against Home and it became clear that not only Quintin Hogg, but Maudling, Boyle, McLeod and Powell were now firmly behind Butler.

Obviously there was no longer any impasse. Butler telephoned Macmillan in hospital to tell him of the new situation but Macmillan refused to accept the call. Instead he precipitated matters by sending off his own resignation to the Queen and nominating Home as his successor before the Cabinet had time to act.

At 9.30 that evening came the final drama. I had gone round to St Ermin's Hotel in Caxton Street to have a chat and a drink with the Butlers (they were staying in the hotel because their own home was being redecorated), but as I arrived Rab left for Downing Street to see Home. I went up to room 531 – a drab little sitting-room with a shabby red suite, a tiny table and two hard-backed red chairs. The telephone kept ringing incessantly and some of it was good news. Sir Michael Fraser of Tory Central Office rang to say that in no circumstances would Powell, McLeod or Boyle serve under Home. I suggested that I ought to break the story to the *Express* and thus force Home's hand. For the news of the dissension might prevent his forming a government at all.

I was on the point of picking up the phone when the door opened and in walked Rab. He looked completely punch-drunk. He said to Molly, 'Do you mind if I take my coat off?' and took off the black jacket which with his striped trousers was his habitual dress.

Without his well-tailored jacket, he looked a fat, shapeless old man. 'It's all over,' he said. 'Alec has won.'

Apparently the meeting at Downing Street had been a four-some – Maudling, Home, Hogg and Butler. Both Maudling and Hogg had capitulated. 'Quintin,' he said, 'has agreed to serve.'

Rab was in no doubt that Home would be able to form a government. He was also afraid of the possibility of a dissolution if the crisis continued much longer. I pleaded with him in a very direct fashion at least not to accept office until Monday on the grounds that if he held out until Monday the anti-Home forces would have time to regroup. But he just looked at me like a spaniel that has been whipped and shook his head sadly. The next day, Alec Douglas-Home kissed hands at the Palace.

A year later, and only a day or two after the 1964 general election had returned a socialist government with Harold Wilson as Prime Minister, I lunched with Rab at the Savoy. When he had been in government Rab had had official cars, he had had private secretaries arranging every single one of his movements. And it was quite clear that without all this he was utterly lost. For instead of arriving at the Savoy Hotel's front entrance in the Strand he arrived at the Embankment entrance by taxi. He had to stumble his way up the back stairs and along the corridors before finally reaching the Grill Room. He looked a shattered man that day and I knew he would never really recover from the blow.

And I knew how Molly Butler felt about Rab's decision not to serve under Home. She had said that she wondered whether it was not all prompted by a nobility of spirit which she had always found in him, a selflessness which made it impossible for him to put himself first in public life. 'Through all the heartache I have suffered,' she had said to me, 'one thing has comforted me, and that is your magnificent tribute to me in your great newspaper. I shall always owe you a debt of gratitude for what you tried to do for my husband – and tried so hard.'

I did not even meet Alec Douglas-Home, the man I had tried so hard to prevent becoming Prime Minister, until after the Tories had lost the 1964 election. At the beginning of his prime ministership I had been invited by Tony Lambton to join a group of editors at Lambton's home to lunch with Alec. But not caring for that group type of lunch, I refused and did not have another chance to meet him.

But after the 1964 election I was lunching with Jock Massereene. Afterwards we walked together into St James's Street and there was Alec Douglas-Home walking briskly in the same direction. Massereene, who clearly knew him well, introduced me to him and we walked on together.

It was the start of an association which has continued through-out the years in and out of office. For Alec Douglas-Home is in many ways the most likeable politician I have met. He has an aristocratic pedigree as long as your arm and yet he still has an instinctive knowledge of what ordinary people are thinking.

He is one of the few politicians who insist that for every lunch you buy him, he buys you one in return. He has a lovely dry sense of humour and is completely lacking in pomposity. Long after leaving office he continued to travel by Underground, avoiding Piccadilly Circus station as he was once mugged there. 'My wife doesn't like me travelling by Tube at all,' he told me, 'but I don't see any reason why I should not do so.'

When Alec was Prime Minister, the story is told of a high-ranking writer from the *Guardian* who took the night train to Edinburgh one Saturday in order to write a profile of how the Prime Minister spent his Sundays in Scotland. On arrival in Edinburgh the writer breakfasted in the North British Hotel and read the Sunday morning papers to prepare himself before driving in his hired car to the Prime Minister's home.

He opened his interview by asking the Prime Minister for his views on a story which appeared on the front page of that morning's *Sunday Times*.

'I'm awfully sorry,' replied the Prime Minister, 'but I haven't read it. We only take the *Sunday Express* and the *Sunday Post* at the Hirsel.'

Alec was to become a frequent contributor to the *Sunday Express*. His articles were usually in his own handwriting and always contained fresh and original thinking.

I once said to him it was a pity that when he became Prime Minister his speeches had not contained the same fresh imagery they had contained when he was Foreign Secretary. He grinned. 'That was my error. When I became Prime Minister they handed me over to Nigel Lawson and Eldon Griffiths. They were supposed to be red-hot on public presentation, but in fact they wrote the dullest speeches. I should have chucked them out but I felt the experts knew best.'

It is almost impossible to get Alec to say anything unkind about anyone. He sees good in everyone – except perhaps for Denis Healey.

I remember lunching with him in March 1981 at the Carlton

Club. After lunch we moved into the smoking-room for coffee.

As he stirred his coffee, Alec turned to me and said, 'What do you think of Denis Healey?'

'Well, he was once a communist,' I replied, 'and I don't believe he has ever lost his blinkered attitude to politics.'

'Neither do I,' said Alec Douglas-Home.

But of another Denis, Denis Thatcher, he spoke most highly. 'He came with Margaret to North Berwick and it was a revelation to see how he went round the constituency talking about fish to fishermen, about farming to farmers, about industry to small industrialists. He does a great job.'

And there is one other thing he said to me that day. 'The trouble with Margaret, of course, is that she cannot make a joke. No sense of humour, just like Neville Chamberlain. His jokes were awful. We had to erase them from every speech he made.'

I don't know if Alec Douglas-Home ever changed his mind about Denis Healey. I know I did, after a day I spent in Brighton with two of my grandchildren. I was surreptitiously and illegally feeding a parking meter when suddenly I heard a voice ringing in my ears, 'I saw you. Don't think you're going to get away with it!'

Startled, I looked up. But it wasn't the law. It was Denis Healey. He, like me, was doing some last-minute Christmas shopping.

I cannot even begin to say how kind he was to the two boys. He embraced them in the conversation, he made them feel important. When we parted, I said to them, 'Do you realise he was for years one of the most important ministers in the Labour government and if things had gone the other way could so easily have become prime minister?'

As I spoke, I reflected that no one had attacked Denis Healey over the years more than I had and perhaps I had even played some little part in denying him his ambitions. Isn't it one of the most wonderful things about our political system, and indeed our society, that you can attack a man's politics without losing his personal friendship?

In July 1983, Alec Douglas-Home's eightieth birthday was celebrated by an informal dinner party in the boardroom of *The Times*. It turned out, for me, to be a wonderful evening.

There were about twenty people around the dinner table. Rupert Murdoch, as proprietor of *The Times*, was there with his wife, although I suspected that he hardly knew Alec. Sir Edward Pickering was also there, as a director of *The Times*, with his wife. I was reasonably sure that neither of them had ever met Alec before. Duke Hussey and his wife, who was Lady-in-Waiting to the Queen, were there and, of course, Alec surely knew them both. Duke Hussey had been, until quite recently, a director of *The Times*.

The Editor of *The Times* and Alec's nephew, Charles Douglas-Home, sat in the chair as host of the dinner and his uncle sat opposite him. Lord Hartwell was there, although I suspected he was there as owner of the *Daily Telegraph* and had been invited as a friendly gesture by the owner of *The Times*.

But what fascinated me was that the other guests just had to have been Alec Douglas-Home's personal choice. They consisted of Quintin Hogg, Sir Anthony Acland, the Permanent Under-Secretary of State at the Foreign Office, Willie Whitelaw and myself.

When the ladies had left the table – an event which Rupert Murdoch afterwards told me had been a mistake since all that had happened was that Anna wanted to have a pee and when she had arisen, all the other women had assumed it was time to withdraw and did so with her – the conversation became fascinating.

Because Quintin, Alec Douglas-Home and I started to discuss that night in November 1963 when Alec had become Prime Minister. Suddenly all the years rolled away and I was back in the room in St Ermin's Hotel with Rab Butler, scheming Alec's defeat. Willie Whitelaw had been at that time a minor figure and he listened just as entranced as the rest of them.

And I suddenly realised not just the extraordinary honour which Alec had paid me in inviting me to be one of his handful of personal guests. I also realised that this was the very end of an era. Willie Whitelaw was finished in the House of Commons and had gone to the Lords with his viscountcy. The day of the old Establishment – of benevolent Tory landowners all from the same school, Eton – was over. And somehow or other they had included me in that old Establishment.

Had I realised it, two decades earlier another era was ending. In February of 1964 Lord Beaverbrook went off to the South of France. He was now in continual pain. When I went down to see him, also there were Michael Foot and Beaverbrook's long-time friend Brigadier Michael Wardell, whom I confess I had always considered to be somewhat of a slug in a strawberry bed. But at Cap d'Ail I was moved by the real affection which Wardell had for Beaverbrook, by the way he fussed around him, tried to protect him.

I was also impressed by the real affection which Michael Foot had for Beaverbrook. One day Michael and I went out walking along the sea front and I said to him, 'The old man is clearly dying. I must have an obituary ready in case he dies on a Saturday. Would you be prepared to write it? And if you would, I promise that no one will know you have written it. It will be kept in my desk against the day Beaverbrook dies.'

Michael looked at me and hit the top of the grass with his walking-stick. And then he said, 'No, I can't do it. I love that old man. And although I believe you when you say he will never know about his obituary, I would not want to do anything which might make anyone think I am pushing him towards his grave.'

Beaverbrook came back to London. For Roy Thomson was to give a great dinner party at the Dorchester on 25 May to celebrate Beaverbrook's eighty-fifth birthday. Everyone who mattered in London would be there. The great question was – would Beaverbrook be there? He was now almost confined to a wheelchair, for when he walked the pain was excruciating. Some days he was a little up, often he was quite a long way down. The night before the dinner he did not think he could appear. He was going to send a tape-recording of his speech. But in the event he turned up.

I sat at my table which was right next to the top table and directly in front of where Beaverbrook was going to sit. Behind his seat there was a service entrance and I assumed that he would be using that, perhaps taking the wheelchair right to the service door. But instead he came in at the main entrance. He had to walk perhaps a hundred yards and in the most trying conditions because he had to walk between the upstanding top-table diners and their protruding chairs to a fanfare of military music. When he reached his chair he turned to Roy Thomson and whispered 'Can I sit down now?' and Roy Thomson replied, 'Not yet, Max. We still have to have the National Anthem.'

I wept for him. But at that dinner, after pedestrian speeches from Roy Thomson and Lord Rothermere, Max Lord Beaverbrook stood up and made a speech with such vigour, such wonder, that tears of pride came to my eyes.

'The man who is not true to himself is no journalist. He must show courage, independence and initiative. He must also, I believe, be a man of optimism. He has no business to be a pedlar of gloom and despondency. He must be a respecter of persons, but able to deal with the highest and the lowest on the same basis, which is regard for the public interest and a determination to get at the facts. I take more pride in my experience as a journalist than any other experience I have had in my long and varied life.'

His theme, he said, was that he had always been an apprentice. First an apprentice to finance in Canada. Then in London. 'And there I decided to become an apprentice in politics. After the war I became an apprentice in Fleet Street. And that was a real exciting experience.' And now in his eighty-sixth year, he went on, 'It is time for me to become an apprentice once more. I have not settled in which direction. But somewhere, sometime soon.'

He walked out of that dinner and went home to bed and to die.

I had already taken part in a television programme, recorded, which appeared on the night of the dinner. In his bedroom at Cherkley he had the film of the television programme shown to him. On the following Saturday night when I was at dinner he telephoned me from his bedroom to say, 'I have seen the television programme. Thank you very much indeed, John, for all the kind things you said about me.'

Three days later he was dead.

About eighteen months later and shortly after his Unilateral Declaration of Independence I flew to Rhodesia to see Ian Smith. I had to travel via Johannesburg and I was appalled by what I saw at the airport while I awaited my connection to Salisbury. It was vastly different from conditions there today. Black airport workers walked around with sullen unsmiling faces and looking like zombies. There were large signs everywhere separating blacks from whites – lavatories, buffets, the lot.

Salisbury, now Harare, was so completely different. On my first evening there John Monks, who was there for the *Daily Express* on a more or less permanent basis, took me for a drive into the country. Everywhere we went smiling black children at the wayside waved and cheered at us. Many of them had bicycles and quite a few of those were shining and new. In the native villages too we were treated with warmth and friendliness. I was staying in Meikles Hotel which at the time just had to be one of the best hotels in the world. A jacaranda tree grew up through the foyer, the restaurant was superb, the food and wines were brilliant and all this was in a country said to be under siege.

I warmed to Ian Smith. At the end of our talk he began to reminisce about how during the war when he had been a fighter pilot with the Royal Rhodesian Air Force he had often come to Fleet Street on a rare night out in London and had stared fascinated at the Daily Express building which had seemed to him to represent the very centre of the sophisticated world. He spoke nostalgically of a restaurant at 57 Fetter Lane where he had been able to eat steak and chips even in the midst of wartime rationing. We struck a common bond when I told him that at the very same time, as a naval pilot, I had eaten there too.

I was to see Ian Smith on many subsequent occasions, including when I went back to Rhodesia to visit him much later during the guerrilla war. At the time of the Lancaster House Conference where he had to bow the knee and give up everything he had fought for, I was having a private talk with Margaret Thatcher. I asked her if she had had the chance to see him privately.

'No, I haven't,' she replied. 'I would love to, but it would be misunderstood by Mr Mugabe and the others. So I daren't. But at the Armistice service the other day I knew he was there just behind me and I longed to turn round and look, but of course I couldn't.'

Every time he came to London thereafter Ian would come to see me and we would lunch together.

The last time I saw him was in October 1988. He had aged a bit since our last meeting. And I thought I detected just the faintest shake in his hand. But his brain was still crystal clear.

He had been in the United States making speeches in which he had attacked the idea of sanctions being imposed against South Africa. His campaign had caused much anger in Zimbabwe. The Zimbabwe *Herald* had published a leader attacking him as a traitor and suggesting that he ought to be jailed or expelled from the country. This worried him, for all his money was in Zimbabwe. He had been born there. It was his home. And he had not the slightest intention of leaving.

'Are you fearful for your own safety if you return there?' I asked him.

He reflected for a moment and then said, 'My family think that one day *they* will come and get me, but I think it would cause too big a stink if they bumped me off. I have too many black friends. When I walk down the streets of Harare there are as many black as white people who come up and shake my hand.'

Smith is an enormous admirer of Margaret Thatcher. But he did not like Peter Carrington, who he felt sold him down the river. And he told me of a chance meeting he had had with his old adversary at the time of UDI – Harold Wilson. Smith had been in the VIP lounge at Heathrow when a steward approached him and said, 'Excuse me, Sir, there's a gentleman who says he is an old friend and would like to meet you.'

Smith looked across and there was Harold Wilson, now Lord Wilson of Rievaulx.

Wilson embraced him and said, 'Ian, it's good to see you again.'

At the end of our lunch Smith was heading for Bush House to speak on the BBC World Service. As I watched him walk up Fleet Street I reflected on his life – Spitfire pilot at twenty, architect of Rhodesia's independence at forty. Still fighting for the things he believes in in his late sixties.

'Do you known who that was?' I asked the newspaper seller at the corner of Bouverie Street.

He nodded his head vigorously. 'Ian Smith. Bloody fascist.'

Whatever he might have been he was not that.

And nor was the man who had embraced him in the VIP lounge of Heathrow Airport and who in 1964 had become the Prime Minister of Great Britain.

Yet one thing has always bothered me about the prime ministership of Harold Wilson. Just what influence and just what part did Marcia Williams have in his life?

Clearly the answer is that she did have a good deal of influence over Wilson. He liked to be surrounded by people who agreed with him and who were close and affectionate. I think that was Marcia's strength.

After the Profumo affair in the House of Commons in 1963 there was an odd incident. Barbara Cartland, not the most political of people, was speaking at a Women's Institute meeting or something like that in one of the Home Counties and in her speech she sounded off in red-hot anger against the socialist Front Bench for having condemned Profumo. The angle of her attack was that there were men on the socialist Front Bench who morally were no better than Profumo had been. I write from memory, but I recollect that the speech was pointed in a way which clearly made it a personal attack on Harold Wilson.

And, unusually for a Barbara Cartland speech, a copy of it was sent by the Press Association to every newspaper office in London. And no doubt in every newspaper office, as in mine, a good deal of deliberation went on. But in the end, no newspaper printed the speech.

Shortly afterwards, I lunched with Harold Wilson and we discussed the Barbara Cartland speech. He told me that he had taken advice on it and decided that since no newspaper had printed it, it was not worth taking action against Barbara Cartland herself. But he insisted that if there were any question of the suggestion being made in a responsible newspaper that he had ever acted in an immoral fashion, then he would swiftly sue.

I then pointed out to him the danger which could exist in the future. Was it not possible, even probable, I suggested to him, that right in the middle of an election campaign a group of anti-socialist businessmen might induce Marcia Williams' husband to give an interview to the press?

Wilson shook his head. I did not proceed any further with my questioning.

The first time I had even indirect contact with Harold Wilson was one evening in 1949 when my wife Pam and I went to have dinner in Hampstead with the late Gurney Braithwaite, then a Tory MP, and his wife.

Gurney was a lovable old rascal who always wore striped trousers and a black jacket, and had the reddish type of face which one associates with good drinking although he was not a heavy drinker. As we had drinks before dinner in the back garden of his new house he told us with certain satisfaction that he had just pulled a fast one over a new young Labour minister.

'I had our old house on the market for £4750 and there were no enquiries,' he explained. 'So the estate agent came to me and said, "Mr Braithwaite, I think you are going to have to pull down the price a bit." Then out of the blue this chap Harold Wilson comes to me in the Commons and says, "Mr Braithwaite, I hear that you have a house to sell. I might be interested. Could I go and have a look at it?" Well, Wilson went and had a look at the house, liked it very much and came back and said, "I'm very interested".'

Gurney chuckled. 'I said to him, "Why don't we do a deal that saves the agent's money? I am asking £4750 and I dare say I will have to pay the agent £250 of that. Why don't we split the difference and take that off the price of the house?" Harold agreed, so that meant I got far more than the agent ever dreamed I would.'

And Gurney laughed again at the memory. But of course in the end it was Wilson who had the last laugh. For I expect that when he sold the house it was worth far, far more than he paid Gurney.

One other interesting point in this transaction was that Gurney told me that the cheque had been paid by the Co-operative Insurance, which meant of course that Wilson had, quite rightly as a socialist, gone to the Co-op for his mortgage money.

I was soon to get to know Wilson very much better. For many years we were regularly to lunch together at the Escargot in Greek Street.

He was a most agreeable companion with a quicksilver mind. Had he chosen journalism instead of politics he would have been one of the greatest journalists of our times. He had the capacity to remember not just what he had said five or six years previously but what you had said. Indeed he could quote your own article at you word for word. I do not believe that this was deliberate and prepared flattery, but I do believe that he had a photographic memory.

His one great, enormous weakness was his utter incapacity ever to admit that he had been wrong on a major issue. Every single speech he made, every single action he took, no matter how wrong it turned out in the end, he was always absolutely convinced was not only right at the time but was still right. And if anything had gone wrong then the fault was due to someone else.

Over the years he wrote many articles for the *Sunday Express*. I did my best in the paper to help him when the leadership of the Labour Party was in contention. I do not pretend that our help did much good but at any rate it did him no harm. And I liked and admired the way he accepted criticism. You could kick him in the teeth – and my goodness the *Sunday Express* kicked him in the teeth so often that his teeth must have rattled themselves silly – but this never altered or changed his personal friendship. In fact I find it difficult to explain how one can like a man so much personally and dislike his politics so completely.

On occasion for lunch Wilson would take me to the House of Commons and he came once with Mary to dinner at my home. Pam didn't like him. She didn't like the way he treated his wife. 'He ignores her,' she said. 'He doesn't pay any attention to what she says.' But then couldn't the same be said about many men? Including myself?

During the 1964 election campaign the *Sunday Express* knocked hell out of Wilson week after week but after he was returned as Prime Minister I wrote to congratulate him on his victory. He wrote back a dry, humorous letter saying, 'Dear

John, Many thanks for your letter. I am glad to see that you are now saying nicer things than you said during the election.'

After his election as Prime Minister I was to see a great deal less of him. Sometimes, along with other editors, I would go to 10 Downing Street when he gave a press conference for editors. I would also see him at the occasional dinner and he was always friendly. Then towards the end of 1968 we had a great occasion coming up for the *Sunday Express*. The fiftieth birthday of the newspaper was to be celebrated in January 1969 in the Savoy Hotel with a great and distinguished gathering.

I decided to invite the Prime Minister to be the guest of honour. To my delight Wilson accepted. Shortly afterwards his Press Secretary, Trevor Lloyd-Hughes, was on the telephone to ask if I would come to Downing Street and discuss the details of the dinner, the speaking arrangements and the seating arrangements with the Prime Minister.

Here is an account of what I wrote at the time:

On Wednesday 16 January 1969, I went to 10 Downing Street and spent a couple of hours drinking whisky and chatting with Harold Wilson in his study – a modern wood-panelled room with a model of a ship at one end and a very fine Lowry at the other. He told me much later in the evening how an MP called Hervey Rhodes had financed Lowry in his early days by giving him £25 for a picture when Lowry was hard up, which was often. Rhodes now has a collection worth half a million.

Trevor Lloyd-Hughes stayed with us for the first half-hour or so and then excused himself. I noticed that he treated Wilson with quite an easy familiarity and only used the appellation Prime Minister after he had heard me so doing.

Wilson, once Hughes had gone, knocked hell out of his colleagues. His main target was Callaghan who must once again be showing signs of ambition. Said Wilson: 'John, he hasn't got a single vertebra in his body. Time after time I have to go in and put a poker up his back to stiffen it.'

Judith Hart – she wanted her bottom spanked. Roy

Jenkins he was less venomous about – obviously he does not regard him as a current danger.

Wilson's utter vanity is still strongly showing. 'I made one mistake. In 1965 to steady the pound I went to Green's Playhouse and made a speech saying there would be no election this year. I immediately realised that this would give Tories a chance to get rid of Alec Douglas-Home. Then one day the telephone rang. The voice at the other end told me Heath had succeeded Home. I was worried and said, "I don't like that. He's an abrasive character." "Nonsense," said Marcia, "He's another Gaitskell." '

He told me that the night he made his devaluation broadcast he was tired and had lain down for ten minutes on top of his bed before going to the studios. An attempt, I thought, at self-excuse.

He then said how in general the job was easy – 'but the power is terrific. All you have to do is press a button and it's done. At first I didn't realise that and acted impulsively. But now its wonderful and quite often there is nothing to do.' In fact the telephone did not ring in two hours and the only interruption was a uniformed attendant asking for the PM's red box which Wilson locked.

He was drinking a reasonable amount of whisky – VAT 69 – and boasted about the way he slept and the amount of exercise he took. Eight hours a night and do you know how many rounds of golf I played at Chequers last year – eighty-five?

I said that when he stopped being PM he must come and have that long-delayed round at Walton Heath.

'John,' he replied, 'by that time you will be too old to play.'

He also told me that *Sunday Express* stories were leaked to Keith Renshaw, our lobby correspondent, via the Chief Whip – but the stories came from Wilson himself.

'The other week I read a story that I was going to sack all junior ministers over fifty-two. Wondered where it came from and then suddenly remembered I'd leaked it myself.'

He talked a lot about Max Aitken. 'I'd trust him with my life.'

He described how Max had gone to Rhodesia. 'I didn't send him, oh no. He came here and said, "PM, you're looking very well." I replied, "I am very well apart from my deafness. For instance I didn't hear you saying you were going to Rhodesia." Max looked puzzled but was quick on the uptake. "I suppose then you didn't hear me say when I was going?" "Oh yes, I heard that. The second week in August if you can tear yourself away from Cowes." '

He described how he liked Ian Smith but that Smith was a terrible liar. He told how at the Commonwealth Conference just before UDI Smith claimed he hadn't been invited to a reception at Buckingham Palace when in fact he had been. And how Smith had complained to Lester Pearson that Wilson wouldn't see him when in fact he had spent forty-five minutes with Wilson that very afternoon.

I asked him if he'd like me to put him up for the Royal and Ancient. 'Yes, but I wouldn't like to be blackballed.'

As he walked down with me to the front hall he told me the story he'd told political correspondents at Chequers when they passed the painting of Charles II: 'They'll never kill me to make James king.' Obviously he is still worried about Callaghan.

Wilson duly arrived at our fiftieth anniversary dinner and made a brilliant speech which enthralled the distinguished guests. There was only one slight mishap. Max Aitken introduced him as 'The Right Honourable Harold Macmillan'. I did put him up for the Royal and Ancient, too. And he was blackballed.

After that dinner my meetings with Wilson remained infrequent, although after he lost the prime ministership in 1970 he was good enough to come to my daughter's wedding. And while Ted Heath was still Prime Minister, I took Harold Wilson to lunch at the Boulestin in Southampton Street.

He was bitter about Heath whom he regarded as cold and uncompassionate. 'Do you know, John,' he said, 'he goes home at night to that house all alone and all he has to amuse is himself.'

But not long afterwards Wilson was back in Downing Street as Prime Minister and looked like staying there forever. Then came his sudden and unexpected resignation.

Why did he quit?

He himself swears that he'd decided to do so a long time in advance. But I wonder. Nor do I subscribe to Hugh Scanlon's theory that it had something to do with the slag heaps scandal.

My mind keeps going back to the old business of Commander Courtenay, the Tory MP for Harrow East whose career collapsed when the Sunday *People* published a front-page picture of Courtenay in his long-johns in a Russian hotel room moving towards a buxom lady who lay awaiting him in that Russian hotel-room bed. The *People* had not paid a penny for that picture. It had been planted on them by the KGB. But why? Why should the Russians have wanted to ruin the career of a completely unimportant, obscure Tory MP?

I don't pretend to know the answer to that question but it is perhaps significant that Wilson resigned while the Jeremy Thorpe scandal about his affair with Norman Scott was at its height and Scott was alleging that Jeremy Thorpe had tried to have him liquidated.

Wilson surprisingly came to Thorpe's defence and spoke about a dirty tricks department which the South African government were operating in England against British politicians. At any rate it was shortly after that speech that Wilson quit office and handed over to James Callaghan.

As far as Harold Wilson's qualities as a prime minister are concerned, I have no reason to go back on a judgement I made in my column at the time of his resignation. After saying that I had never doubted his compassion, his intellect or his patriotism I went on to say, 'All I ever doubted was whether between his backstud and his backside there was anything but his braces.'

There was an occasion when he issued a writ because of something I had said about him in the column. He sought exemplary damages because of the harm done to his good name. Our counsel was a barrister who was not only brilliant but had a sense of fun, David Hurst QC. At a meeting we held in his chambers long before the case was due to come to court, he exploded with mirth when I suggested that we pay £100 into court before the case began. This would mean that if Wilson went ahead with his case and the jury awarded less than a derisory £100 Wilson would have to pick up the costs for both sides.

'Why not?' said Hurst. The next thing we heard was that Harold had picked up the money and the action was finished. As I remarked at the time, it suggested that he did not value his good name too highly. But that was an unfair judgement. I suspect that the answer is that Harold's heart had never been in the law suit and he just wanted out at any price.

Years later, when the *Sunday Express* and Wilson were in litigation again, His Eminence Cardinal Hume, the Archbishop of Westminster, requested the pleasure of my company at a reception in the presence of his Holiness Pope John Paul II. I arrived to find an airless and crowded room containing Ted Heath, Harold Wilson, Sir Hugh Fraser, David McNee, James Callaghan, Sir Bernard Braine and almost every other name you can think of. The drinks, offered on trays, were either tepid orange juice or tepid red wine.

The Pope arrived, stayed for precisely five minutes in the room, blessed us all and went on his way into the next room. We were then told that because of security requirements none of us would be able to leave the room or the building until the Pope had left. It was fifty minutes later when I made my own exit. I don't know what the others had expected when they came there, but I can hardly imagine that Ted Heath or Harold Wilson had come without at least a vague expectation of being presented to the Pope. As it happened they would have been lucky to have seen even the tip of his head.

And yet that evening was redeemed for me when Harold Wilson spotted me and walked over to have a long and friendly chat. And even though the *Sunday Express* and myself had been saying some pretty hot things about him, he still bore no animosity of any kind.

Alas for Harold the last few years have been largely downhill.

He has had a major operation and the old clarity of mind seems to have gone too. The last time I saw him for any length of time was on 26 November 1985 when I arrived at Bob Edwards' retirement party at the Café de France nursing a tummy bug which meant that I would be able neither to eat nor to drink.

There were about fifty guests apart from Wilson. They included Michael Foot, Peter Shore, Lord Goodman, Frankie Howerd and Jimmy Savile, together with Louis Kirby, Charles Wintour, Jocelyn Stevens, Richard Stott, Mike Molloy, Michael Cummings and many other newspaper celebrities. I was glad to see that Bob had invited three of his children. Bob Maxwell had also invited two of his own daughters – both quite strikingly attractive women. And there was not the slightest doubt about the affection and warmth in which the daughters held their father.

I was sitting between Michael Foot and Harold Wilson and I came to the conclusion quite early on that either Harold had had much too much to drink or he was losing his marbles. He kept telling me the story of how his wife Mary had been delighted by an article about her in the *Sunday Express* on Halley's Comet but deeply offended by a mocking reference to her on the same subject in *The Sunday Times*. He also kept asking me the same question: 'If you were on a desert island and could only get one newspaper a day, which would you take?'

I replied that I would take the *Daily Telegraph*. 'So would I,' he said. 'What about Sunday?'

'Why, the *Sunday Express*, of course,' I replied.

'So would I,' he said.

Every five minutes he turned to me and asked precisely the same question. It was the fact that he kept on so doing that worried me. I also became very bored by it all. First because he wouldn't let me talk to Michael Foot and secondly because the old brilliant clarity of the Harold I had once known had disappeared completely.

Not long afterwards I went to the Hyde Park Hotel to a reception given by Charles Forte for his son Rocco and Rocco's wife. It was for the benefit of people who had not been able to attend their wedding in Rome some weeks previously.

I found myself in a corner chatting with Peter Walker when Ted Heath arrived, saw us and made a bee-line towards us. He was in the most jovial form. Almost straight away he began talking about Wilson.

'Do you think the old boy is losing his marbles? Geoffrey Howe was at a dinner the other night at which Wilson was in the chair. At the end of the dinner Harold stood up and said, "Gentlemen, the Queen". Everyone got to their feet and toasted the Queen. Then a few minutes later Wilson got to his feet again. Everyone thought, "Oh God, now he's going to make a boring speech." But not a bit of it. Once again he said, "Gentlemen, I give you the toast to the Queen." And do you know something? He did the same thing three times more.'

And Ted's shoulders convulsed in laughter. For my own part I was reflecting on what a sad end it all was to a great career.

When I first became friendly with Woodrow Wyatt he was married to Lady Moorea Hastings, daughter of the Earl of Huntingdon – a delightful woman although she was not to remain his wife for too long.

Woodrow by this time was the star of *Panorama* and a considerable public figure. It was his exposure on that programme of the crookedness and corruption in the electricians' trade union which ended communist control of that union. Had it not been for Woodrow the communists could have had the ability to close down British industry every time Moscow told them to do so. It was as a result of Woodrow's exposure that the union came under the control of moderate leaders like Frank Chapple and later Eric Hammond.

As a socialist MP Woodrow was a maverick – very far to the right.

He was an agreeable friend. We played a lot of tennis together at weekends on my home-made grass court by my cottage at Mickleham. But at a party we held there one Saturday night he upset some of my local friends by saying to Moorea in a loud voice, 'Let's go into the other room, darling. All the interesting people are in there.' It was quite a sight to see him dancing with an attractive lady, shuffling round the floor with a cigar still in his mouth.

He liked to live and to entertain in great style, although I often doubted whether he had the money to finance it. He had a palatial mansion in Little Venice and plenty of servants too. But sometimes things did not go quite as planned.

He invited me to lunch one day and insisted on offering me champagne as an aperitif. When the Portuguese butler arrived carrying a silver tray on which were two glasses and a half-bottle of champagne, there was only one snag. When Woodrow tried to pour the champagne he found that it was frozen solid inside the bottle. The butler had kept it in the deep freeze instead of the refrigerator.

In some ways his sophistication masked an enormous insecurity. In between his marriages, the *Sunday Express* gossip column planned to run what I considered a quite inoffensive story about him. On the Friday night I received a phone call from Woodrow. He seemed almost on the point of tears and begged me not to publish the story. It was the manner in which he did so which startled me. He said, 'You've achieved so much in your life and I've achieved nothing. Would you be surprised if I told you there are times when I almost feel like suicide?'

Years later and even though he was no longer a Labour MP, Woodrow's political power began to grow when in 1973 he started writing a column for the socialist *Sunday Mirror*, then edited by Bob Edwards. In his column he took a robust right-wing view which must have influenced many of his readers. The column certainly interested Margaret Thatcher, who spoke to me about Woodrow. I told her what a likeable person he was and that she should get to know him.

Then one day she telephoned me and said, 'Would you like to come and lunch with us in Tite Street on Sunday? I've invited Woodrow Wyatt.'

Not for anything would I have given up my golf and driven to London on a Sunday so I declined. But from that point Woodrow never looked back. In some ways he became Margaret Thatcher's guru.

And then there was Victor Feather, the most charming, personable, agreeable, delightful companion. He told entertaining stories in his gritty, North country voice and was the most jovial of luncheon companions. He was also, in himself, a most reasonable person.

The only trouble was that he had neither judgement nor guts.

I remember lunching with him on 11 June 1970. The general election was just one week away. All the public opinion polls were showing a Labour victory. I ventured to say that I did not accept the judgement of the opinion polls, although I confessed I did so with not too convinced a spirit.

Vic Feather brushed me aside. 'I can tell you it's all over and done with. Wilson has won, and believe me once next Thursday's election is finished he is going to act as if he could walk on water. I tell you, John, that the only guardian of democracy we will have in this country is the TUC.'

As it happened, Vic Feather turned out to be wrong, very wrong.

With a Tory government in office, Hugh Scanlon and Jack Jones began to run the TUC. Vic Feather wanted to be reasonable but never got the chance to be so and did not have the courage to speak out. I remember Tony Barber telling me, 'It really is funny. Vic Feather comes in to see us in 10 Downing Street. He whines away about how difficult life is for him, that he quite sees our point of view, that he wants to be reasonable. But then he says "But what can I do? I've got Jones and Scanlon against me. It's all very difficult for me." '

'And then,' went on Tony Barber, 'the devil of it is that he steps out of the front door of Downing Street, has a microphone put in front of his mouth, the television camera points at him and some reporter says, "What did you talk about Mr Feather?" And dear old Vic Feather will say in that voice of his, "I thumped my fist on the table. I told them what we in the unions wanted." '

Some time later, when the government was about to introduce its wage freeze after many weeks of futile negotiations in Downing Street between Ted Heath, the CBI and the unions, I had lunch with Frank Chapple.

Chapple had once been a communist. He was married to a Czech and had seen what had happened in that country. Now he was fiercely anti-communist. He was a likeable man with a tremendous number of four-letter words which he scattered throughout his conversation like another man might put salt and pepper on his steak. He was scathing in his condemnation of Jones and Scanlon. And he was almost equally scathing in his condemnation of Vic Feather.

'Feather,' he said to me, 'has got no guts at all. He comes to me and he says, "Why don't you argue this point with Jones and Scanlon? Why do you let them get away with this. Why don't you say this, that and the next thing?" '

Chapple looked at me. 'I tell him,' he continued, ' "What right have you got to ask me to do any standing up? Why don't you occasionally get up off your own effing knees and speak your own mind to Jones and Scanlon?" '

That lunch with Chapple took place just before Ted Heath introduced his pay and prices freeze on 26 October 1972. The electricians' wage claim was still undecided and the one strike which the government could not face was a power-station strike. At that lunch Chapple said something of the greatest significance to me. 'If we get an offer of £2.60 and I put it out to ballot,' he claimed, 'I will stake my career that my chaps will accept it.' This was at a moment when the power workers were publicly demanding something more than £5 extra a week.

The next day, Ted Heath called the national newspaper editors to Downing Street and told them what had been going on in his talks with the TUC and the CBI. He made it clear that the talks had been unsuccessful, that Jones and Scanlon were unwilling to settle and that the government must now move on to a temporary wage and price freeze.

After he had finished talking, he invited questions. While the others were putting their questions I took the pad which had been placed in front of me on the Cabinet table and I wrote a message: 'Frank Chapple tells me he will stake his career on an offer of £2.60 being accepted by his men.'

As we got up to leave the Cabinet Room I handed this folded piece of paper into Ted Heath's hands. He looked at it and said, 'Do you think he really means that?'

'I am sure he means it,' I replied.

Within the next few days the offer to the power workers had been accepted. The threat of an electricity strike had ended.

And providing the power workers continued to work there was little the militant union leaders could do to bring the country to a standstill.

While it is comparatively easy for a British editor to lunch with a British union boss, British Cabinet minister or even a British prime minister, it is a damned sight more difficult to lunch with the President of the United States of America. It happened to me in 1968 when the Vietnam War was at its height and Lyndon Johnson was in the White House.

Lyndon was in a huff at the time with the White House press corps who had been savaging him over his conduct of the war and was seeing none of them. Indeed I suspect it was partly to spite them that he had agreed to give me an interview at all.

My interview was scheduled for 12.30 p.m. on 15 February at the White House. I presented myself five minutes ahead of time and was taken to a room known as the Fish Room where I sat and sat and sat. I knew that King Hussein of Jordan was in Washington on an official visit and I assumed the President would be lunching with him. At 1.15 p.m. as I still sat there I was gloomily coming to the conclusion that there would be no interview at all. An aide would soon come in and tactfully explain that the President's previous appointments had overrun and that unhappily my appointment had been cancelled.

But not a bit of it. Ten minutes later a smiling aide told me that the President was ready to see me now. I was then taken to a room where the President was sitting in a rocking chair. He rose, greeted me affably and enquired whether I would like to join him in some root beer. I had no idea what root beer was but happily assented. When the root beer arrived he resumed his rocking and the interview began. All the time we were talking a Japanese photographer was busy taking pictures of us. I deduced that Lyndon probably found it a good public relations ploy to send newspapermen home to their families clutching photographs of themselves chatting familiarly with the President.

After about five minutes the character of the interview changed. We began to talk about Vietnam and the barrage of criticism to which Johnson was being subjected. He spoke glowingly about the help he was getting from Australia and how much he admired the great Australian Prime Minister, Robert Menzies, who had once told him that every night he had prayed for his critics. 'Yes,' he told Johnson, 'every night as I pull the covers over my head I say God-damn you all.'

'I do the same,' Johnson said.

I asked him if he had ever thought of going on to the offensive with his critics.

'After all,' I pointed out, 'it was not you who took the US into this war and it would be the easiest thing in the world for you to take them out of it. And that's precisely what you would do if you were only after political popularity. That you don't do so is because you are putting your duty to your country before personal popularity.'

At this point he leaned forward in his chair. 'What are you doing for lunch?' he asked.

'Absolutely nothing,' I replied.

The next hour and a half was fascinating. He showed me the Oval Office and we then walked through the White House grounds to the private apartments. On our way there he suddenly asked me, 'What size do you take?' I was bewildered for a moment until I realised that he was talking about off-the-peg suits. 'My arms are so long that I have to have special ones,' he informed me. I didn't have the heart to say that I hadn't bought an off-the-peg suit in years.

It was one of the most interesting lunches of my life. Once inside the private apartments Lyndon telephoned one senior White House aide after another and asked if he would like to join us. There were about twelve of us round the table when we eventually sat down to a simple lunch of soup, chicken sandwiches and rice pudding.

One thing I learned during the course of lunch was that Lyndon had not the highest opinion in the world of Harold Wilson. He was particularly indignant about a story which had received much publicity in England during the Soviet leader Kosygin's recent visit there. It was to the effect that Wilson and Kosygin together had made an attempt to stop the Vietnam War and that in the middle of the night Wilson had spoken to Johnson on the telephone with exciting proposals. Lyndon denied flatly that he had ever spoken to Wilson during the Kosygin visit and implied that Wilson would do anything for publicity.

Since at the time Harold Wilson had made a great play of his dramatic telephone call to Johnson, this story intrigued me. Although everything I learned from Lyndon was obviously off the record and not to be used in the newspaper, on my return to London I told some of my friends what Lyndon had said.

For example, I told Reggie Maudling. I told Quintin Hogg and I told Duncan Sandys. And at dinner one night at the Savoy I also told Bob Edwards.

The very next Saturday evening, an hour before the *Sunday Express* was due to go to press, I received an anguished telephone call from the American Embassy.

One of their First Secretaries was on the line. A report had reached Washington, he said, that I intended publishing in the *Sunday Express* the fact that the President was denying having spoken to Wilson on the telephone during the Vietnam crisis. Would I please give an undertaking to do nothing of the kind? To publish such a story would be very embarrassing.

The note of urgency in the diplomat's voice was very real. It was quite clear that he had received urgent orders from on high. I reassured him. I told him that I did not and had not any intention of publishing in the *Sunday Express* what I had learned from Lyndon Johnson. Satisfied, he rang off.

But immediately I began to wonder why and how on earth Washington had got to know that there was even a chance of my taking a decision to publish. I asked Quintin Hogg on the telephone. Had he mentioned to anyone what I had said to him? No he had not. A telephone call to Duncan Sandys produced the same answer. So did one to Reggie Maudling.

It was only after some time that I began to realise what had happened. Bob Edwards had passed my story on to the political correspondent Terry Lancaster who was close to Wilson. Lancaster must have told Wilson and Wilson had taken swift action. Hence the telephone call from the American Embassy.

In the years after Beaverbrook's death in 1964 Max Aitken seemed to have so much going for him. He not only had great personal charisma, he was genuinely liked, respected and indeed almost worshipped by members not only of the editorial staff but also of the machine-room staff – although that of course never stopped them trying to screw him for money.

Our Sports Club secretary, Tom Glynn, himself a machine-room hand, once told me of the occasion when the Glasgow office had been playing the London office in the final of a football tournament for some shield or other. It had been at White Hart Lane, there had been only a handful of spectators, the rain had been pissing down but throughout it all one sodden figure, a soft brown trilby pulled over his eyes, had doggedly remained on a bench beside the touchline – Max Aitken.

Even before his father's death Max had persuaded a sailing friend and distinguished submariner, John Coote, later to be immortalised by *Private Eye* as Captain John Coote RN (submerged), to quit the Navy and join the *Express* on the management side. One of Coote's first jobs was as manager of the *Sunday Express*. He immediately became enormously popular with most of the people around him. And with reason. It would have been difficult to find anyone less pompous or more reasonable.

I took an immediate shine to him and listened intently to any hints he might give me on sailing in the Solent – a sport I had just taken up. I still have somewhere the instructions he sent me before I embarked on my first trip across the Channel to Cherbourg. They were addressed to Prince Henry the Navigator and said, 'Just remember to turn left at the Needles, steer 180 degrees all night and you will find Cherbourg in front of you in the morning.' I did too.

The only trouble with Johnnie was that he was not much good as chief executive, a job he inherited when old wise Tom Blackburn, the man who had been in the job under Beaverbrook, came through age and illness to leave the scene.

And economic troubles were mounting around us. Newspapers were increasing in size and price and so people were buying fewer of them. Commercial television meant that there was vastly more competition for advertising revenue, costs were soaring, we were seriously overmanned and the mechanical unions had their ignorant Luddite hands firmly and permanently round our windpipe.

In Glasgow the stage was soon to be reached when the workforce was constantly threatening production – sometimes because they did not like the political message of a cartoon. I remember the manager in Glasgow pleading with the so-called fathers of the union chapel and warning them that if they carried on like that then one day London would come and close the Glasgow office down.

'Don't give us that, Mr Paterson,' he was told. 'If they want to try and close us down they can come any time they like.'

It would have taken a genius to have found an answer to our problems. Johnny Coote, alas, was not that. Instead he committed what in my view was an almost unbelievable blunder.

In an effort to reduce the numbers of editorial staff he offered a scheme of voluntary redundancy. The result was cataclysmic. Many of the best people on the writing staff applied for redundancy, picked up large cheques in compensation and walked straight into jobs on the *Daily Mail* and other rivals. Those who knew they had no other job to go to stayed put.

But another figure was rising to prominence at Beaverbrook Newspapers. Although not a yachtsman, Jocelyn Stevens was a friend of Max's. He had made a name for himself with the magazine *Queen* which he had built up into the great fashion periodical of the early Sixties. Alarming but no doubt apocryphal stories at the time had spread around Fleet Street that occasionally Jocelyn chewed the carpet in his anger or chucked filing cabinets out of windows. It was to the *Evening Standard* that Max now sent Stevens. But it was not long before Coote was out and Stevens had taken his place as Managing Director of the whole group. And I was to see much, too much, of him thereafter.

When Max told me about the decision to appoint Stevens I was appalled and told him so. He then gave me an assurance that Stevens would never have any personal authority over me or my editorial freedom and that at all times I would be answerable directly and only to him. Nor did he ever break that undertaking.

Meanwhile without Beaverbrook constantly peering over my

shoulder I had the best job in the world. And the best staff too. My deputy was a large fellow-Glaswegian called Victor Patrick. Patrick was mad about cricket. He had played as a youngster for West of Scotland. He organised a *Sunday Express* cricket team and such was his enthusiasm that soon on summer Sundays almost everyone on the editorial staff was taking his wife or girl to follow the team. It all made for quite wonderful office camaraderie.

There were brilliant cartoonists like Michael Cummings and the great and only Carl Giles who lived on a Suffolk farm, drew his cartoons in his studio in Ipswich and descended every once in a while like a mad whirlwind on Fleet Street. His contribution to the success of the newspaper was beyond measure. He made people laugh out loud with his comic genius but there was never either malice or cruelty in anything he drew.

Then there was Thurlow Craig who lived even further away in the Welsh mountains and seldom, if ever, came to London at all. But every Sunday he brought through his column a breath of country air into the homes of all our readers. There was also the brilliant essayist Robert Glenton who wrote about cars in such enchanting and inimitable fashion.

But perhaps the brightest and certainly the bravest of them all was Douglas Clark, friend of Bob Pitman and for many years my successor on the Cross-Bencher column. He had a magical touch with both words and life. He had taken a double first at Oxford and every morning in the train on the way to town did *The Times* crossword in just seventeen minutes. He was the most convivial of men and although he was very far from being a drunk he drank whisky as if it were going out of fashion and was seldom without a cigarette in his mouth.

Still in his forties, Douglas suffered not one but two cerebral haemorrhages. He recovered from the first in the most miraculous fashion but then instead of slowing down he took off again just where he had left off before his illness – living as if there were no tomorrow. Then two years later came the second stroke and once again he was written off. Yet once again he came back and the only discernible difference in his life-style was that it might have taken him perhaps one minute longer to do *The*

Times crossword. The rest of the staff adored him and there was much grief when some time later a third cerebral attack proved sadly that he was not after all immortal.

We had some scintillating writers contributing to the leader page too. Quintin Hogg was a regular contributor, as was Harold Wilson and indeed every prominent politician of the time. However, it was not a political giant but instead what some might describe as a political minnow who of all MP contributors most most captured my admiration – Teddy Taylor, the Tory MP for Southend.

I lunched with him only once. I went with the preconceived idea that he was a useful political lightweight for whom the very top job in politics would have been the Secretary of State for Scotland and that he had lost that possibility for ever when he had failed to hold Cathcart, Glasgow in the 1979 election and had been forced to take an English constituency instead.

For most of the lunch I felt that my preconceived ideas were being confirmed. Then in a passing reference to his having lost Cathcart he described it as 'one of the three great disasters of my life'.

'What were the other two?' I asked him.

He hesitated and then said, 'The first was when my father went bankrupt.'

Then he told me the story of how his father had been a stockbroker's clerk in Glasgow. The stockbroker had quit the business and because Taylor senior knew of no other profession he had taken over the office. But because he was unknown and simply a clerk no one gave him their business. He went bust and was hammered in the Stock Exchange. Shortly afterwards, at about the age of fifty, he died in a public telephone-box calling his wife.

According to Taylor, he and his mother sold what was their only asset, their home, in order to try and help meet his father's debts. From being a reasonably comfortable lower-middle-class family they quite suddenly had nothing. But nothing. Mother went out to work in a textile factory. Taylor, then aged twenty-two, took a manual job. They did not stop until every penny of the father's debts had been paid off.

When he had finished telling me his story I said, 'And what was the third disaster?'

He looked at me as if wondering whether to confide. 'Not many people know this. But in 1968 I had a cerebral haemorrhage. All my life I had had terrible migraines. Sometimes the headaches were so great that I had to sit in the darkness chewing a carrot in an effort to relieve the pain. Then in the Commons after a tremendous row with Ted Heath I collapsed. Dickson Mabon (the Labour MP at that time for Greenock, and a doctor) attended me. I was carted off to Westminster Hospital where it was discovered that I had had a cerebral haemorrhage.

'It was in that hospital that I met my wife. Otherwise I suppose I would still be a bachelor. Ted Heath was so certain that I was going to die that he sent red roses. But I didn't die. Thereafter I had to attend Westminster Hospital every three months for a check-up but after a time I got fed up with doctors telling me what to do and now I never see a doctor at all.'

But can you imagine with that medical background the pressure that must have been on him? And yet in all Westminster there is not one MP more active or more dedicated.

Teddy Taylor may not have reached the top in politics. But could anyone ever reach higher than he has in courage?

As Editor I took then and have always taken the view that I should not sign anyone on for the *Sunday Express* unless I were quite sure that he was going to make the grade and that his face was going to fit. When people left before retiring age it was either because they had been promoted or were taking up some new venture. And because of my reluctance ever to sack anyone, I was especially hesitant ever to take on an older man already well established on another newspaper.

Wilfred Sendall was such an older man. He was in his mid-forties, had a family to support, a mortgage no doubt, and was set up for life as parliamentary correspondent of the *Daily Telegraph*. I was looking at the time for someone to write the Cross-Bencher column and he was quite prepared to take the risk of jumping into the unknown. But the art of writing Cross-Bencher is a very special one and for the first year of his life on the *Sunday Express* Wilfred just did not have that art.

Almost every Friday Bob Edwards, who was then my deputy, would sit down and rewrite the column.

I was getting desperate. There was no way I could sack Sendall. At his age that would have been an awful thing to do. Then suddenly it all came right. Wilfred found the magic touch and began to write Cross-Bencher as if he had been doing so all his life. I congratulated myself on having solved the Cross-Bencher problem for years ahead.

But my self-congratulations were premature. One day, Wilfred, who had been one of the first marines ashore on D-Day and clearly did not lack courage, came into my office to tell me that he had been made an offer by the *News of the World* and had decided to accept it. In vain I offered to top their offer, pleaded for his loyalty, pointed out the dangers at his advanced age of leaving a secure job and in general tried every trick in the book. All to absolutely no avail. He had loved his time on the *Sunday Express* and liked all his colleagues including myself very much indeed. But he felt he needed a new challenge.

'Besides,' he said, 'I'm not really going away. Fleet Street is just a village and I'm only going to the other side of the road. I expect I will be back.'

And he was too. He later moved yet again to become Political Editor of the *Daily Express*.

Sendall gave me a disturbing insight into the character of Winston Churchill. Because of his age and unlike the rest of us Sendall had been a reporter before the war. He said that in those pre-war days Churchill would gladly give the time of day to any American correspondent in London in order to get his views across in the USA but that he treated British reporters with contempt – presumably on the grounds that since he was on terms of close friendship with most of the British newspaper proprietors it was unnecessary to speak to their underlings.

Sendall told me how once before the war he had been sent by the *News Chronicle* to Euston Station to meet the train carrying Churchill from Liverpool where he had been addressing meetings in the East Toxteth by-election.

As the great man descended from the train Sendall introduced himself and asked if he had anything he would like to say to the *News Chronicle*.

Churchill looked at him and thrust out his hand. 'Yes,' he said. 'You can go back and tell them you have shaken the hand of Winston Churchill.'

Enoch Powell was another contributor to the *Sunday Express* at that time.

I had been trying for some years to persuade him to write for us although I had in fact never met him. I invariably made the approach through the *Sunday Express* Features Editor and every time an approach was made the reply would come that Mr Powell was already committed, that he was writing an article for the Wolverhampton *Express and Star* and that he regretted that he would be unable to write for the *Sunday Express*.

I did not bother overmuch about this, but one day a few weeks after Beaverbrook's death my secretary told me that Mr Powell was on the telephone wishing to speak to me. On a hunch that it might be *the* Mr Powell and not simply an irate reader I accepted the call. It was *the* Mr Powell.

And we had the most extraordinary conversation. He explained to me that a book of his speeches was about to be published the following Monday and he wondered if I might care to have the book reviewed in the next edition of the *Sunday Express*?

I replied that a book of political speeches was not quite the thing a Sunday newspaper reviewed inasmuch as all the speeches had already been published and there was not a great deal a reviewer could say which had not already been said by leader writers at the time the speeches had been delivered. But, I went on to say, I would be delighted to have the occasional contribution from Mr Powell on the leader page of the *Sunday Express*.

Powell then said the most extraordinary thing. 'Yes,' he said, 'I would be prepared to write for the *Sunday Express* now that he has gone.'

Not quite sure that I had heard properly I said, 'What do you mean, now that he has gone?'

'Now that Beaverbrook has gone,' Powell replied. 'He was a

165

most evil man. I could never have written for the *Sunday Express* while he was still alive.'

I became coldly angry. 'In that case, Mr Powell,' I said, 'I don't quite see how you can write now. Because everything that Lord Beaverbrook stood for, I still stand for. His policies are being continued on the *Sunday Express*. For I happen to believe in his policies.'

But Powell did in fact start writing for the *Sunday Express* and from time to time he and I had lunch together.

It was always an interesting experience. To begin with it was quite clear that he was conducting a massive campaign to woo selected British newspapers. There was not a suitable editor on whose door Enoch Powell did not knock or to whose desk did not come a copy of Enoch Powell's latest speech. But at the same time it must be added that the speeches were magnificently compiled and were always essentially newsworthy. Nor was Powell venal. He would extract a good price for an article but he was always more eager to have a speech printed as a speech in every newspaper – for which he was paid nothing at all – rather than to make 100 guineas or even 200 guineas by turning the speech into an article exclusive to one single newspaper.

It seemed to me when I first met Powell that he had an enormous intellectual arrogance. It was not so much people speaking to each other as Enoch Powell lecturing me. But with the passage of time that changed and I found that I was able to have a real dialogue with him. The intellectual arrogance was still there but I found increasingly that he respected, if not accepted, my instinct on political matters and on the times we differed it happened that I was right more often than he was.

Powell's wife Pam and his two daughters were absolutely devoted to him. When once they came to visit us in the country during a half-term holiday I was very impressed indeed by the way in which they spoke to him and the air of equality which existed between father and daughters. It was not a family in which the father was a dictator. They held in our presence a discussion as to which cinema they would go to on the Monday of the half-term and the decision was taken in true democratic fashion by a show of hands.

The picture which appeared on my election address when I fought Kincardine and West Aberdeenshire in the general election of 1945. I failed to win the seat by 642 votes.

The Sports Staff of the *Sunday Express*. In front of the group is Dick Francis, then a famous National Hunt jockey and now renowned as a thriller writer.

With Lyndon Johnson in 1968. 'What are you doing for lunch?' he asked. 'If you are free, come and lunch with me.'

Alongside the quay at Barfleur in the hot August sun. For three glorious weeks, the stresses and strains of Fleet Street are far, far away.

The President of the Gambia, Sir Dawda Jawara, spends a day sailing on board *Outcast*. Ted Heath came aboard to say hello.

With Reginald Maudling on the morning after the general election of 1970. Only hours before, Reggie had been appointed Home Secretary.

The Prime Minister and Lord Hailsham at the dinner to celebrate JJ's twenty-five years as Editor of the *Sunday Express*.

Powell was desperately keen that his children should think well of him. I remember a lunch when he said to me, 'My daughter, Jennifer, is home for half-term this weekend and we will all be going to look at old churches on Sunday. But I want to do something before then. I want on Friday night, when she has gone to bed, to go and sit beside her bed and to explain to her what it is I am trying to achieve, why I say the things I say, why I do the things I do.'

He looked pensive and added, 'We try to be a normal family and it's very difficult. Sometimes I think she understands. We were having a discussion at the lunch table one day among the whole family about some unimportant subject and I said, "Don't try to engage my sympathy, I am not a compassionate man. I'm not prepared to listen to compassionate arguments." Jennifer just looked across and said, "Daddy, you are a compassionate man. You are a compassionate man because I have often heard you argue with Grandma on behalf of mentally handicapped children. And anyone who was not compassionate would not argue the way you do."'

A fond light came into Enoch's eyes as he explained to me that his wife's mother, a fine woman with whom he got on very well, was inclined to protest from time to time about the amount of money which was being spent on criminals who merited the death penalty and on medical care for children who would always be mental abnormally. He was obviously delighted that his daughter should have seen that behind his sometimes hard mask there was someone with very human and compassionate feelings.

I suggested to him that instead of going into his daughter's bedroom and explaining his motives, he would do much better to write down his motives in a form that afterwards could be read by posterity. But he shook his head.

It was at lunch one day in April 1973 at his home in South Eaton Place that I suddenly received a blinding insight into how Enoch Powell's character and motivation had been formed.

Somehow during lunch the talk had come round to children's illnesses. His wife said that she had just had a piano tuned by a piano-tuner who was completely blind – the result, so he said, of scarlet fever as a child.

'Not scarlet fever surely,' said Enoch. 'It must have been measles – I had them at the age of four. I remember it because I had to give up reading the *Encyclopaedia Britannica*, at the time.'

We laughed but he insisted that he was serious. 'My mother and father started to teach me to read at the age of two,' he said.

He began to talk about his parents: 'My mother was the driving force. I was never afraid of my father but I was of my mother. She was a big woman in every way except physically. Do you know that when she was an old woman and I was a grown man I still used instinctively to duck if she made a sudden movement?'

He relapsed into thoughtful silence for a second and then added, 'A wet towel can be very painful.'

The only thing that worried me about Enoch Powell was whether he was always completely in charge of his trolley.

There was the occasion on the M4 when he was being driven by his wife at 70 m.p.h. in the fast lane when a chauffeur-driven car, after several abortive attempts to persuade Pam to move over, passed them on an inside lane. Enoch looked up from his newspaper, took the offending car's number and secured the successful prosecution of the chauffeur. I thought that not only vindictive and self-righteous but also oddly arrogant since it assumed that his own car's speedometer was accurate.

The other occasion which gave me pause was the day Enoch emerged from his South Eaton Place house and found his garage exit blocked by a car. That is something which would make even a saint angry but Enoch appears to have gone almost berserk, according to reports published at the time, and went round the car beating it up with his umbrella.

During the general election of February 1974 Powell came close to urging people to vote socialist rather than re-elect a Heath government which had committed us to the Common Market. He himself had withdrawn his candidature of Wolverhampton South-West rather than stand as a Heath supporter.

The first time we lunched after the election, he told me how he had felt when the results were announced.

'People imagine that I worked it all out deliberately but the truth is quite the opposite,' he said. 'I was convinced that Heath would win the election with perhaps a majority of sixty seats. So I thought I was committing suicide and that I would never enter politics again when I announced that I was not going to fight my seat. The night of the election, 28 February, the girls had some friends in for supper. I went to bed at a quarter to eleven and told Pam I did not want to be disturbed no matter what happened. I read for twenty minutes and then fell asleep.'

'Did you take a sleeping pill?' I asked.

'Never,' he replied. 'I went straight to sleep and I wakened the next morning about seven o'clock and went downstairs to make a cup of tea. In the hall *The Times* was slanted through the letter-box. I could just read the second headline which said, "Wilson Praises Maturity of Electors". I thought, "Well, that seems interesting" and I pulled the paper out of the box. There was the main headline: "Heath Gamble Fails". I went upstairs and had a bath and while I was in my bath I sang the *Te Deum* in its entirety.'

When he became an Ulster MP I was to see a good deal less of Enoch. But on a night in July 1982 we met at the Howard Hotel for dinner. He told me that after Mountbatten's assassination the Queen was very disturbed and said to the Prime Minister who was then Margaret Thatcher, 'Isn't this ever going to stop?'

Powell had come to the Howard by Tube, travelling on his free old-age pensioner's pass. He travelled back the same way.

I asked whether he was afraid he might be a target for assassination.

He smiled. 'No, I don't think so,' he said. 'For if they were to kill me they would tighten the screw and unleash anger against themselves. The people they kill are those whose deaths are designed to loosen the screw and bring extra pressure on the British government to seek a solution which involves a federal Ireland.'

'Do you take any personal precautions to protect yourself in Ulster or while travelling to and from there?' I asked him.

'Only one,' he replied. 'I make sure I never tell the police my travel arrangements.'

VI

IN MARCH 1970 I set off for a trip to Singapore, Taiwan, Hong Kong and Vietnam carrying in my hand luggage a very new and very broken camera.

I was sore about that camera. I had bought it only days before my trip had been decided upon and it occurred to me that if only I had delayed I could have bought the same model much cheaper in Hong Kong. There had been an even greater calamity. The weekend before my trip it had slipped out of my hand and fallen on to the kitchen floor. To my horror the lens cover seemed jammed in its screw.

Enquiries the next day of camera specialists in London produced the gloomy news that it would take two weeks to put it right and would cost rather more than the camera was worth. Nevertheless I carried it with me on the assumption that there were bound to be more repairing facilities in the countries to which I was going.

On my arrival in Singapore, where I was to have an interview the next day with the Prime Minister, Lee Kuan Yew, it seemed that I was right. Almost the first building I saw was a large Konica workshop. But when I showed them my camera, oriental heads shook sadly. 'Sorry,' they said, 'at least ten days to put it right.'

Exactly the same thing was to happen in glittering, prosperous

Hong Kong. But in Saigon where the war was its height, where every night you could hear the sound of the enemy guns, where because of shortages there was nothing in the shabby shops – Saigon, as it turned out, was different. Saigon was different in every way. Saigon was magic. I fell in love with it and its people at first sight. There was an air of gentle, civilised decadence. The French influence was everywhere. And the Vietnamese women were breathtakingly beautiful.

Bert Okuley, the UPI staff man who met me at the airport, was to become my guide, mentor and chum during my few days there – wonderful days in which I flew by helicopter gunship to outlying villages within rifle fire of the Viet Cong front line. Wonderful nights too. There was a little French restaurant in the same street as my hotel and every night all the US war correspondents would gather around the same round table to eat and drink and exchange experiences. They were an interesting bunch. One of them had so fallen in love with the country that when his newspaper had called him back to the US he had jacked in his job and opted to stay in Vietnam as a freelance – an occupation which at that stage of the war could not have been producing rich pickings.

But of all the men at the table it was Sawada San I best remember. I am not sure if that was his real name. It was what Bert Okuley called him. He was a Japanese photographer working for UPI and strangely for a Japanese was about six feet tall and burly. Bert whispered to me that the previous year he had won a Pulitzer prize for his war pictures. He also had another claim to fame. He had once been caught in a Viet Cong ambush but instead of surrendering when held up at gunpoint he had simply turned his broad back on the patrol and walked steadily away. He had taken the view that he would rather be killed than taken prisoner. The Viet Cong were so dumbfounded that they did not fire.

During the meal I told Sawada the sad story of my camera. He listened and then said, 'Let me have a look at it.' The next night at supper he gave it back to me. Working perfectly. And this in a city where there were no spare parts for anything. I was to see Sawada only once again – the next morning at the airport. I was heading for Hong Kong, he was heading for the Cambodian border on another assignment for UPI. He never returned from it. Bert Okuley later wrote to tell me he had been killed. Perhaps having once again turned his back and tried to walk away?

I found Lee Kuan Yew to be a fascinating man. He told me how he had ended the tyranny and turmoil caused by Red agitators in Singapore during his early days in office not by banning them but by letting them talk their heads off in Raffles Square with TV cameras always in attendance. Close-ups of their wild, contorted faces could be seen in every family sitting-room. It put the fear of God into viewers and concentrated their minds powerfully about the need to keep the Reds out and Lee Kuan Yew in.

There was just a shade of anti-Australianism in his talk. He was emphatic that at the time he wanted not an Australian military presence in the area but a British one. I was to learn afterwards from Peter Carrington exactly why he suspected Australians.

Just before the Japanese took over Singapore, Lee, then a child of eight or nine, had been standing outside his house as a detachment of disenchanted, defeated Australian soldiers straggled by. One of them took his rifle, threw it at Lee and said, 'Here, you take this. It's your fucking war now.'

Lee was never to forget that.

Of two other things from that interview, one was the good-natured contempt in which Lee held Harold Wilson. 'If he had implemented his trade union legislation, "In Place of Strife", he might have put at least a thumb-print on British history. But unhappily he is just incapable of ever taking a decision about anything.'

My second memory? After the interview had been going for more than an hour I asked politely if I might be permitted to light a cigarette. Lee was the essence of graciousness. 'Of course,' he said. But then added: 'But do you mind if I have the air-conditioning switched on? The cigarette smoke so irritates my eyes.' My cigarette case stayed in my pocket.

Taiwan, outside of the capital Taipei, in some ways reminded me of Scotland with its wild beaches and sand dunes. But no one could ever have confused Sauchiehall Street with the garish, brightly lit streets in Taipei. And at that time Taiwan, under the firm control of Chiang Kai-shek, was in some ways a spooky place.

Gill Alder, our Naval Attaché, told me that Chiang Kai-shek's secret police were everywhere and he was convinced that all the telephones were bugged. Outside all the restaurants were cages which contained snakes. You picked a snake as you might a trout from a tank and it was then cooked for you. I was not tempted.

I visited a pottery factory and was asked if I would like to buy anything. Not having very much hope that anything I purchased would ever be delivered to England, I bought a cylindrical blue table-lamp standing about two feet high and domed. It cost me less than £5 including freight charges. I was also asked whether my electric current in England was AC or DC. I replied AC firmly believing that the question would be academic.

To my utter surprise the lamp duly arrived one month after my own arrival home. It was in perfect condition, worked immediately and was quite outstandingly beautiful.

Gill Alder and his wife were delightful people and entertained me most hospitably during my time in Taiwan. Unhappily a few years later they were to become headline news back home in England. An intruder broke into their Sussex home and killed them both with a shotgun. The most awful thing of all is that the man subsequently tried and found guilty of the crime was their own teenage son.

I remember one other thing vividly of my trip to Taiwan and that was the return flight to Hong Kong. I had been made aware during my trip to Vietnam that the descent into Hong Kong airport in bad weather was extremely hazardous since there were skyscrapers on either side of the approach.

When we left Taipei airport in a Royal Thai airliner I was comforted by the thought that the pilot was most probably a Scandinavian. That comfort disappeared when after take-off and we were at our cruising height the pilot announced, 'This is Captain Tuklan speaking. The weather over Hong Kong is atrocious but we will try to get in.'

As we neared Hong Kong surrounded by swirling cloud I sank into my seat. My neighbour, an American businessman selling perfumes in the Far East and who had been served kosher food during the flight, looked at me speculatively.

'Don't worry,' he said. 'I fly hundreds of thousands of miles a year and these things are as safe as houses. You probably don't fly very much do you?'

I didn't try to tell him about the number of friends I had lost in 'stuffed' cloud. And he was right. We were safe as houses. The Thai pilot whom I had envisaged as a tiny chap perched in the cockpit on a pile of telephone directories so that he could see out of the windscreen got us down safely.

The tempest was still blowing the night I left Hong Kong by Qantas jet for Australia. The rain was pelting down and the winds were at gale force, but inside the Qantas jet was warm and comfy.

I was at the back when one of the later arrivals came in to the fore part of the cabin. She was carrying an armful of tennis rackets which she slung into the overhead luggage compartment. She looked around the whole plane and in so doing her personality lit up the entire 707.

I didn't recognise her but I was aware instinctively that here was a great personality, a person with quite extraordinary charisma. I asked a steward who she was later in the trip and was told that she was Virginia Wade, then at the beginning of her brilliant career. I thought of going up the aisle and introducing myself to her and then decided against it.

When I arrived at Sydney Airport I was met by my friend Jack Cannon who at the end of the war had shared a flat with me in London after having served throughout it as a rear-gunner in the Royal Australian Air Force. By now he was Sports Editor of a Melbourne newspaper. During the war Jack had made some sort of history by surviving when his RAF Lancaster bomber had crashed and exploded in Norfolk on its way back home from bombing Germany. The entire rear gun-turret with Jack still in it had come down on its own from 300 feet.

I told him that Virginia Wade had been on my plane and asked him if he could find her hotel number so that I could contact her. He was horrified. 'She is a big star playing in a big tennis tournament,' he said. 'You can't do that.'

So I didn't.

Some three years later Virginia and I met in London and became good friends. I told her about the first encounter and her reply was, 'God, I wish you had come up to me on that plane and telephoned me at my hotel in Sydney.'

She is quite a girl. Warm and vibrant. We lunched together a few times, but, alas, remained only good friends.

Over dinner that first night in Sydney Jack told me that he had arranged the following day, Sunday, for his friend the great Australian cricketer Richie Benaud to drive us in his car to the Blue Mountains. We took a long time getting there. Richie, a delightful man, was not only a slow bowler. He seemed to have the same technique driving. There were many times when milk floats seemed to be passing us.

But we did get there and the view was fantastic. We went into lunch in a hotel in a place which had some extraordinary name like Katatoomba, but I knew everything was just like home when I saw the menu. Brown Windsor soup was the starter.

By the time I returned to England it was evident that a general election would not be too long delayed. Nor was it. Within three months Ted Heath was in 10 Downing Street.

I first began to get to know Ted Heath when he was Leader of the Opposition. He invited me to lunch at his flat at the Albany in Piccadilly. The meal was a good one, cooked by his housekeeper, although I noticed with a lack of enthusiasm that the wine consisted of a half-bottle of Mateus rosé. Over the years his taste in wine was to improve dramatically.

I found the conversation hard going. We seemed to have so little in common, although he came to life when I asked him if he ever suspected that his telephone was tapped. For at the time I believed that my own was tapped.

Heath said quickly, without hesitation, 'Think it's tapped? I am sure it's tapped.'

After the Tories finally did win the 1970 election, Reggie Maudling became Home Secretary. I asked him whether there ever had been any telephone tapping and he assured me that it had all been imagination on the part of Ted Heath and myself, that there had never been any tapping of private lines of journalists or politicians.

But back to Ted Heath. We remained on coolish terms but we lunched occasionally.

Then he took up sailing and one day at lunch he told me that he was thinking of buying an ocean-going yacht. I suggested to him that he might like a Hillyard. He was interested and even more interested when I suggested that I might ring the owner of Hillyard's boat-building yard to find out what sort of discount could be offered. In the event Ted decided to buy an American-designed boat by Sparkman & Stephens which, of course, became the first *Morning Cloud*. I expect he negotiated a big discount on that too.

The next time we lunched *Morning Cloud* was almost completed and Ted was discussing where he was going to find a mooring for her. I told him that I kept my own boat at Fairey Marina at Hamble. I told him that I was reasonably certain that I could get a mooring for him alongside mine right at the mouth of the River Hamble. I explained that Peter Twiss, the manager of the yard, was a friend and that I would ring him that very afternoon if he wished. And indeed he did so wish.

When I got back to the office I forgot to ring Peter Twiss for perhaps a couple of hours, and when I did so Peter said, 'Everything is already fixed up. I had Ted Heath's secretary on an hour and a half ago.'

Which shows that Ted is pretty quick off the mark. On all subjects connected with yachting he comes immediately to life. He had the mooring next to mine at Hamble for more than a year and during that period I got to know him and like him reasonably well.

By the time the 1970 election came around we were, if not friends, at least good acquaintances. Once again I lunched at the Albany in the first week of the campaign.

The opinion polls were heavily against the Tories. I told him that my own opinion poll, the sale of the *Sunday Express* which always increased when there was a move towards the Tories, was indicating a Tory victory.

But the campaign according to the public opinion polls seemed to go from bad to worse. Then on the second-last Sunday of the campaign we published – thanks to a tip from Tony Barber – a lead story to the effect that the then Minister of Health, Dick Crossman, had told the BMA in confidence that it was quite impossible to give the doctors an increase in salary because of the frightening economic situation which the country faced. There were some people who felt that this exposure of the fragile nature of the economy might have helped the Tories considerably. Certainly Heath was good enough to ring me up and say quite simply, 'Thank you, that may have turned the tide.'

Even so, in the final week of the 1970 election there was scarcely a Tory leader, Heath and Tony Barber apart, who thought they had any chance of winning. The opinion polls still showed the Labour Party miles ahead.

I had arranged for Quintin Hogg to write the leader article on the last Sunday of the election campaign. He had been campaigning in the north and was due to ring me early on Saturday morning on his return to London so that we could discuss what he should write.

Quintin phoned in a state of near panic. He did not think he should write anything at all. He was convinced the election was lost and that instead of writing for the *Sunday Express* he should be on the streets of Marylebone knocking on the doors of constituents and canvassing for votes in order to hold his own constituency.

I pointed out to him that if he were going to help his own campaign in Marylebone, if he thought he was really in danger of losing a seat with such a massive majority, which he clearly did think, then far and away the best thing for him to do was to have an article in the *Sunday Express*. Such an article would do a great deal more good than all the knocking-up of voters that any one man could do on a Saturday morning.

Reluctantly he agreed and his article duly appeared.

The results of the 1970 election began to come through just about midnight. In common with many other Fleet Street people and businessmen, I had gone to the Savoy to a party given by Michael and Pam Berry, Lord and Lady Hartwell. To begin with there was gloom and despondency among the Tory supporters present. On the other hand the Labour supporters were in a happy, buoyant mood. I was standing in a group with Lord and Lady Melchett when the first results began to come through. Melchett's face was a study in agony and so was his wife's. They both clearly had been hoping for a socialist victory. The gaiety went out of that section of the Savoy party.

During the election campaign I had lunched with Reggie Maudling once or twice and we had fixed another lunch for the Tuesday after the election. I began to wonder whether it was worth while carrying on with the agreement since by this time it seemed almost certain that the Tories would lose. But Reggie in his calm, quiet way said, 'Never mind. Let's have our lunch anyway.' And of course when he arrived at that lunch it was as Home Secretary.

After the election there came the affair of the Arab girl guerrilla, Leila Khaled, when we were blackmailed into releasing her in return for the safe conduct given to a hijacked airliner in Jordan. I resented the giving into blackmail of this kind. I resented even more the way in which Downing Street was guiding the newspapers on the Saturday night before Leila Khaled was released. Downing Street was intent on suggesting that the lives of the hostages in Jordan were in active danger.

All the Sunday newspapers ran the same story. The mobs in Amman, it was said, were reaching such frightening proportions and were moving off in the direction of the hotel in which the hostages were held that the British Ambassador in Amman had counselled Her Majesty's Government to give in immediately to the guerrillas' demands.

The next Tuesday the *Daily Telegraph* carried a report from their man in Amman which indicated that he had been hauled in by Arab guerrillas furious at the suggestion which had appeared in Britain's Sunday newspapers that mobs had threatened women and children. 'We don't act in that sort of way,' said the

Arab. It became clear that the story had not emanated from Amman at all but from 10 Downing Street.

I rang Donald Maitland, then Ted Heath's Press Secretary and very much his right-hand man, and spoke roughly to him about his manipulation of news. I said that in all Harold Wilson's time at 10 Downing Street, he had never done anything like this.

As a result Keith Renshaw and I were invited to come and have a drink with the Prime Minister. I came to the conclusion during that drink that Ted Heath did not really understand what I was getting at. He seemed to think that what Maitland had done with the newspapers was the most natural and right thing in the world. He is curiously blinkered in a way. He sees straight ahead and is unable to distinguish greys on either side.

Not that Donald Maitland then thought so. Shortly after the Tory election victory he explained to me why he thought that Heath would make a quite extraordinarily good prime minister.

'There are some politicians who can analyse brilliantly the problems which may lie ahead if they adopt a particular policy,' he told me. 'They will say to themselves and to their colleagues, "If we pursue this particular policy then the moment it begins to bite we can expect massive hostility from public opinion. Our poll ratings will drop. But as long as we don't panic and keep pushing ahead then it is all going to come right and the hostility will be replaced with praise." '

'But then,' added Maitland, 'there are some prime ministers who even though they have analysed it all in advance still panic at the first blast of public anger and do a U-turn. But I don't think Ted will be like that. I am sure he will be a strong leader who will never go back on his policies.'

In the event of course Ted Heath was to do more U-turns than almost any prime minister in our history.

Heath could also be extraordinarily naive, as I was to find out later in his prime ministership when during the Lord Lambton scandal another Conservative minister, Lord Jellicoe, was forced to resign after having admitted that he too had had an affair with a prostitute. The incident had nothing whatsoever to do with Lambton. There was no security involved. Yet such was the public wrath that poor old Jellicoe had to go.

Ted Heath told me that he just couldn't understand why there had been such public animosity towards Lord Jellicoe.

I explained that it was perhaps because Lord Jellicoe had committed the cardinal sin during his wife's absence from London of having sex with the prostitute in his own marital bed.

'I don't think people like the idea of a man taking another woman to his wife's own house.'

'Oh, you mean she owned the house?' asked Heath.

I gave up the attempt to explain.

In that session with Heath about the Arab guerrillas – the first session I had had since he became Prime Minister – we drank whisky and he seemed tense and unrelaxed. But once business was over and we started to talk about sailing his whole attitude changed. He became warm, relaxed and friendly. I'm told he is the same when discussing music, although I wouldn't know about that since my idea of a real song is 'Alexander's Ragtime Band'.

He told me that night a story concerning how he had come to win a race at Burnham-on-Crouch. The course had been over a series of buoys, but ten minutes before the race was due to start a notice had gone up indicating that the race course had been changed to a simpler and shorter one – one which meant that the yachts went straight out from the harbour, round a buoy and then virtually back into Burnham again.

Heath was puzzled by this sudden change in the rules and insisted on one of his crew going through the rule book. They then realised that the change of course did not apply to the race on which they were embarking, but to the race which was following them.

Heath's big rival in the race took up a lead as they went out to that first buoy. The first leg was virtually into the wind and of course on the way back the spinnaker would have to be used. Ted knew that the other yacht was going far faster to windward than he was. He watched it round the first buoy and then to his joy and amazement he saw that instead of heading at a course of right-angles towards the second marker buoy this leader yacht was coming back towards Burnham. He quickly realised that the owner of the yacht had made the same mistake which he, Heath, had nearly made.

Quick as a flash Ted came to a decision. 'Get out the spinnaker and prepare it along the starboard rail,' he told his crew.

The result was that as he approached the marker buoy and the other yacht was coming away from it the captain of the other yacht saw Ted ready with his spinnaker and naturally thought no more of it. He assumed that Heath would be following him some distance behind. So on he went sailing happily with the spinnaker up back to Burnham while Heath, rounding the buoy, headed for the second and correct marker and of course won the race.

He roared with laughter as he told me this story of how he had fooled the other yachtsman.

I saw another side of Ted Heath in March 1971 when Tony Barber was about to produce his first Budget. Everyone was wondering whether he was going to make a mess of it because his performances in the House had been very shaky indeed.

The Sunday before the Budget I took my own yacht, *Outcast*, from Littlehampton to the Hamble for the beginning of the sailing season. It was a six-hour trip on a bracing, cold spring day. We arrived in a state of elation at the end of the first sail of the season. And there we found, when we repaired to the yacht club, the Prime Minister sitting on a settee holding a cabinet meeting, a cabinet meeting not of financiers and politicians discussing the Budget but of his sailing crew discussing his new boat which was going to be launched in two weeks' time – the boat with which he won the Admiral's Cup.

He joined us for a drink and was most agreeable, as he always is on sailing occasions. From that time onwards I was to see quite a lot of Ted Heath during his prime ministership. Sometimes in unusual circumstances.

I was once sitting having a drink with Tony Barber and his wife Jean in 11 Downing Street when we suddenly heard a pounding of feet on the stairs and a voice calling out 'Chancellor, Chancellor'.

'Who is that?' said Barber, jumping to his feet. And in walked

Ted Heath. He had come straight from a television statement he had made on the Ulster crisis following his announcement in the Commons earlier in the day about the imposition of direct rule. He had a whisky from a special bottle of Glenlivet not on public view (I myself had an ordinary blended whisky from a decanter).

He spoke freely of Ulster. Did I know, he demanded, that the British Government had had no say in who should be interned and that we had not even had a sight of the dossiers of those who had had been interned?

He told me that they had great communication difficulties with Ireland. If they went through Londonderry the IRA knew what they were saying before the people in Belfast. If they went on the scrambler telephone their messages were picked up and decoded by the Russians in Highgate. They had decided that the direct telephone (STD, I presume) was the safest means of communication.

'Another whisky, Prime Minister?' Barber enquired. 'No,' replied Heath and then almost immediately changed his mind. 'Perhaps half a glass. But what I am really looking around for are some nuts or biscuits.' Jean Barber rushed to the kitchen to get a plate of biscuits. But for all that Heath looked in reasonably good form.

'Who is going to be on your leader page?' he asked me. 'No, don't tell me. It will either be Powell or Angus Maude and I expect it will be Angus Maude.'

Not long afterwards I went at Heath's invitation to see him at Number 10 Downing Street. It was 5.45 p.m. on a hot sunny evening and he suggested that we sit out in the garden. It has occurred to me since that a prime minister sitting out in a garden adjoining Horse Guards Parade and in an area surrounded by comparatively high buildings could be a target for a sniper. Donald Maitland was with us for the first quarter of an hour or so, but when a servant bought a decanter of whisky and a jug of water and glasses Maitland did not take a drink.

Heath had won the Round the Island Race the previous Saturday on the eve of his birthday and was clearly delighted with his victory. We then discussed the Industrial Relations

Court and I asked him whether he had been prepared to face a dock strike if the seven picketing dockers, who had recently been up in court before Sir John Donaldson, had been sent to gaol instead of being taken off the hook by their barrister, Peter Pain, who had emerged as the prisoners' friend.

Heath staggered me by saying that he had never envisaged their going to gaol at all; that what he had always imagined was that they would get a good rollicking from the judge and that would be the end of it. I thought this a little naive.

I mentioned Jeremy Thorpe's recent allegations about corruption in public life and said something to the effect, 'Isn't Thorpe an absolute nuisance to stir things up like this?'

I suddenly became aware that Heath did not think that Thorpe was a nuisance. He said, 'Well, it's a dreadful business, an appalling business this Poulson affair.'

But it was Reggie Maudling and not Jeremy Thorpe who was involved in the Poulson affair. I had no doubt at all as to where Heath's thoughts were heading. I prompted him by saying, and without mentioning Maudling's name, that you would think people would have more sense than to associate with a man like Poulson. He gave me a brisk nod of agreement. I knew there and then that Reggie was going to get no support from the Prime Minister.

I left Downing Street feeling a bit depressed over Maudling's future.

I next met Ted Heath in June 1973 when we lunched together in the White Tower restaurant in Percy Street. But he did not come alone. Also in attendance, as a safeguard no doubt against misquotation, was the newly knighted Sir Donald Maitland, soon destined to become our Ambassador to the United Nations.

Heath was in a wonderfully relaxed mood, suntanned and brim-full of confidence. He spoke about Princess Anne and her fiancé Mark Phillips and he said to me, 'Everyone wants me to make him an earl or something. I suppose you would take a very dim view if we made him a duke?'

I replied that we would take a dim view, but I also said that some of us were rather worried about Ted Heath's unwillingness to creat hereditary peers because – and I looked at Donald

Maitland – 'Some of us remember our own Scottish James I who said "No Bishop, no King" and some of us feel "No new peers, no Queen".'

I added, 'A club can only remain providing it is not entirely exclusive. The Royal Yacht Squadron, for example, must allow every now and again some humble peasant to join the congregation.' I was of course referring to the fact that Heath had recently been made a member of the Royal Yacht Squadron.

I continued, 'As long as the humble peasant is admitted now and again then the whole club can continue. But I feel that if we go through ten years of Tory rule without a new hereditary peer being created then it might be impossible ever again to create a hereditary peer.'

Ted's argument was that a peerage inherited by a man who had not also inherited money could bring the whole system into disrepute. He cited the case of Lloyd George's eldest son.

As for food, no one could accuse Ted Heath of being a frugal trencherman.

We had no aperitifs, but instead I had ordered two bottles of Pol Roger champagne which I knew to be his favourite. He once told me that the manufacturers supplied it free to him as they had to another Tory leader – Churchill.

Upstairs in the White Tower there is a most delightful private room and the table had been carefully prepared. A little flock of waiters stood by to take our order. Ted enquired about the possibility of gulls' eggs and was delighted to find that they were already on the table. So we started with gulls' eggs, we continued with Charente melon, then a delicious chicken dish which is a speciality of the White Tower and finished off with fresh mangoes.

After that little plates of petits fours were brought.

I pushed one towards Ted, but he declined. A few minutes later, however, I noticed him looking at the dish longingly and eventually he put out a thumb and forefinger and extracted a piece of Turkish delight. Had I not been on a diet I would have done the same.

Over coffee he told me that he was going to make a trip to China and in three days' time the Chinese Foreign Secretary would be coming to him to extend the official invitation.

He said that when he was Leader of the Opposition he invited the Chinese Chargé d'Affaires to lunch with him in the Albany. During the meal Heath had put the question to him: 'I would very much like to visit China. Could it be arranged?'

The Chinese Chargé d'Affaires looked slightly embarrassed and then said, 'I'm afraid that would be difficult.'

Ted persisted. 'It may be difficult, Chargé d'Affaires, but are you willing to transmit my message to your government – the request that I would like to visit China?'

The Chargé d'Affaires again looked embarrassed. 'It would be very difficult,' he replied.

'But why should it be difficult?' demanded Ted.

'Your government is not acting in a very friendly way towards China.'

'But it is not my government,' said Heath. 'I have nothing to do with the government. I am the Leader of the Opposition. I do not approve of the government's policies. So why should I be prevented from going to China? Is there another reason for your refusing to transmit my request to Peking?'

The Chargé d'Affaires looked even more embarrassed and then finally he said, 'Yes, there is another reason. Do you remember that when there was a Conservative government in power and one of your ministers came to Peking he was met by the appropriate Chinese minister and everything was done according to protocol?'

'Yes, I remember,' replied Heath, nodding his head. 'Well,' said the Chargé d'Affaires, 'after that the Chinese Foreign Secretary came to Geneva and there he met your Foreign Secretary who was then the Lord Home. And on his first night there he received an invitation from Lord Home to come and have dinner with Lord Home at the British Embassy.'

'Yes, I remember, but what was wrong with that?'

'Ah,' said the Chinese Chargé d'Affaires, 'protocol demanded that Lord Home should have waited to receive an invitation from Mr Chou En-lai.'

And as he told the story, Ted's shoulders broke into convulsive laughter.

One thing puzzled me about that lunch – the size of the bill.

Even though we had eaten well it still seemed a little high.

I was soon to find out why. On the following Monday my home telephone rang. It was the *Express* switchboard wanting to know whether it would be all right for them to give my home number to 10 Downing Street.

I eagerly assented.

Within seconds the telephone rang again. I rushed to it wondering what the Prime Minister might want to say. I was a little crestfallen to find that on the other end was a Sergeant Crew, who was the Prime Minister's bodyguard. And who apparently had been sitting downstairs in the White Tower while we were in the private room. He wanted to apologise because by accident the cost of his lunch had been put on my bill, whereas he had meant to pay separately.

I told him not to worry and asked him if he had eaten well at lunch.

'Oh yes,' he said, 'absolutely delicious. I thought you probably knew what you were about so I told them to bring me exactly the same as you were having.'

Six weeks later I went to see Ted Heath at 10 Downing Street at six o'clock in the evening. We met in his library, a Piper painting above the fireplace, a bottle of champagne on the table. He had long since moved on from Mateus rosé.

The purpose of our talk was an interview he had given to the *Sunday Express* on the economic situation in question-and-answer form. But that part of the proceedings took only twenty minutes and we then had a further forty minutes of very little but relaxed small talk.

I told him that on my way to town that morning I had come across Quintin Hogg at some traffic lights driving his own car, that I had opened my window and yelled 'Good morning, Quintin' and from that time onwards I had followed him into Central London and had observed how good and careful a driver he was.

This was nothing less than true. Quintin had driven a meticulous twenty-nine and a half miles per hour using the traffic indicator with enormous accuracy and constancy. He also inhibited me from passing him since I felt it would be unwise to break the speed limit in front of the Lord Chancellor.

Ted hooted with laughter at the story and said, 'God, was he driving himself?' Clearly he thought that the Lord Chancellor should not be driving his own car. He went on to say that he had been forbidden to drive a car when he became Prime Minister and he had tried his best to dissuade his eighty-five year-old father from driving too.

His father had looked at him sharply and said, 'I don't see why I should stop driving. I don't see why you being stopped has anything to do with me.' And so apparently the old boy had continued as before.

Heath then told me a story about driving back to London while he was still in opposition beside Peter Carrington in his Jensen car.

'I was sitting there beside him absolutely petrified, holding on for dear life,' said Ted. 'We were doing a hundred-and-twenty miles an hour at times. At one stage I said to him, "Aren't there any police around here?" But Peter simply grinned and said, "Not on a Monday morning, they are all going in the opposite direction."'

Heath and Carrington apparently arrived without incident in London but in the very last stage of the journey, when they were travelling at about two miles an hour, they bumped into a car near Buckingham Palace. Quick as a flash Peter Carrington according to Ted Heath said, 'Nip out quick.' And according to Ted Heath that is exactly what he did. He nipped out of the car before the police or anyone else arrived.

I sat next to Ted Heath at the Yachtsman of the Year luncheon in November of that year when he told me an amusing story of the recent visit of the Japanese Prime Minister, Mr Kakuei Tanaka.

Apparently when Ted Heath had first gone to Tokyo some time before he asked, on the eve of his departure, what present had been arranged for him to take to the Japanese Prime Minister. To his astonishment he was told 'a set of golf clubs'. Then it was explained to him that the Japanese Prime Minister was mad on golf and that nothing would give him greater pleasure than for him to be able to boast in Japan that he had a set of British golf clubs.

The visit and the present were a great success.

Then Mr Tanaka came to England and announced hopefully that he had a weekend to spare between his meetings in Paris which ended on a Friday and his meeting with Ted Heath which was scheduled for the Monday.

Ted Heath immediately took the hint and invited him to spend a weekend in England. The Japanese Ambassador then let it be known that the Prime Minister and his Foreign Minister would like to play golf. 'We can't let these two Japanese go off on a Saturday morning looking for a golf course to make up a four ball,' thought Ted.

So it was proposed that two of Britain's professional golfers, Tony Jacklin and Peter Oosterhuis, should play with the guests. But when this was put to the Japanese Ambassador he demurred. 'I should tell you,' he said, 'that our Prime Minister has a handicap of seventeen and that it should really be twenty-two. I think he would be upset playing with such good players.'

So Ted Heath arranged instead for Willie Whitelaw and a friend, Alec Hill, to make up a four ball at St George's.

The Japanese Ambassador also warned: 'In Japan we have not quite the same rules as you have. We are not much interested in where the ball lies as in where the ball is going to go. So we hope that the Prime Minister will not lose face by having it pointed out to him that he is not playing according to your rules.'

The hint was taken and Willie Whitelaw and his friend were informed not to blink if they saw the Japanese Prime Minister kick his ball out of the rough. It was then carefully worked out how the Japanese Prime Minister was to be allowed to win.

Lunch was arranged half-way round at the ninth hole and Ted Heath arrived by helicopter to join the party.

There apparently had been a slight crisis at the seventh hole where they had allowed the Foreign Minister to win. He had been so encouraged by this that he had gone on to win the eighth and ninth hole as well which was not according to plan and made the Prime Minister on the losing side at the turn.

Lunch was a typical Royal St George's clubhouse lunch ending with a golden-syrup pudding. As the two Japanese left the clubhouse to begin the second nine holes the Japanese Prime

Minister turned to his Foreign Minister and said in Japanese, 'You see, we are being accepted socially at last. Did you see that syrup pudding on the menu? The English are at last beginning to treat us as equals.'

It says a good deal for syrup pudding and as Ted Heath pointed out it also gives a wonderful insight into the Japanese character.

Ted Heath had a very good story which dated back to Harold Macmillan's time. The Bolshoi Ballet were coming and the woman Russian minister in charge of the concert – she was said to be Khrushchev's mistress – had to be entertained in London. Heath's department was responsible for the entertainment.

She was a very bloody-minded woman, enormously difficult to please. Time after time efforts were made to take her to museums and either she would fail to turn up or was rude beyond measure to the people with whom she was dealing. Eventually Heath decided to take her on a tour himself. He took her to the Royal Academy of Music where they entered without warning and there on the stage was a beautiful black girl in full song.

The Soviet lady looked astonished. 'You have black women in England?' she said.

They then visited an art museum and finally Heath asked her whether she would like to see his flat.

'Yes,' she replied, 'I would.'

Heath took her round to his modest little flat in Albany. 'Do all the other government ministers live here, then?' she asked.

'Oh no,' replied Heath, 'they live in many parts of London or in the country.'

'But the government pays for all their houses, doesn't it?' demanded the Soviet lady.

Heath explained that in this country ministers traditionally paid for their own housing.

She was silent for a moment and then she said, 'I have been to England many times but this is the first time I have been inside an English house.' And for the rest of her trip she was quite a changed and happier woman.

As Heath told the story it occurred to me that the Soviet lady had indeed been honoured. There cannot have been too many women ever invited alone to his flat.

In the days when Jim Prior was still his Parliamentary Private Secretary and had not received office off his own bat, he was constantly hoping that Ted would find a nice suitable lady and show a healthy interest in her. One night at a Commons reception he was delighted to see Ted apparently engrossed in the company of a good-looking bird who was just about the right age for him.

Hovering on the fringe of their conversation he overheard Ted asking her where she was going after the reception and might he give her a lift?

Shortly afterwards Ted and the lady left the reception, with Prior like a good PPS still hovering discreetly in the background. But his hopes were to be dashed. For while Ted gallantly held open the rear passenger door for the lady, he then slammed it shut and jumped himself into the front passenger seat beside the chauffeur.

Near the end of Heath's prime ministership there were times when I got from him the faint but unmistakable whiff of panic. On 25 January 1974 I got back to the office about 9.30 p.m. to find that Ted had been trying to get hold of me by telephone.

Eventually at about half-past eleven he came through at home. But I found that all he wanted to say was, 'Where are you, John? Oh, you are not in the office. I'm so sorry to have disturbed you, but I wasn't able to have a press conference this afternoon and I wondered if there were any questions that you would like to ask?'

This of course was all on the eve of the miners' strike. Until that point they had been on an overtime ban but now they had voted for a complete strike. It seems to me odd that the Prime Minister should be spending his evening ringing around newspaper editors basically drumming up support for his case – but, of course, it was the beginning of the end. Soon he was to be out of office.

After the Tories had been defeated in 1974 Peter Carrington told me a rather touching story.

Apparently two weeks after the election, Willie Whitelaw went to see Ted Heath and said to him in effect, 'Look Ted, you have qualities which I can never possess. You have so many qualities. But I think there is one quality which you do not have but which I think I do have and that is a way with people. So why don't you use me to complement yourself? Anything I can do I will.'

Sometime afterwards Peter Carrington went in to see Ted. He was standing looking out of the window in rather a thoughtful mood.

He turned to Peter and said, 'Why is it that people hate me?'

But as Leader of the Opposition Ted was soon bouncing back.

Pam and I went to a birthday party given for him in Chipstead. Ted was resplendent in a new tweed suit which looked like a bookie's suit. His brother and sister-in-law were there. So were his father and step-mother. I had a conversation with the brother who was a very dull chap indeed. Pleasant but commonplace. As was his wife. And yet at the party were people like Toby Low, Lord Aldington, Peter Carrington, Sir Michael Adeane and a great host of other nobs.

A week or two afterwards I expressed my admiration to Peter Carrington for the way in which Ted had invited his comparatively humble relatives to his birthday party.

'Oh, but he is terribly good at that,' said Carrington. 'He invites them everywhere. There is only one thing. Do you ever see him speaking to them?'

Ted Heath, of course, was absolutely crushed when he lost the Tory leadership to Margaret Thatcher. His venom towards her was enormous. But he was still a Tory and he knew his duty at election time.

On the first Sunday after the 1979 general election had been announced I went sailing with Tom Boswell and on the Sunday night went to the Royal Southern Yacht Club for dinner. Ted Heath was there and joined us at our table. I asked him to write for the *Sunday Express* during the campaign and pointed out to him that no matter what he thought of Margaret Thatcher personally it was his duty to the nation to support the Conservative cause to the utmost.

He agreed. His article arrived for publication on the last Sunday before polling day. That Saturday afternoon I received a telephone call from Carrington.

'How are things going?' he asked. 'Do you think the campaign is going well?'

I replied I thought the Tories were going to win.

He sounded a little diffident. 'I'm with Margaret,' he said. 'She would like to know who is writing tomorrow's leader page.'

'Ted Heath,' I replied. There was a sudden silence at the other end, and then I added, 'And do not worry. He has written a marvellous piece which should help Margaret substantially.'

Shortly after the election Ted asked me to lunch at his home in Wilton Street. I was much impressed by the marvellous style and quality of the furniture and the precious paintings which adorned the walls. I found myself wondering where he had made his money. After lunch and the inevitable bottle of champagne he posed the question as to what he should do.

'You must be like de Gaulle,' I replied. 'You must retire to your Colombey-les-deux-Eglises. But your Colombey-les-deux-Eglises is the back benches. You must sit there and you must be absolutely silent. No matter what happens you must not criticise the government. For if you do that it will be taken as plain envy. If your time ever does come it will be because the nation turns to you and it will only do so if you have nothing to do with the downfall of the Prime Minister.'

He agreed, but alas it was not very long before he had started to criticise both government and Prime Minister. It was a tragedy that by so doing he effectively ended his political career.

Sometimes a lunch with Ted provided a fascinating insight into the affairs of other countries. Here is my diary entry for 26 July 1979. It revealed to me a great deal about Jimmy Carter's Presidency.

'Ted Heath told me today that there had been a conference in Vienna last week under the chairmanship of the Austrian Chancellor Mr Kreisky and that he had suddenly been called away from the conference just before lunch. He came back after lunch and apologised to the diplomats and political leaders present, including Willie Brandt, but explained that he had had to see Yasser Arafat of the PLO.

The American Ambassador then said that he too would like to see Arafat. Kreisky expressed surprise and wondered whether it might not be misunderstood in the United States if the American Ambassador had consultations with someone as anti-Jewish as Arafat. The American Ambassador considered this and said that on reflection perhaps he ought to have clearance from the White House.

The next morning he approached Kreisky again and said, yes it was OK. He would still like to see Arafat. Kreisky said, 'Are you quite sure? Did the White House really sanction your meeting?'

'Oh yes,' said the US Ambassador. 'I spoke personally on the telephone and got clearance from Mrs Rosalyn Carter herself.'

Many years later on, 19 November 1987, I was to get a footnote on Ted Heath's prime ministership.

I had not lunched with Nicholas Ridley for perhaps fifteen years. Nor had any chance of a conversation with him during that period. So we had a lot to catch up on. The first time I had ever met him was at a Brighton Tory Conference when he had been a junior minister in the Ted Heath government and was finding himself at odds with almost everything that the government did. I learned that day in 1987 for the first time how he came to leave the government.

He explained that he had been in Portugal on an official visit when he received a telephone call from his boss, the late John Davies, who was then Secretary of State for Industry. Davies did not waste words. 'You are to come home immediately,' he said. 'You are going to get the sack and you have to be in Downing Street tomorrow morning.'

Despondently, Ridley replied that he would catch the 7.30 p.m. plane which was the last scheduled flight from Lisbon that night. He then went to see the British Ambassador to explain that he would be cutting short his visit.

The British Ambassador was aghast. 'You can't do that,' he said. 'Have you forgotten that there is an official banquet tonight and you are making the main speech?'

When Ridley explained that he was under orders to come home the Ambassador telephoned the then Foreign Secretary, Alec Douglas-Home, explained the situation and pleaded that Ridley be allowed to stay at least until after his speech. The upshot was that Douglas-Home sent out an RAF Britannia to pick up Ridley at midnight, which meant that he would have time to make his speech and still be home for his appointment in Downing Street.

Ridley told me that he then had a drink or two which means, I expect, that he had five or six. He claimed that he had no idea what sort of speech he made but he did know that he had had a miserable trip home alone with his secretary in a huge and otherwise empty Britannia. It was cold and miserable and he didn't sleep.

The next morning, angry, resentful and exhausted, he presented himself at Downing Street and was shown into the presence of the Prime Minister.

Ted was sitting at a desk signing letters to constituents. He did not look up. He did not say good morning. He kept on signing letters until the pile was finished. Then he turned in his chair and looked at Ridley.

'I am sorry I had to bring you home early,' he said, 'but I want your job.'

'Fair enough,' said Ridley, 'but what have you against me?'

Heath replied that he did not think Ridley was making a good enough show of presenting the government's policy.

Ridley's anger simmered over. 'How could anyone make a good case of presenting this government's policies? You have gone back on everything the Tories ever stood for. It's the policies which are wrong and they need changing.'

Heath brushed his protests aside and said, 'Are you interested in the arts?'

'I am,' replied Ridley, 'but if you are thinking of asking me to become Chairman of the Fine Arts Commission or the Royal

Opera or something like that then I'm not interested. I mean to stay in Parliament.'

'That's not what I had in mind,' said Heath. 'I want you to become Minister for the Arts.'

If he had been treated from the beginning of the interview in a different way Ridley might have reacted differently. As it was he said, 'I don't want any part of this government.' And he stalked out.

'That was the wisest decision I ever made in all my life,' he reflected. 'It shows that sometimes the decision you take in anger is the best one.'

On becoming Prime Minister Ted Heath had of course sent Reggie Maudling to the Home Office. I would have trusted my life to Reggie. But I expect that if I had done so I would have lost it. Not because there was any evil in him. He was one of the most decent and compassionate men I have ever met. What he lacked was judgement in his personal life.

He had a magnificent brain. Other ministers have told me that when Reggie chaired a Cabinet committee, his capacity for getting quickly to the point, his ability to sift facts and figures and to get to the very heart of an argument was quite fantastic to watch. He was utterly without malice. I never heard him speak ill of anyone – not even Ted Heath.

His trouble lay in his fondness for the good things in life – he came to be known as the caviar kid. Nor did he seem to mind just whose caviar he ate. Another weakness was the way he doted on his wife and children. They could do no wrong in his eyes.

Rab Butler, although he was very close indeed to Reggie, did not like his wife Beryl. 'You know I'm godfather to one of their children?' Rab once told me. 'God, Beryl irritates me. I find that a couple of weeks before the child's birthday I get a letter from her saying, "Dear Rab, I know you're an absent-minded old thing. So I thought I had better remind you that it will be Edward's birthday a week on Thursday." That sort of thing annoys me.'

Brian Walden was similarly annoyed when he met Beryl by chance in the street and she immediately confided in him that the next day was Reggie's birthday. 'I know you will want to send him a present.' she said. Nor was she joking.

Reggie wanted to give his family all the best things in life. That was why he mixed with people like Poulson. But I would be very surprised if he ever did anything either corrupt or dishonest.

Yet he did want to build up a fortune.

He had been Chancellor of the Exchequer in the Tory government which lost the 1964 general election. Sometime afterwards we were having lunch and I was enthralled when he told me of a certain way to make money.

At that time overdrafts were tax deductible.

Maudling's plan was very simple.

All you had to do, he explained, was to go to your bank and ask for an overdraft facility for, say, £100,000 with which to buy unit trusts. The bank manager would look at you and say politely, 'And what collateral are you offering against the overdraft?' You would say to your bank manager, 'The unit trusts I will buy are those issued by your own bank. They would remain in the bank's name. You surely trust your own unit trusts, don't you?'

Reggie's plan was that you would then leave the unit trusts for a year or more during which time they would surely appreciate by maybe as much as 50 per cent. During that time you would get tax relief at the top level of your income on the money you had borrowed and then at the end of a year or more when you sold you would pay only 30 per cent as Capital Gains.

It seemed absolutely foolproof to me and I rushed back to the office determined to put the plan into action. But being a cautious soul I first of all telephoned my friend Hamish Falconer in Edinburgh and explained the plan to him.

Hamish, who was one of Scotland's top investment advisors, was horrified.

'Have nothing to do with it,' he said. I argued with him and pointed out that Maudling had one of the best financial brains in the country and had, after all, himself been Chancellor of the Exchequer until recently.

Hamish was unimpressed. 'I don't give a damn what he was

or what he is. Have nothing to do with it. Never borrow money for shares which you cannot instantly afford to repay.'

I was impressed by the urgency in his voice and did nothing, and thank God I didn't. For shortly afterwards Roy Jenkins, the new Chancellor of the Exchequer, ended tax allowances on overdrafts.

Robert Carr, later to become Home Secretary, was another man who had mixed views about Reggie and Beryl Maudling.

He and Reggie had been close friends and neighbours over many years. They lived in adjoining houses in Reggie's constituency of Barnet. Carr had found his house first and when Reggie was nominated for Barnet back in 1950 he had suggested that Reggie buy the house next door.

One tiny little rift developed in their relationship.

At that time they were both young, both eager to succeed in politics, both Tory candidates and both, like many other people, had a great ambition to meet Churchill. During the 1950 general election Churchill came to Reggie's constituency. The whole place was agog. Beryl Maudling had arranged that the great man should come back to the Maudlings' house for a drink or a meal after his meeting.

The Carrs eagerly awaited an invitation. But no invitation came.

Worse than that. On the morning of the party Beryl Maudling came to Mrs Carr and said, 'Could I possibly ask you a great favour? There are going to be so many cars in front of our house tonight because of Churchill's visit. Would you mind terribly if you did not park your car in front of yours and left us an extra space?'

Robert Carr relates how he and his wife sat and watched through curtains as the great man arrived at the house next door.

But I doubt if Carr stayed angry for long. It was impossible to do so with Reggie. He was like a lolloping, bumbling, good-natured Labrador.

Caroline, his daughter, was the apple of his eye and Caroline was quite devoted to her father. And yet with her illegitimate child, with her divorce, with her dress when she appeared in court in South Africa and with the extraordinary interviews she gave to South African newspapers she got Reggie into considerable trouble.

But Reggie never felt the slightest bit angry towards her. His complaint was always against the newspapers who had given undue publicity to what she had said. It was in vain that one might try to suggest that Caroline might possibly make a mistake once with newspapers, but that surely she ought to have learned more sense than to keep on giving interviews which were publicised throughout the world. In the first interview about her illegitimate child, it is conceivable that she did not know the effect her words would have. I found that difficult to accept with subsequent interviews.

But Reggie never found any difficulty at all.

While I liked Reggie and loved his company I was always aware that he was not, any more than I am, the sort of man who is likely to jump overboard to save you from drowning in a rough sea.

One Friday evening when he was Home Secretary I was invited to dinner at Admiralty House. There were only three of us – Beryl, Reggie and myself – and I arrived there driving my own car. We had a simple meal, helping ourselves from a buffet table, and the three of us then sat hour after hour drinking red Spanish wine and talking politics.

By the time I came to leave it was nearly midnight. None of us was by any stretch of imagination legless. All of us had drunk, however, a good deal of red wine. Reggie came down to the courtyard to see me into my car and I drove back to Fleet Street. It occurred to me as I did so that it would have been easy for him to have had me driven back to Fleet Street rather than run the risk of my being stopped by the police on the way.

On occasion, too, Reggie might miss a lunch by telephoning at short notice. This happened very seldom and when it did it was under real pressure of business.

But there was an occasion when it did cause embarrassment.

The occasion was the Sunday Express Boat Show luncheon of January 1971. Each year at the Boat Show we ran a lunch for about twenty people, many of whom were big advertisers in

198

the *Sunday Express*. I always tried to add glamour by including some television stars like Eamonn Andrews, Robin Day and Cliff Michelmore plus one top politician.

For this particular lunch I had asked Reggie, then Home Secretary, to be guest of honour. The whole idea was that the businessmen would be able to go home and tell their wives what an interesting lunch they had had.

But when I arrived at my office on the morning of the lunch my secretary Pooh told me that Reggie Maudling's secretary had phoned to say that an emergency had arisen and he would be unable to attend.

This left me without a 'crown jewel'. Desperately I began to telephone for a substitute.

First of all I rang Quintin Hogg, then Lord Chancellor. Quintin would have been most willing to help. He always was. But alas he was already heavily committed and he explained that he did not see how he could get out of it.

In desperation I then rang the Chancellor of the Exchequer's office and found that by the greatest of good luck Tony Barber had no official luncheon for that day. But, explained his secretary, he was in an important Treasury meeting. There was no way of getting a message in to him. He had no idea when the meeting would end. It might go on until well after one o'clock.

None the less, I explained the situation to him, told him that if he could get a message to Tony Barber when his meeting finished and that if Barber was agreeable to coming I would arrange to have him met outside Olympia and shown straight to the Green Room where the lunch was being held.

Shortly after this I myself had to make my way to Olympia to be ready to greet the first guests. When I arrived a waiter came to me and said, 'Your secretary has been on the telephone. She asked me to let you know that the Lord Chancellor would in fact be coming to the lunch.'

Good old Quintin, I thought. How super of him to have made the effort and got out of his engagement. I dispatched a messenger to the front of Olympia to meet him and to bring him through the milling crowds to the Green Room.

But Quintin never arrived. We were just about to begin our

lunch when a figure entered the Green Room door – Tony Barber.

Pooh had made a mistake. She had mixed up the Lord Chancellor with the Chancellor of the Exchequer. Barber had arrived at the front door of Olympia. No one had recognised him. No one had been there to meet him. He had virtually to slip past the commissionaire, climb over a turnstile and thread his way through a vast crowd in an effort to find the Green Room.

I felt more than slightly embarrassed. But even more embarrassed before the lunch had ended. Two-thirds of the way through the door opened and with a fanfare of trumpets an *Evening Standard* circulation representative marched proudly into the room with an armful of the first editions and presented one to each guest.

We all opened our *Evening Standard* and turned to the leader page. And there in the main leader position was a violent attack on Anthony Barber, then struggling to make his name as Chancellor of the Exchequer.

Happily Tony Barber is one of the nicest men in politics. He grinned, shrugged his shoulders and said, 'Don't worry. I'm used to this sort of thing.'

Afterwards of course Reggie was, as always, suitably penitent.

The last years of his life were overshadowed by his libel action against Granada Television over the *World in Action* programme which had virtually accused him of corruption. It seemed to me then and it seems to me now monstrous that an honest man of moderate means can bankrupt himself taking legal action to clear his name against a multi-million company which, even if it loses, can put it all down as a tax loss.

During that period people who used to seek his company were quite prepared to insult him. I remember receiving an invitation to lunch at company HQ from Ambrose Congreve, the Chairman of Humphreys & Glasgow, the great pharmaceutical company.

On the morning of the lunch Reggie rang me to ask if I were free to lunch with him. When I explained I was already committed Reggie said, 'Ambrose is an old friend. I will get myself invited too.' And he did. But he must have regretted it later. Congreve spent most of the lunch insulting him in the full hearing of all the other guests. I felt sick at his humiliation.

About this time pressure was being put on me to stop Reggie writing leader-page articles for the *Sunday Express*.

'It doesn't do the paper any good,' I was told.

But I refused to deal that final blow. Reggie was still writing for us when he died.

Tony Barber, that most likeable of men, was indirectly responsible for the first by-line my daughter Penelope ever received in journalism.

During his time as Chancellor of the Exchequer he had invited my wife Pam and me to lunch with Jean, his wife, and himself at 11 Downing Street. Before lunch his daughter Josephine, aged seventeen, popped in to see us. She would not be lunching with us, Tony explained, because she was too busy studying upstairs for her A levels. The idea of a young girl studying for A levels in Downing Street appealed to me. What must it be like, I wondered, to be studying A level Maths and English when outside your window the high and the mighty in the land are rolling up in their limousines to see the Prime Minister?

When I got home I suggested to Penelope, then a trainee on an IPC magazine, that Josephine might be a good subject for an interview for the *Evening Standard*. The interview subsequently took place, was published in the *Evening Standard* and I still have in my possession the pay slip for £40 which Penelope received. It was her first ever pay day from a Fleet Street newspaper.

Tony Barber I found completely unostentatious and completely unaggressive. But as Ted Heath's Chancellor of the Exchequer I found him also a very tired man. A man who was working much too hard.

I lunched with him at the Boulestin in June of 1973. Tony arrived six minutes late and was quite unnecessarily apologetic. He explained that he was flying to Luxembourg for an important bankers' meeting. It emerged that he would be going straight from the restaurant to the airport and that his wife would be in the car coming to meet him. I asked why he had not brought Jean to lunch with us and he replied simply that he had not wanted to impose on me.

And while he was reasonably confident about the economy he had by that time produced more Budgets than any other living Chancellor. But he had had fewer opportunities for a holiday than any other minister, including the Prime Minister. For with no other member of his department who was also a member of the Cabinet he was always on duty.

And of course he also had his constituency to attend to. He told me how the previous weekend he had gone to an RAF show in order to be present at a commemoration service for a squadron in which he had served as a Spitfire pilot. It had taken him four hours to get there by road.

'Why in God's name don't you use a helicopter?' I asked.

He looked at me sadly. 'Because it was not official business,' he replied. 'And I dare not use a helicopter on party or personal business.'

He went on to tell me how he had recently used a helicopter during a visit to Chevening. But the helicopter pilot who arrived was a free-enterprise pilot who had only just learned how to fly the machine and was far from sure as to how to use the radio direction finder. The result was that at one stage during the flight he turned to the Chancellor of the Exchequer and said, 'Do you mind taking the controls for a few seconds while I try to find out which air space we're in?'

Years later, in August 1984, I lunched again with Tony Barber. He arrived in a brand-new Bristol with his chauffeur at the wheel, although as Chairman of the Standard Chartered Bank he could have had a Rolls-Royce if he had wanted. But Tony, clearly something of a car nut, preferred his Bristol.

He told me about the recent dinner given by Ted Heath to honour Harold Macmillan on his ninetieth birthday. The food had been quite superb – delicious salmon, saddle of lamb and Stilton. And during the meal, Macmillan had turned to him and whispered, 'It's a shame about Ted, isn't it? He is such a good fellow.'

The wines had also been superb. The *pièce de résistance* had been a magnum of Château Lafite which he thought had been the 1874 vintage but which I suspect was the 1894 to coincide with Macmillan's birthday. But when Ted had tried to take out the cork early in the evening to decant it he had been scared off by the unusual old-fashioned bottle neck and was terrified he might break it. So what did he do? He telephoned Charles Forte and asked him to send his head sommelier over to remove the cork.

I had first met Peter Carrington in July 1972 when Ian Gilmour invited us both to lunch at the Epicure. He was then a senior member of the Heath government and spoke about Heath in glowing terms. He was not only the best Prime Minister we had, he said, but also there was no discernible successor in the Tory Party save, perhaps, Alec Douglas-Home who would only accept out of duty. Carrington drank only one gin and tonic and no wine. He impressed me as a most lively, highly intelligent mind and he gave me one interesting piece of information. The Archbishop of Canterbury – and here he held up his hands in mimic prayer – had written to Ted Heath opposing the suggestion then being canvassed that Lord Goodman be appointed Chairman of the BBC on the grounds that the job should go to a member of the Church of England.

From that time onwards Peter Carrington and I became regular luncheon companions. And from him I was to get a fascinating insight into the politics of the time. I learned from him that Heath and Maudling got on badly and that on one occasion Heath had turned to Peter and said angrily: 'Everyone says "Poor old Reggie". Why should it be poor old Reggie? He's never had to work or fight for anything. It's all been handed to him. The right sort of family. The right sort of connections, everything easy. But I've had to fight and struggle for everything I've got.'

He also told me an amusing story about Sarah Morrison, who had apparently decided that the time had come to tell Ted Heath quite frankly that he was getting far too fat. One evening she found herself sitting next to him at an official dinner. Steeling herself to her purpose, she looked straight ahead with fixed eyes, summed up her courage and said, 'Ted, you are disgustingly fat. You really have to do something about it. You just must stop eating.'

She then turned round to see what effect her words were having on Mr Heath. None at all. Ted was fast asleep.

When the Heath government went down the tube in the 1974 election Carrington remained for a time Chairman of the Tory Party. The day he was sacked he was lunching with me at the Boulestin. I had arrived a few minutes early and had been told by a waiter that Lord Carrington's secretary had been on the phone with a most urgent message – would Lord Carrington telephone her the minute he arrived?

When Carrington did arrive I took him to the telephone which was situated in a little room off the main restaurant and was one of those old-fashioned models with buttons marked A and B and left him to it. Some fifteen minutes later when he had still not come to the table I looked to see if he was OK. I found that he was still wrestling with the machine. I then discovered that in all his life he had never used a public telephone-box before.

After Margaret Thatcher toppled Heath from the Tory leadership, Carrington was in a dilemma. He clearly had to work with the new leader and indeed wanted to. But working with was one thing, socialising with was something quite different. And he didn't want to offend Ted Heath. One day at the Ritz he asked my advice – should he ask Margaret to dinner or perhaps even to spend a weekend on his country estate? It seemed to me that he had a vague aristocratic contempt for her lowly background as indeed he had for Ted's too.

For one little weakness Lord Carrington has is snobbery. Lady Olga Maitland told me how her parents had lived in the same part of London – Ovington Square – as Lord Carrington for many years. Carrington had always ignored her father when he was plain Patrick Maitland, though Maitland's brother was an earl.

Then one day Maitland's elder brother, a Sussex vicar, committed suicide by walking into the sea off Selsey Bill and Patrick inherited the earldom. On his very first day as the new Earl of Lauderdale he was astounded to hear Carrington's voice saying in Ovington Square, 'Good morning, Patrick'.

But while Peter Carrington might have had a contempt for Margaret Thatcher's social background, he did admire her courage. He told me how years later he had travelled with her to a Commonwealth meeting in Lusaka at a time when African feelings were running high and angrily against Britain while the Rhodesian issue was still unsettled.

On the aeroplane he noted that she had a pair of large sunglasses on her lap. He afterwards discovered in conversation with her that she thought she might be attacked when she left the aircraft and the one thing which frightened her was that someone might throw acid in her eyes. Hence the sunglasses. She thought she would wear them for protection.

But in the event when the plane landed she took the sunglasses and put them in her handbag and walked out of that plane with her head held high. Her attitude had been, she told Carrington, 'I'm not going to let them scare me.'

Carrington himself came to grief in the Falklands War and went completely out of political life. He went completely out of my life too. When he was in office or in opposition and needing perhaps the occasional spot of help and understanding from a newspaper he was constantly on the phone. After the Falklands I never heard from him again.

Nor do I think I ever will. Not unless of course I succeed to an earldom.

Lunching with fascinating politicians sometimes means also lunching with them in a time of personal crisis. Lord Lambton, for example. He was anguished when in May 1973 he had to leave the government after his part in the call girl scandal when he had been pictured in bed with two prostitutes and smoking cannabis.

Lambton was particularly bitter at one aspect of his downfall. 'Man is a human being and the government consists of an association of men – most of them friends,' he said to me. 'Wouldn't you have thought that in this government of friends, someone might have warned me? Someone might have said to me, "Tony, watch it. Don't be a bloody fool." But, you know, no one gave me any warning of any kind. They knew from April that the police were about to take action against me and not a single soul in the Cabinet gave me any warning of any kind. And after all my first cousin is in the Cabinet. Don't you think he might have warned me?' The first cousin to whom he was referring was, of course, Alec Douglas-Home. And in my mind as I listened to Tony Lambton my admiration for Alec Douglas-Home grew instead of decreasing.

I could visualise what had happened. I could imagine Ted Heath calling in Sir Alec and saying to him, 'Alec, I am terribly sorry, but your cousin Tony Lambton is in big trouble. He is taking drugs, he has been photographed with prostitutes. And I am going to have to sack him. There is also going to be police action against him. I have to tell you this, but I also have to ask you that on no account will you warn Lambton.' And I could see Sir Alec Douglas-Home, as always, putting his country before himself and his own family. I think he was abundantly right to have so done.

Then there was Jim Prior. At that time he was of course in Ted Heath's government, but I shall never forget meeting him fifteen years later at a time when he was back in the Cabinet again and being battered by Margaret Thatcher. But there was no animosity towards her. Just good humour.

And he told me an amusing story. A decision had to be taken by the Cabinet as to whether to go along with Sir Michael Edwardes, the Chairman of British Leyland, in his re-financing plan for that ailing company or whether to put the whole lot into liquidation. Prior had suggested to the Prime Minister that it might be a good idea to have an independent view and to ask another really expert and knowledgeable business man to look over the figures submitted by Michael Edwardes before a decision was taken.

Mrs Thatcher looked thoughtful. Then she said, 'Denis isn't too busy at the moment. I'll get him to look over the papers at the weekend.' The idea of Mr Thatcher being regarded, even by his wife, as an expert in business caused Prior to roar with laughter. I laughed dutifully at the time but it does occur to me that Denis Thatcher knows a damn sight more about business than Jim Prior has ever done.

Then there was Selwyn Lloyd who instead of becoming prime minister, as at one time it seemed he might, ended up in 1971 as Speaker of the House of Commons. But Selwyn Lloyd, Chancellor of the Exchequer in Harold Macmillan's government and the Foreign Secretary in Sir Anthony Eden's at the time of Suez, was never one of my intimates.

He had married a woman much younger than himself and she had created a bit of a scandal by running away and leaving him. Rab Butler told me that he had asked the wife why she had left Selwyn. And her reply was according to Rab, 'Would you like to go to bed with a man who wears a pullover over his pyjama top?'

So Selwyn was in some ways a figure of fun – especially among left-wing Conservatives. But he was still a good politician and a brave one too.

Public life is in fact littered with men who would have made good prime ministers if the breaks had gone the other way. Duncan Sandys was another one of them. He had two misfortunes. One was that he was the son-in-law of Winston Churchill and I suspect that that acted against him because many people felt that any job he received would be as a result of that relationship. His other weakness was his inability to stand fools and his unwillingness to mix with rank-and-file Tory MPs, or even constituents, in an effort to build up popularity.

But Duncan was an exceptional politician, uniquely capable in his own way of taking decisions. Those twinkling eyes, that reddish hair, that active brain, masked an enormous capacity for summing things up and then instinctively and quickly taking the right decision.

One thing about Duncan fascinated me and that was his belief in flying saucers. He had been Minister of Aviation and had held a series of other jobs in government and although he would not talk too much about it he was absolutely convinced that flying saucers really did exist.

Over the years I found myself enormously moved by the tragedy of Duncan. All his life he dedicated his talents and his career to public service. And he held many offices. He had been Minister of Defence, he had been Minister of Commonwealth Relations and for Colonial Affairs. He held many more distinguished offices under Tory prime ministers. During all that time, I do not expect he made a penny for his private purse.

Then came the Tory election victory of 1970. Edward Heath became Prime Minister and Heath had no further use for Duncan Sandys. So Sandys, in his sixties, was tossed on to the scrap heap. That is how he came to join Lonrho soon afterwards. And that is why he came to be involved in the Lonrho financial scandal of the time.

Over lunch in 1973, in a voice which was not always steady, he told me how it all happened.

Once he realised that politics was finished for him, he explained to me, he knew he would have to embark on some business career. So the Lonrho people approached him. Angus Ogilvy, Tiny Rowland and Alan Ball came to see him and said that they would like Sandys to act as a consultant on Africa. Sandys knew Africa well, and because of his previous office in government he also knew many of the rulers of Black Africa well.

His first job with Lonrho was for £10,000 a year. He proved eminently successful. So Ogilvy, Rowland and Ball approached him again and they said in effect, 'You've done a great job. Now we would like you to do more. Why not take on a full-time consultancy? We will pay you £50,000 a year.' Sandys was attracted as any man would have been attracted. It was also pointed out to him that since his work as consultant would be outside the United Kingdom, there was really no need to pay tax on most of his income.

He considered the proposition. It was within the limits of United Kingdom law. So he accepted an arrangement whereby £49,000 of his salary was paid into an account in the Cayman Islands and only £1000 was paid to him in England.

After a time they came back to him again and they said, 'You've done a great job. Now we would like you to be chairman of the company.' Sandys said no. But he added that he would be willing to help them find a chairman. He approached two other well-known men and each man refused the job.

In the end he agreed to accept the job himself at a salary of £38,000 a year. The Lonrho people then said to him: 'This means that you are giving up your consultancy at £50,000 a year. It was agreed that we would use you as consultant for six years, so clearly we must pay you for the time which you are not acting as consultant.'

And Sandys weakly agreed. And that is why Duncan Sandys found himself in the middle of a devastating scandal, the essence of which was that a UK company, Lonrho, appeared to be avoiding UK taxation by paying salaries to some of its directors in the Cayman Islands. In just about the only memorable phrase he ever uttered, Ted Heath, described it as the 'unacceptable face of capitalism'.

When the scandal became public knowledge Sandys returned every penny of the money to which he was entitled. But the damage was done. And he said something to me that day which touched me enormously. 'All my life,' he said, 'I have tried to serve the public. I won't say I have become a first-class public figure, because I haven't. But at least I have become a respected second-class public figure and now it is all gone, all finished. And the terrible thing is that I have done nothing wrong.'

I looked at him and I saw to my dismay that his eyes were filling with tears. I tried to tell him that he was being too subjective, that he was too close to the centre of the affair and that no one who knew him really thought that he had been in any way dishonest.

But he would not be convinced. 'I know I've done no wrong,' he kept saying. 'But no one believes that. They read the headlines and think that I have been dishonest. Do you know that I'm no longer willing to go into the street? Until recently I used to walk around and people would come and shake my hand and say, "Good morning, Mr Sandys. How are you, Mr Sandys?" Now I'm ashamed to go into the street. Do you know that we have kept our little daughter away from school so that people would not stare at her?'

Duncan Sandys was a man who could have been a great prime minister, a man with enormous powers of decision and above all a man of enormous personal integrity. And I saw that day a man washed up at the age of sixty-five simply through having accepted what he thought was an honest offer.

There was never a danger of anything of the kind happening to another figure whose public career has continued long past the age merely of sixty-five – Lord Goodman. For Lord Goodman was and is the great Fleet Street fixer of my time. I first heard of him, when he was plain Arnold Goodman, in the early 1960s. George Wigg was a great fan of his and every time George felt he had been libelled, which was frequently, it was invariably Goodman to whom he rushed. Wigg was constantly extolling Goodman's virtues and my guess is that it was about this period that Harold Wilson through the good offices of George Wigg became a client of Goodman's.

When Wilson became Prime Minister in 1964 one of the first things he did was to impose import quotas on all imported goods including newsprint. There was a surcharge of 10 per cent and this threw Fleet Street managers and proprietors into a tizzy. For overnight the price of their newsprint was going up by 10 per cent at a time when it was impossible to increase the selling price of the newspaper. They all quite rightly shrieked in protest at what they considered to be a surcharge on news and many attempts were made to persuade Harold Wilson that even if all the other import levies were retained at least newsprint should be free of tax.

But how to get through to Wilson since none of the Fleet Street proprietors or managing directors felt they had personal access to him? Like a blinding flash of light came the answer – Arnold Goodman, of course. For Goodman, it was said in all the right places, had the 'ear of the Prime Minister'.

The process of sucking up to Goodman began. As far as the Express Group were concerned it was conducted with gusto by Tom Blackburn, our Chairman. His reason was that if he could convince Goodman of the iniquity of the surcharge then Goodman might in turn convince Wilson. Goodman became a real power in Fleet Street.

Around this time the William Hickey column of the *Daily Express* made a reference to the Arts Council, of which Goodman was Chairman – a reference at which Goodman took umbrage. There was no libel involved and yet Hickey was forced to publish an apology which had been, so I was assured by the *Daily Express* legal manager, Andrew Edwards, dictated by Goodman himself.

Andrew Edwards told me that on another occasion he was

instructed by Blackburn to consult Goodman on a legal matter. Goodman graciously agreed to see Edwards, but only if Edwards arrived at the restaurant where Goodman was lunching at the time when he was due to leave and drove with Goodman in his car to Goodman's next appointment.

Goodman did not show much interest in Blackburn's problems until he learned that Edwards was a man of some standing, that he was the son-in-law of Norman Wates, the building millionaire, and that Edwards' own brother owned a prep school to which two royal children went.

'The moment I started dropping names, Goodman's whole attitude to me changed,' said Edwards. 'He leaned over to me and said, "Mr Edwards, your brother owns that prep school. I have a client who is very keen to have his son go there." '

'It is not only a fact that my brother owns the school,' Edwards replied with great satisfaction. 'I also have shares in it. But I can assure you that the list is full for the next seven years and it would be absolutely impossible for me to do anything for you.'

Until Beaverbrook's death in 1964 Michael Foot and his wife had been constant visitors at Cherkley. They went there once or twice after his death and on one occasion Lady Beaverbrook, who had taken up horse racing, asked Michael if he knew of anyone who could give her advice. Michael immediately thought of George Wigg who was a racing fanatic and suggested his name. Indeed he introduced George Wigg to Lady Beaverbrook. Later on it transpired that Lady Beaverbrook also wanted a good lawyer. Many months afterwards Michael went back to Cherkley for dinner and there sitting at the dinner table and acting as if they were the most frequent visitors were Lord Goodman and George Wigg.

In this same period I was playing golf one morning with Norman Wates, Andrew Edwards' father-in-law. He began to tell me how he had met such a charming and generous man one evening the previous week. Arnold Goodman. Wates explained that the then Minister of Housing, Richard Crossman, had no expense allowance with which to entertain leaders of the building industry but that this marvellous man Arnold Goodman had arranged a dinner party in his flat so that leaders of the building industry could meet Crossman over a social meal. Around the table had been the boss of Bovis, the boss of McAlpine, the boss of Trollope & Colls and every other big building man in the country.

'Was the evening a successful one as far as influencing Crossman was concerned?' I asked.

'Most disappointing,' replied Wates. 'I got the impression that he wasn't the slightest bit interested in our arguments.'

He went on to tell me that he had left the dinner party rather earlier than the others and that Goodman had come with him to the front door, helped him on with his coat and while so doing said, 'I thought the Minister was very impressed with your argument, Mr Wates.'

'Well, I didn't think so,' said Wates. 'He gave me the impression of not even listening.'

Whereupon Goodman put his arm round Wates' shoulder and said, 'Well, I thought you made a good argument.'

Goodman is a man who operates enormous influence on a personal basis. His life's work has been getting to know everyone of importance in public life. There is no area – left or right – where he does not have his contacts.

Shortly afterwards Lord Goodman, at Harold Wilson's suggestion, went to Rhodesia with Max Aitken. He may not have persuaded Ian Smith into signing a peace settlement but he secured for himself the friendship and devotion of Max. Not least because at that time Goodman was helping Max with a domestic crisis. For Max, I had heard from a colleague, had fallen madly in love with an Australian girl, Patricia Tudor, an ex-Miss Australia and a Qantas air hostess. There seemed little doubt in fact that he had proposed marriage. And Arnold Goodman was walking gloomily around looking as if he were going to have to conduct the most dreadful divorce case ever.

But affection waned. Indeed the turning-point might have been at a party where Max announced that his new yacht was going to be entirely black, with black sails, and that he would insist on all the crew wearing black uniforms.

'But I don't know what to call her,' Max said. 'Has anyone any suggestions?'

'Yes,' Miss Tudor piped up loud and clear, 'I have a brilliant idea. Why not call her *Black God*?'

From that time there was an enormous cooling. But the relationship had been pretty hot and Max caused considerable embarrassment on arrival with Goodman in Rhodesia by sending compromising messages over the telex from Salisbury – especially since all of them were picked up by the authorities.

It might have been thought that when Wilson went out of office this would have been the end of Goodman. Not a bit of it. After the 1970 election it became known that he was a friend of Ted Heath and a confidant of Alex Douglas-Home. He went on from strength to strength.

In fact I had had my own little contretemps with Goodman. In May 1972, the *Evening News* in London had published a brilliant exposé of the way in which British Lion was selling Shepperton Film Studios to a developer called John Bentley. Shepperton had only been handed over from the State to British Lion on condition that the land would never be used for building development. Because of that condition the shares of British Lion languished. Lord Goodman, in addition to all his other duties, also happened to be Chairman of British Lion – and he had arranged this deal with Bentley. The *Evening News* mounted a campaign against the sale of Shepperton studios.

The *Sunday Express* chimed in with a leader on 17 May in which we said that it would be morally wrong for money to be made by shareholders out of the sale of land. The next day I went sailing, and when I arrived back in the clubhouse at Hamble I learned that John Coote, the *Daily Express*'s Managing Director, had been telephoning me all day long. Goodman had been on to him. It transpired – something I had not known – that Goodman was flying the very next day to New Brunswick where he was to receive an Honorary Degree from the hands of the University of New Brunswick's Chancellor, Max Aitken.

Goodman told Coote that he would be sorely embarrassed unless an apology appeared in the *Daily Express* the next day. Unless such an apology appeared he would not be able to fly to Canada. Coote replied that it was quite impossible to ask one newspaper to apologise for the sins of another. Goodman thereupon demanded that on the Monday morning I should have a leader writer in his office to take to his dictation the leader which he wished published. I told Johny Coote to tell Goodman that I had no intention of doing any such thing.

In the end Goodman did go to Canada. Three days later I had an anguished call from Max Aitken in New York.

'I am having a hell of a time here,' he said. 'I'm fed up with the whole business. Won't you please print something?'

And in the end I printed a statement which contained no apology tucked away at the bottom of a news page. But I did so only to save Max embarrassment.

One further point. At the time *Private Eye*, and in particular Paul Foot, were pursuing a relentless campaign against Goodman. But on one occasion they boobed badly.

They printed a story about Goodman's bank account and the fact that his bank manager had asked him to pay an outstanding overdraft. In fact they had written about the wrong Goodman and were completely in error.

Paul Foot and Richard Ingrams, the Editor of *Private Eye*, were summoned to Goodman's office and he read the riot act to them, threatening untold litigation. At the end of the meeting Goodman turned to Paul Foot and began to speak to him of the Hanratty murder case, about which Paul Foot was then campaigning because he believed that Hanratty should never have been hanged. 'I am very interested in your views on the Hanratty case,' said Goodman almost as an aside. 'Would you like me to raise it in the Lords?' But the matter did not end there. Goodman asked Paul Foot to drive him out to see the field in which the murder which Hanratty is alleged to have committed took place.

When he stepped out of the car and saw the field he said to Paul Foot, 'I am completely convinced that this man did not really have a case against him. Why should he be in a field of this kind in the middle of the night? What could he possibly be doing here?'

Foot drove Goodman back to London and as Goodman was about to leave the car Foot said to him, 'I do hope that you are going to be able to do something about this, Lord Goodman. For time is running out and the whole case to try and prove Hanratty's innocence is in danger of falling flat.'

Goodman's parting shot to Paul Foot was, 'Foot, when I get my teeth into anything I never let go.'

The next time Lord Goodman swam into my ken was several years later, in October 1984, when he invited himself to lunch with me. He came into the Howard Hotel restaurant on the arm of his driver and looking very old and despite his weight a bit haggard. He explained to me that he had an ear complaint which was affecting his balance but which was not Menière's disease.

The purpose of our talk was simple and appeared straightforward enough. Goodman was writing his memoirs and one possible place in which to serialise them might be the *Sunday Express*. He was not prepared to divulge any professional secrets or to let any of his clients down, he said, but he made it clear that he still had some pretty good stories to tell.

He told me how, when Lord Snowdon had separated from Princess Margaret and the announcement of the divorce had come through, Snowdon was in Australia and travelling back to London. His secretary rang Goodman in some anguish lest Snowdon be badly treated at Heathrow Airport and not given his customary VIP treatment.

Goodman rang the Airport Authority and was assured that Snowdon would be given VIP treatment in exactly the same way as he always had been.

Only later did Goodman discover that when he arrived at the airport Snowdon had had to carry his own bag. Goodman immediately wanted to know why the promise of VIP treatment had not been fulfilled and was told by the Airport Authority that his instructions had been countermanded by the Palace. Who in Buckingham Palace could have done that?

Goodman also told me how he had been invited to dine by Lord and Lady Rupert Nevill and found that there was only one other guest – the Queen.

He said during our lunch that Central TV was planning a rehash of the Christine Keeler story. Jack Profumo was one of his clients. If this programme were ever screened might it not once again crucify a man who had made his atonement? Might I not wish to attack the projected series in my column?

And that indeed was just what I did. I received a grateful telephone call from Profumo. But I never heard another word from Lord Goodman about his book.

An incomparably better writer and certainly a friend who was to become a frequent lunch and dinner companion from the early 1970s was John Betjeman. Indeed he was to become a friend of all my family. He was a natural flatterer, which is perhaps why he kept saying that my daughter was a most beautiful woman. Maybe he even meant it. One of my most treasured possessions is a sketch he did of her from memory one night when he and I were dining in town.

He was very frail and walked with tiny doddering steps. But there might have been just a little bit of play-acting in that walk. My Swiss daughter-in-law, also beautiful and whom he called the Helvetian, and I arranged to lunch with him on board one of the paddle-steamers moored near Waterloo Bridge. The tide was fully out and the gangway down to the boat was precipitously steep and slippery. Suzi and I both had difficulty negotiating it and we wondered how John could possibly cope. When he arrived at the top of the gangway clutching a bundle of books I realised this meant he could not even hold on to the guard rail. I tried to shout a warning but he didn't hear and to the astonishment of Suzi and myself came down the slippery gangway with the sure-footedness of a cat.

John was the greatest of fun and told the most wonderful stories. Once when we were in the White Tower he told me how the great Edwardian artist Sickert used to lunch there as an old man, often accompanied by the then young and ambitious Augustus John. One day as they walked up Charlotte Street to the restaurant, Sickert stopped in front of an ironmonger's shop. Without saying a word he stared long and hard at the contents of the window. Anxiously Augustus John stared too in the hope he might see what had captured the old man's attention and might even inspire his next painting. Finally the old man turned away and looked at John.

'Augustus,' he said, 'wouldn't it be marvellous to have a brass cock?'

Betjeman also told how many years later when Augustus John was himself rich and famous and the restaurant was owned by a bohemian character Emil, who was also a bit of a drunk, he turned up one day and after the meal was presented with a bill for £43 – a then quite staggering amount, perhaps thirty times more than normal.

Augustus John summoned the proprietor and demanded an explanation. 'Well,' said Emil, 'it's not just what you've eaten today. It's that dark young Welshman who has been eating here for weeks. He told me you would pay.' And Augustus John did. The Welshman was Dylan Thomas.

Betjeman also had a delicious story about himself. When he became engaged his future father-in-law, the fearsome Field Marshal Lord Chetwode, who had commanded the Army in India, discussed with him how after the marriage Betjeman should address him.

'I've decided that for you to call me by my first name would be far too familiar. On the other hand "Lord Chetwode" would be a bit formal. So I think the best answer would be if you were just to call me Field Marshal.'

John was touching about his own father and about the day his father died. Betjeman was working on the *Evening Standard* Diary at the time – a choice of career which explained in part why he and his father were not then on speaking terms. Betjeman had been out on a Diary story and on the way back to Central London his Tube train stopped for a much longer time than usual at Chalk Farm. Betjeman's father was in a hospital near the Tube station and the thought crossed Betjeman's mind that God might be hinting that he should get off and go to see his father. He shrugged off the thought as fanciful. The train started again. Betjeman later discovered that his father had died that afternoon.

There was a time in 1971 when I feared I was going to become Editor of the *Daily Express*.

I say 'feared' because it was a job which I did not want. It was a job which, because of the tax situation, could not have meant any more money for me but could have meant even less leisure than I was enjoying on the *Sunday Express*. It would not even have meant more power, since in my view the *Daily Express* was a less powerful newspaper politically than the *Sunday Express*.

Derek Marks was at that time Editor of the *Daily Express* and the suggestion came up because he was having a rough spell. Max Aitken suddenly said to me one day in the office, 'Why don't you take it over? Why don't you come in and run the *Daily Express*?'

I explained to him that I thought I was temperamentally unsuited for the job, and that I had no capacity to devolve responsibility, which was something a *Daily Express* Editor must have. I also pointed out that there was no immediate apparent successor to me on the *Sunday Express* and it would be crazy to ruin one good and profitable newspaper without the certainty of helping the *Daily Express*.

But Max was insistent. 'Think about it,' he said, 'and I will ring you when you get back from golf next Monday morning' – Monday being my day off. And Max knew that I got back from golf at about 1.30 p.m.

Well, I thought about it. I went to see my doctor and he assured me that my health would be sufficient to take the strain of the enormously difficult working conditions on a daily newspaper. I spoke to my wife Pam about it and I discussed it with my children. It would have meant my having to live in town during the week. It would have meant an end to all my present social life. But by the weekend I had convinced myself that it was my duty to accept. I had even begun to look forward to the new tingling excitement of trying to make the *Daily Express* once again soar upwards in circulation.

On the Monday I finished my game of golf and I came home to await the call. At exactly 1.45 p.m. the telephone rang and I rushed towards it.

It was Max. 'Max, the answer is yes,' I said to him straight away.

But Max was not listening to me. He was saying instead, 'Did you see this morning's Scottish *Daily Express*? Isn't it a wonderful newspaper?' And I knew that I was no longer on the point of being made Editor of the *Daily Express* and that the next incumbent of that job would be Ian McColl.

Ian McColl was someone whom I had known well in my youth in Scotland. He had been a fervent young Liberal in pre-war days. Until the age of fifty he had been a teetotaller and also I suspect a virgin under the strong influence of his mother – who was not only a rabid Liberal but also a rabid teetotaller and highly religious to boot. Then she died and Ian blossomed out. Before he came south he had been Editor of the *Daily Express* in Scotland, had married his secretary, started a family and had taken up not only drinking but smoking too.

In October 1972 I drove with him to that then great annual occasion, the Vintage Dinner, where the world's greatest wines were served to a celebrity gathering. On the way he confessed to me how much he loved these dinners and how remarkable it was that he stayed sober at them. This he put down to the fact that he liked the mineral water that was served in between the wines. We were placed at different tables for the meal but when afterwards I fetched up in his car I realised that his articulation was far from being perfect. He looked at me and he said a wise and wonderful thing. 'Do you know something?' he said. 'This year I forgot to drink enough mineral water in between the wine.'

And my God he had, too.

But not even Ian McColl, full as he was of mineral water and Celtic passion, could fail to stem the downward slide in the *Daily Express*'s circulation. When the time came for him to go, it was not I mercifully who was offered the job again but someone whose name I suggested to Max, Alastair Burnet, then Editor of the *Economist*. Max liked the idea, which I felt would move the *Express* up-market. But he hankered even more over someone else – Larry Lamb, then at the height of his fame as Editor of the *Sun*. Max suggested that before we made a formal approach to Burnet, I should lunch with Larry Lamb and sound him out.

This I did. Larry came to lunch with me at the Boulestin. He was on the wagon at the time and drank not at all but ate quite prodigious quantities of rare roast beef. He appeared to be quite attracted to the idea of editing the *Express* and told me that he had no contract of any kind with Rupert Murdoch and so technically would be free to come at any time. The lunch ended with his agreeing to see Max privately to discuss the matter further. This they did a day or two later in Max's Marsham Court flat. By this time Lamb had abandoned the wagon, they drank two bottles of champagne between them and the evening ended with Larry saying he would think further over the matter.

A few days later came the reply which all along I had known would be inevitable – that Larry had decided he could not leave Rupert. I suspected then that he had used his conversations with us to demonstrate to Murdoch just how highly he was valued elsewhere and just how easy it would be for him at any moment to leave the *Sun*. Who knows, he might even as a result have been given a salary increase and a lengthy contract?

At any rate it was not Larry but Alastair Burnet who became the next Editor of the *Daily Express*. Dear Alastair. He was and is such a lovely man. So gentle, so decent, so compassionate. But he was not cut out to be the editor of a popular national daily. He and I often used to arrive in the front hall of the Express building at the same time in the morning and often Alastair would have tucked under his arm a bottle of whisky he had bought in a supermarket on the way to work and from which he would dispense hospitality to members of his staff. Alastair's method of control was very much a civilised hands-off one. One Sunday night I had put my car on the night train to Scotland and had then a couple of hours to while away until the train itself was due to leave. So I decided to visit the *Express* and see Alastair at work. It was just before first edition time and the editorial floor was bustling with activity. Tape machines were spewing out reports from all over the world. Messengers were running about hither and thither. Reporters' typewriters were clattering furiously but of Alastair there was no sign. On the back bench where the senior executives sit his place was vacant. When I asked where he was I was told that he was in his office. And there in that oasis of peace and tranquillity I found him immersed in a document.

An article for the *Daily Express*? No. He was working on the speech he was going to give at the following month's Conservative Party Conference. I knew then that he could never survive as Editor. And there was a further problem with Alastair. He was at that time a committed supporter of Ted Heath. The snag was that it was Margaret Thatcher who by this time was leader of the Tory Party. So we had the ridiculous situation that the newspaper appeared to be supporting the past rather than the present Conservative leader. I had words with Max Aitken on the subject. And although he was a friend of Heath's he agreed with me.

Max then did something which took even me by surprise. One night while on a visit to Canada he issued a personal statement to be published on page one of the next day's paper giving full support to Margaret Thatcher. Alastair was at dinner at the Savoy when the statement arrived. Robin Esser, whom he had left in charge of the back bench, was instructed by Max to publish it without delay. Alastair returned from supper to find himself editing a newspaper with a different policy.

The next Editor of the *Daily Express* was Roy Wright, who had been Charles Wintour's number two on the *Evening Standard*. He was an excellent technician and a good handler of news stories. But he lacked the charisma a good editor needs. His stay in the top chair was not to be a long one either.

Nor were the princely salaries paid to some journalists always adequate compensation for loss of office. Certainly there were journalists, especially on the *Daily Mail* and the *Daily Express*, who earned enormous sums. Those who worked for Lord Hartwell's *Daily Telegraph* were less lucky.

Harry Boyne was for years one of the most respected and distinguished lobby correspondents in Fleet Street. Although a Tory of conviction, he was knighted by Harold Wilson. There is not a touch of envy in him. But he confessed to me that when he retired in 1981 from the *Daily Telegraph*, he was receiving just a little less than £8000 a year – a quite derisory figure. But he also told me with pride and with gratitude that Lord Hartwell had given him a good-will pension of £2000 a year. I pointed out to him that this was so very much less than other journalists in other organisations received by right. But he would have none of it. He was quite content with the way in which he had been treated.

He told me how many years before his wife had seen an advertisement for a flat in Marsham Court, Westminster, and had pointed out to him that if only they could raise the £7500 to buy a 68-year lease, it would mean very much less travelling late at night for Harry when he left the House of Commons. But how to find the money? They reckoned that the house in which they lived at that time would not fetch more than £3500. So Harry, prodded by his wife, went to the Bank of Scotland, who cannily suggested that they might possibly put up half the money if the *Daily Telegraph* put up the other half and guaranteed the whole.

Harry then went to see the Company Secretary of the *Daily Telegraph*, a Mr Stevens. But Mr Stevens shook his head sorrowfully. There was a firm company policy taken by the Board that no more loans would be given to employees. When Harry told this to his wife, who for years had worked at Harrods to help make ends meet, she urged him to go and see Lord Hartwell himself. Harry arranged an appointment and the loan was immediately given. Another example, Harry pointed out to me, of Lord Hartwell's generosity. For my own part I thought it damnable that Boyne should be treated so meanly when many other political correspondents were having Westminster flats provided for them rent-free by their newspapers.

And yet I have enormous respect for Lord Hartwell. For he it was who in 1961 launched the *Sunday Telegraph*, which threatened to be a most serious rival to the *Sunday Express*. At that time Lord Hartwell was printing the *Sunday Times* on the *Daily Telegraph*'s presses. When that contract stopped it made economic sense that the presses should not stay idle on Saturdays. So the idea of having a Sunday newspaper of his own materialised.

Market research showed that some 60 per cent, possibly an even higher percentage, of *Daily Telegraph* readers bought the *Sunday Express* on Sunday. Hartwell reasoned that if there were a *Sunday Telegraph* they would buy that instead. And I have to confess I thought they might too. To meet the arrival of the new paper I decided to take the *Sunday Express* a little more up-market. And I introduced a two-page foreign news spread with people like Henry Fairlie and other top names contributing columns from America.

Then came the night when the first edition of the new paper arrived on my desk. I danced a little jig of joy. I knew that it was not going to be a serious competitor to the *Sunday Express*.

I was proved right. The first *Sunday Telegraph* was a dull, drab affair and from the complete sell-out which the first edition of any new newspaper gets it quickly dropped to a level of around 660,000. It has since improved enormously in its content but has never really recovered from that first failure all those years ago.

With another potential rival it was a different story. The first edition of the *Mail on Sunday* in 1982 was so terrible that again I felt like dancing. But after the first few weeks the Editor, Bernard Shrimsley, was sacked and Sir David English, the Editor of the *Daily Mail*, stepped in. He reconstructed the paper virtually overnight. And quite miraculously saved it from disaster – although the fact that Lord Rothermere was pouring money into it to the extent of losing up to £15 million a year helped a little too.

But it is quite extraordinary that the *Mail on Sunday* is even now selling less than the previous Associated Newspapers' Sunday paper, the *Sunday Dispatch*, was when it raised the white flag to the *Sunday Express* in 1961.

Which leads me to ask: What sort of Editor was I? This extract from an article in the *New Statesman* by Alan Watkins of September 1972 presents a picture which is not completely accurate. Watkins had worked for the *Sunday Express* from 1959 to 1964 and was at one stage Cross-Bencher.

His *New Statesman* article was written shortly after the appearance of A. J. P. Taylor's biography of Lord Beaverbrook in 1972:

One day in February the Editor, John Junor, called me into his office. 'Have you ever heard of Anthony Praga?' he asked. I confessed I had not heard of him. The Editor explained who he was. In the 1930s, so it appeared, Praga had written a series of articles for the *Express* in which the plots of well-known, unread, lengthy novels were summarised 'like short stories', said the Editor.

The series had been successful. Beaverbrook, at any rate, had been pleased with it. Some thirty years later he wanted to revive the idea. The Editor read to me part of his dictated memorandum. He wished for a start to have summarised, in short story form, *East Lynne, Lorna Doone, The Scarlet Letter* and *Seven Days* by Elinor Glyn. He was particularly keen on Elinor Glyn, maybe on account of her relationship with Lord Curzon or perhaps for some other reason. However, he foresaw trouble owing to her advanced views.

'Elinor Glyn,' Beaverbrook wrote, 'may present difficulties but we should be able to overcome them with tactful treatment.'

The assignment, I confess, did not greatly appeal to me. The prospect of reading *Lorna Doone* was particularly distasteful. This was a book I had been at pains to avoid. It had been on the school reading list and I had failed to progress beyond the first chapter. To have to read it now, in Fleet Street, at the request of Lord Beaverbrook, would be to suffer some kind of defeat in life.

'What about Bob Pitman?' I asked. The late Robert Pitman was then the Literary Editor of the paper. 'Bob is much too busy with other things,' said the Editor, which seemed a comprehensive enough reply. 'You are the only other person on the staff with enough literary ability to do this job.'

The flattering effect of this opinion was slightly spoiled by what came next. 'I may say,' the Editor went on, 'that this series will appear in the *Sunday Express* over my dead body, but as the idea comes from Beaverbrook we have to go through the motions at first.'

It was one of the Editor's several virtues that he was by no means an obedient follower of his proprietor's frequently incomprehensible instructions. One of Pitman's functions was to decode the strange garbled messages which would issue from Cherkley, Montego Bay or the South of France.

'Bob has a genius for seeing what's in the old man's mind,' the Editor would say.

When the instructions were deciphered he would sometimes procrastinate or deliberately misunderstand them. However, he was rarely as frank about his ultimate intentions as he was on this occasion. I cannot say I was wholly discouraged by the promise of non-publication. I had no wish to acquire a reputation, however slender, as a compressor of the works of Elinor Glyn. 'He wants the first piece to be on *East Lynne*,' said the Editor, 'just to see how it goes.'

I bought a Collins Classics edition of Mrs Henry Wood's work and, hour after hour, sat reading it at my desk. Occasionally the Editor would pass on his errands of encouragement or reproof to his staff, 'You're a slow reader, I see,' he would say, and laugh as if he had made a joke.

Eventually I produced a piece of about 1500 words which was dispatched to Beaverbrook. 'He thought it was all right,' said the Editor some days later. 'Now he wants you to have a go at Elinor Glyn.'

Happily I never did have a go at Elinor Glyn. I pretended to forget the task, the Editor made no more references to the matter and Beaverbrook, as far as I am aware, showed no further interest. Elinor Glyn, like *Lorna Doone*, remains a gap in my reading.

As so also it remains in mine.

VII

'I DO NOT think you have ever met Margaret Thatcher. Would you like to? And if so are you by any chance free for lunch today?'

The voice on the other end of the telephone was that of Gordon Reece, a former *Sunday Express* reporter who was now acting as a personal adviser to Mrs Thatcher. And the timing of the call? Just six days before polling day in the 1974 general election – an election which Ted Heath was to lose to Harold Wilson.

The timing struck me as odd. Margaret Thatcher had never seemed to me to be a powerful political figure – perhaps because in my male chauvinistic fashion I regarded all women politicians as essentially second-rankers. Indeed some time previously I had shot down the *Sunday Express* political columnist, Robin Oakley, when he had had the temerity to suggest that Margaret Thatcher might be appointed Chancellor of the Exchequer. Absolute nonsense, I had snorted. And besides I already had a lunch appointment. So I declined the invitation but said I would be happy to see her after the election. And after the election when the whole Tory world was in ruins the invitation was renewed.

Reece came with her and we lunched at the Boulestin. This was because Reece asked me in advance which was my favourite restaurant. When I arrived a bottle of champagne was already in an ice-bucket on the table. The champagne was none of her doing. But Reece drank nothing else. My first impressions of her were mixed. She did not seem quite as attractive as her pictures suggested. Indeed she gave me at that first meeting the impression of being entirely asexual.

Nor was I over-impressed with her as an intellectual. Our lunch took place only a few days after a speech made by Keith Joseph in which he had appeared to suggest that lower-class income groups were not fit to have children. Margaret Thatcher, then a keen Joseph supporter, explained that it had all been most unfortunate; that what had happened was that Joseph had inserted that section into the speech himself. The rest of the speech had been written by economists, including Samuel Brittan and Alfred Sherman.

I asked her why she didn't herself make a speech on Tory philosophy. She did not immediately reply but a few minutes later she asked me what my view was on Hugh Trevor-Roper. I replied that I had not a very good view of Trevor-Roper.

There was silence for a moment and then she said, 'What do you think of Robert Blake?' I said that I thought Robert Blake was a fine historian and a most agreeable man.

'Why do you want to know about Blake?' I asked.

'Oh,' she replied, 'I was just wondering who could prepare a statement for me on Tory philosophy.'

'But why on earth don't you write your own speech?' I asked.

She explained that that was a procedure which would take far too long and that it was much easier to have an academic prepare a speech. I found myself reflecting that people like Quintin Hogg, Alec Douglas-Home and Reggie Maudling had never used anyone to prepare a speech laying out their own privately held and publicly held political views.

If I had thought Margaret Thatcher lacked sex appeal that first time I met her, my views were to change in time. So were those of many others.

Of course there were some who had always found her sexy. Douglas Clark, when Political Editor of the *Sunday Express*, attended a Tory Conference at Blackpool when she was Minister of Education in Heath's government. After a night of drinking with delegates in the various hotel bars and receptions rooms he retired to his bedroom in jolly mood and still not ready for his sleep. Suddenly he found himself thinking of Margaret Thatcher and in a mad impulse picked up his bedside telephone and asked to be connected to her room. When a sleepy and utterly virtuous Margaret Thatcher answered she gave a very dusty answer indeed to his suggestion that she might care to come to his room for a nightcap. The next morning that lovely man Douglas in an act of contrition sent a huge bouquet of flowers to her room. At the expense of the *Sunday Express*, of course.

And as the years pass Margaret Thatcher's sex appeal has actually increased. Jim Prior told me how one or two ministers had, as he inelegantly put it, tried unsuccessfully to get a leg over. Which proves, I suppose, the truth of the old adage that power is the greatest aphrodisiac of all.

I was wrong too about her intellect. Her mind is razor-sharp. And she was absolutely right to delegate the things which didn't matter to someone else. Harold Wilson's tragedy was that he spent all his time thinking about his next speech and being utterly ineffectual in between speeches. The country is not restored to prosperity by politicians making speeches but by politicians taking the actions and giving the incentives which make prosperity possible. So Margaret Thatcher was dead right to tell her speech-writers precisely what she wanted to say and then let them get on with preparing the phraseology.

But Margaret could be sensitive to what people thought and said of her. I remember lunching with her privately in the House of Commons in the large gaunt room allocated to the Leader of the Opposition. The table was set for two. The meal was a help-yourself collation of cold chicken and salad laid out on a sideboard. On the sideboard was a bottle of white wine, a bottle of whisky and some glasses. She poured herself a whisky and asked me if I would like one. I said I would prefer to wait for the wine.

I asked her if she had read Paul Callan's interview with David Owen in that morning's *Daily Mirror*. She hadn't. So I told her that Owen had described to Callan how he had been sitting one night in the Members' dining-room when she had left her own table to return to the Chamber. 'As she brushed past me,' he had said, 'I was conscious of a sexy scent of perfume and whisky.' I went on to explain that the whole tone of the interview had been far from unfriendly to her and that Owen clearly admired her. She made no comment but I noted that she did not have a second whisky.

If there were neither airs nor pretensions of grandeur before Margaret Thatcher became Prime Minister, there were not that many either after she did so. In her first few weeks of office I received a formal invitation to lunch at Chequers. It was an enormous honour and it was one I would have loved to have been able to accept. But for the Sunday in question I had already made another commitment – to take my boat round from Littlehampton to the Hamble – and I had fixed up a crew of friends to accompany me. I did my best to explain my dilemma to the Prime Minister's personal secretary, the lovely and super-efficient Caroline Stephens. The next time I saw the Prime Minister she was surrounded by friends but she still pointed an accusing finger at me and jestingly said, 'Here's the man who turned down a date with me.'

I had the good fortune to be forgiven and invited to Chequers several times during the next ten years. What impressed me there was the way Margaret Thatcher looked after both the staff and her guests. If it were a buffet luncheon she would fuss around making sure that everyone had enough to eat and drink and had someone to talk to. And in her attitude towards the staff she made it clear that she regarded them as just as important as any of the VIPs.

It was typical of Margaret Thatcher that even after I had left the *Sunday Express* in 1989 and it had not yet been made public that I was joining the *Mail on Sunday* she should have sent me an invitation to attend her Boxing Day party at Chequers. In so doing she was simply showing her loyalty.

From my point of view it was an unforgettable experience. Among the guests were Sir Geoffrey Howe, Nicholas Ridley, Kenneth Baker, John Major and Cecil Parkinson. She could not have been more friendly and when the time came for me to leave the party she insisted on walking downstairs with me and fussing around me until I drove off. There is no one who is ever going to convince me that this is not a woman who is caring and compassionate and fiercely loyal to her friends.

Margaret came to the dinner given by Victor Matthews at the Ritz to celebrate my twenty-fifth anniversary on 25 November 1979 as Editor of the *Sunday Express*. At the same round table as the Prime Minister and myself were Ted Heath, Quintin Hogg, Manny Shinwell, Enoch Powell, Victor Matthews and the South African Ambassador, Dawie de Villiers. The last named I chose quite deliberately. He was a personal friend and I didn't give a damn what anyone thought about his being invited to sit at the same table as the Prime Minister. At the very end of the dinner and after all the speeches had been made, a division was called in the Commons and all the MP guests had to rush away. Many of them did not return, nor indeed was there any reason why they should. But Margaret did and stayed chatting with fellow guests for perhaps another hour. Simply because she was enjoying herself.

At that dinner one tiny and irrelevant incident puzzled me. In my own speech, I had posed the question: What makes a man or woman succeed in politics, what separates a great prime minister from the others? And then one by one I had named some of our leading political guests, including all the ones at my table, and discussed their qualities. I suggested that being prime minister was in some sense like being editor of a newspaper. And that if she wanted to stay prime minister for as long as I had stayed editor it might not be a bad idea to follow the same principles – namely by sticking true to your beliefs, never following the herd but always standing by what you believed to be true and right for the country even if what you were saying was temporarily unpopular. Readers will stay with a newspaper they believe to be honest and truthful. They will also stay with a prime minister of whom they think the same.

I learned afterwards from another guest who had been sitting at the same table as him that Willie Whitelaw had been much displeased by my speech and indeed had gone as far as to describe it as 'disgraceful'. Yet the very next time I saw him he was as always fulsome in his praise. I sometimes think that Willie would not be two-faced if there were a third one available.

At that anniversary dinner Ted Heath had shared our table. Not long afterwards I asked Margaret why she would not have him in the Cabinet. I pointed out that it might lessen her difficulties enormously. She looked at me and replied, 'I couldn't. He wouldn't want to sit there as a member of the team. All the time he would be trying to take over. I have to tell you this, John. When I look at him and he looks at me I don't feel that it is a man looking at a woman. More like a woman looking at another woman.'

Poor Ted. If only he had been able to contain his wounded pride he would have been of real service to the Tory Party during the early years of Margaret Thatcher's leadership. As it was that fell to others.

One was Quintin Hogg, my friend for so many years. His eldest son Douglas, whom Margaret Thatcher made a government minister, once asked me, 'How did you and my father become such close friends?' It was a good question, and one to which I really don't know the answer. Next to Beaverbrook, Quintin has far and away the best brain I have ever met. Intellectually he could have gobbled up before breakfast many post-war prime ministers, including Attlee, Eden, Heath and Alec Douglas-Home. His mind is laser-sharp, the depth of his knowledge – and over the widest possible range of subjects – is massive.

Yet in many ways Quintin is a most unostentatious and unassuming man. No matter how high his office he was always early for every appointment. I remember him and his wife Mary coming to a party at our house in Surrey. There was limited car parking space in the drive and stable yard. So I asked my son Roderick, who was then about fourteen and who had not at that time met Quintin, to organise the car arrangements as people arrived. About fifteen minutes before the party was due to start and while I was still getting dressed for it, to my horror I heard the sound of a car arriving. To my greater horror I heard through my bedroom window Roderick saying, 'Would you mind, Sir, dropping your passenger here and then parking on the grass verge further up the road?' I looked out and there was Quintin at the wheel of his familiar shabby Austin. 'Not at all dear boy,' he replied. 'I've a fold-up bicycle in the boot and will cycle back.' And he did too.

Quintin went everywhere on that cycle when he was out of office and had no official car. He told me once about an altercation he had had with a van driver in the Piccadilly under-pass – surely the most hazardous cycle-way even for fit young cyclists, far less for an arthritic old age pensioner. 'He used the most foul, shocking language to me,' said Quintin. 'And what did you do in response?' I asked. A happy smile crossed his face: 'I gave him a real earful in return.'

He is a devoted Anglican and a convinced Protestant and he loved to argue about religion with the late Father Tom Corbishley, who had been at Oxford with him and was the most brilliant of Jesuit priests. Corbishley told me that once in wartime London Quintin and he had spent the whole evening discussing religion. When the time came to say good night Corbishley had a train to catch from St James's Underground station, so Quintin and he walked through the blacked-out park together. On the way to the station Corbishley remarked, 'Quintin, you see it is I who am carrying the torch.' Quickly Quintin replied, 'Yes Tom, but it is I who know the way.'

When he was Lord Chancellor in Heath's government Quintin was offered the use of Chevening, the stately home near Sevenoaks left in a bequest originally for Prince Charles and failing that some other senior member of the Crown.

Heath, after Prince Charles had refused it first of all, offered it to Tony Barber but the Chancellor of the Exchequer discovered that he had eliminated himself on a technicality through having passed a Bill granting funds for the restoration of the building. So at the very last minute, before the bequest became invalid, Quintin took it – 'to save it for the nation', as he said.

When Quintin and his family arrived they found that the main building – on which some half a million pounds had been spent – was absolutely uninhabitable. It had been in crumbling disrepair for years and the money had been spent simply to strengthen the walls so that the place would not fall down. Only three rooms were fit to live in – in the servants' quarters. Which meant that the whole family could never all come down on the same weekend – there was only one spare room for the daughter, Mary Clare, or else a married couple.

'What about the shooting?' I asked Quintin when he told me of the problem. I knew that Quintin loved to wander around with a gun even though he seldom hit anything.

Quintin looked rueful. 'Marvellous shooting, dear boy, absolutely marvellous. But it is all let to a syndicate. However, they did come to me and offered me a gun. "But we must warn you," they said, "that it is a little bit expensive of course. It is £1450. Would you be interested?"'

Quintin rocked with laughter. '£1450? The only possible way I could join that syndicate would be if they let me in as a beater.'

There was no swimming pool at Chevening, he told me, but there was a huge artificial lake probably built by Capability Brown in the eighteenth century. It was choked with weeds but the water was beautifully clear and even though the bottom was a little soft Quintin loved to swim there. Years later when I visited Chevening as a guest of Sir Geoffrey Howe a member of the staff told me that Quintin used to arrive on a Friday evening in his official car, dash through the house divesting himself of his clothes on the way and plunge straight into the lake.

I never met Quintin's first wife. Nor did he ever mention her. But I knew the story of how during the war he had come home unexpectedly on leave during his time in the army and had found her in bed with a Free French officer. Mary, his second wife and the mother of his children, was a delightful as well as a lovely lady although it has to be said that while she was still alive Quintin spent a good deal of time moaning about her. It was only when she so tragically died – thrown from a bolting horse when they were on an official visit to Australia – that he started talking about how much he had loved her and how desperately he missed her. And for years afterwards tears would come into his eyes every time he mentioned her name.

But then tears come easily to Quintin. I remember one day discussing human happiness with him and suggesting that in fact everyone got exactly the same amount of happiness out of life, that there was a perfect balance inasmuch as some people got great happiness out of even the tiniest pleasures while others, oddly, were happy even in their unhappiness. In reply he began to tell me the story of an old aunt of his who – and he must have been a young man at the time – was incapacitated and in an old people's home where she lay in bed all day hardly able to move and, according to Quintin, praying only for death.

'One day I went to see her,' he said, 'and the poor old dear told me that she had had the most splendid dream. She dreamed that she had died and was in heaven. Then she wakened and found she was still in bed and in pain. Poor old dear. She had such an unhappy life.' I looked at him and his eyes were full of tears. That same night, 14 February 1974, he went to Oxford and made one of the most vigorous, hard-hitting speeches of the general election campaign.

There were plenty of times, of course, when Quintin used tears to his advantage and played up like a ham actor on his loneliness after Mary's death. I remember Margaret Thatcher saying to me, 'John, I can't sack Quintin. Without his job he would just crumple up and die. He has nothing else to live for.' Quintin's third marriage in 1986 changed everything. Margaret no longer had any compunction about retiring him as Lord Chancellor and giving Michael Havers the chance for which he was financially desperate and for which he had waited so long. But according to Havers, Quintin had still put up quite a fight. Again according to Havers, when Margaret had broken the bad news, Quintin had burst into floods of tears and pleaded that he would die if he were deprived of the office in which he still had so much to do. But Margaret had been unrelenting. And Havers found that Quintin still turned up every day in the Lords just waiting for him to make a mistake. Poor Havers. If that were so Quintin did not have to wait all that long.

Havers also heard that Quintin was very much disliked by his staff and that on one occasion he had actually thrown a jug of water over one of them. Much as I like Quintin I am prepared to believe Havers on both counts. Quintin could on occasion be extraordinarily rude to inferiors, as from time to time one of my secretaries would testify. But is there any great man without warts? And Quintin is by far a greater man than most.

And then there was Willie Whitelaw. Willie was nobody's fool, a most adroit politician. And a good deal more ambitious than he pretended to be. One Sunday I attacked him in my column in the most savage terms and then, on the following Tuesday, I lunched with Ian Gilmour in White's Club.

After lunch Ian and I were having coffee in leather chairs at the bottom of the great staircase which leads down from the dining-room when to my horror I saw Willie coming down the stairs and looking straight at me. There was not the slightest question that he had seen me.

'Hello John,' he said, in a great booming voice which everyone around could hear. 'You know, when my wife read what you wrote about last Sunday she turned to me and said, "He's quite right, Willie."'

It was a magnificent lesson in how to disarm someone and turn a critic into a supporter.

But none the less Whitelaw is an odd character. You can never be sure just which side he is on. Nor am I by any means the only person to hold that view. To the friends of Margaret Thatcher he protests his undying loyalty to her. And yet one becomes aware in meetings with other journalists that he is quite capable of putting the knife into her back when he thinks he is in the right company in which to do so.

Cecil Parkinson was once scathing to me in his comments on Willie Whitelaw. 'When the Sara Keays affair was all over and I came back to the Brighton Conference, I quite unexpectedly received a standing ovation. In the middle of it, Whitelaw got to his feet, lumbered up to me and embraced me in full view of the TV cameras at the Conference. He did it all just to impress the Conference, whereas I discovered later that he had been going around delegates and friends saying, "He didn't deserve a standing ovation. There was nothing in his speech. I can't understand why he got one."'

Parkinson pointed out that it was not until the 1983 election was over that Whitelaw had decided he wanted to go to the House of Lords. 'And why do you think that was? Why do you think he delayed so long? I'll tell you. It was because he wanted to make sure that there was no chance of him still becoming leader of the Tory Party. If Margaret had lost the election, he would then have been available. When she won it, he realised that he had no further chance of becoming leader and that was why he then decided to go to the House of Lords.'

And there was Gordon Reece, who had so much to do with the reshaping of Margaret Thatcher's image. She responded with warmth by inviting him to spend Christmas with her and her family at Chequers. But Reece is someone who for many years deserved better from the world than he had so far received.

I remember lunching with him in 1984 at the Savoy Grill. There was a bottle of champagne beside him on the table. The bill would be on an expense account picked up either by British Airways or by Tory Central Office. But that was no reflection on Reece. He had never had a bean. His marriage had broken up when his wife had fallen in love with a younger man and in the collapse of the marriage he had lost his six children too. To Gordon, a devout Roman Catholic, it was utter catastrophe.

He had taken up a job with the American oil tycoon Dr Armand Hammer. But it was clearly an empty job and he disliked Hammer. 'I'm back here on a sabbatical from Hammer,' he told me. And back, no doubt, to float along earning a crust here and there. He was at the time doing a four-month job for Lord King of British Airways.

'Saatchi & Saatchi have suggested something to me,' he said.

'What sort of money are they offering?' I asked him. 'A hundred thousand?'

'Double that. Should I take it?'

'No.' I gave him the hard answer. 'For it would be said that it is a pay-off for what you have done for Saatchi & Saatchi in giving them the Tory account.'

He did turn the offer down. There are not too many men whose basic decency I trust. Gordon Reece is one of them.

The first indication I had that all was not well with Max Aitken was when he failed to turn up for the Sunday Express Boat Show luncheon in January 1977. His wife Vi took his seat opposite me at the table where we were entertaining some thirty prominent industrialists, advertising agents and show business personalities. Margaret Thatcher, then Leader of the Opposition, was guest of honour and was seated on my right. Jimmy Goldsmith was one of the guests and had arrived at the party with a startling piece of news.

He bounced in, buttonholed me and in a state of great excitement said, 'I've been trying all morning to get hold of Max. But since he's not here I'll tell you. I've bought Rupert's shares in Beaverbrook.' For me it was the most sensational and most depressing news. For although Rupert Murdoch's three million Beaverbrook shares were non-voting shares, there was not the slightest doubt that under Goldsmith they would be used as a launching pad for a takeover. I saw the long face of our then Managing Director, Jocelyn Stevens, when a few minutes later Goldsmith confided the same intelligence to him and I could see that he was equally shaken.

At that stage I did not know how ill Max was. When later in the week he did in fact attend a Boat Show reception and walked round like a zombie with Jocelyn Stevens and Charles Wintour on either side of him acting as minders, I decided that Max must be very ill indeed. That night I rang his doctor, Alan Everett, who also happened to be an old friend of my own. 'Mark my card, Alan,' I said to him. 'Will Max ever recover? For if he doesn't I certainly will not survive.'

Everett thought for a moment and then replied, 'You've had a good innings anyway.' It was the beginning of the end. Although Max recovered sufficiently from his stroke to return to the office, the game was up and before the year was out the new proprietors of Beaverbrook Newspapers were Trafalgar House. Our new boss was Victor Matthews. He was in many ways to be the best thing that ever happened to me.

And one of the remarkable things about Victor is the late age at which he emerged as a figure of even minor consequence in public life. It was in 1964 when he must have been about forty-four that his name came to prominence. The story of how he first started on the upward path to fame and wealth is a fascinating one.

He had been offered a job with a company called Clark & Fenn. The Chairman of the company was a man called Victor Fost. And what attracted Victor Matthews to joining Clark & Fenn was that Mr Fost offered him a seat on the board and a company car. He got the seat on the board all right, but there was never any mention of a company car in the coming months.

Then one day at lunchtime Victor was out in the street with the company Chairman when a smart Jaguar passed. Mr Fost looked at it admiringly. 'My brother has got one just like that,' he said. 'That's the sort of car you should have, Victor.' He then added in some discomfiture, 'My God, we promised you a company car, didn't we? We must get you one. But not a Jaguar. That's too flashy. I tell you what. When we get back to the office, go and see the transport manager and get him to get you a good second-hand Humber Snipe with a low mileage.'

And so Victor got his car. He also produced profits for Clark & Fenn. They were involved at that time in the building of the Shepherd's Bush BBC TV Centre and they had secured the contract for the sound-proofing of the studios. Victor engaged subcontractors. And the money in profits began to cascade in. So much so that Mr Fost was able to take an extended holiday in the West Indies. While he was away Victor had the usual trouble and moans from subcontractors – the moans, he explained to me, which every builder has.

When the Chairman came home and was due to start work on the Monday, Victor set off on his own holiday driving his Humber Snipe to a furnished house in Tenby. When he arrived at the house there was a telegram awaiting him. From his Chairman. It said 'Telephone Me Immediately'.

There was no telephone in the house and so Victor went to the telephone kiosk in the village. When he got through to London he found the Chairman in an angry mood. He had come back, he complained, to a pile of complaints from subcontractors. He had never known anything like it in his life. Victor must come back to London straight away to deal with them.

Victor told him to get stuffed. And that was how he came to start up in business for himself. He had a little luck in the first

238

business. He put in an estimate for a job and employed a surveyor to do the estimate for him. The estimate was accepted and it was only later that, whereas Victor had estimated in square yards, the man who had accepted the contract thought it was in square feet. Victor was on his way. He then joined up with Nigel Broackes and soon, like Broackes, was counting his cash in millions at Trafalgar House.

The extraordinary thing is that although at Trafalgar House they had a quite brilliant working partnership they were as jealous as hell of each other – perhaps because each thought the other was getting too much credit for Trafalgar House's success. Victor was particularly anxious that Broackes should not be in any sort of contact with members of the *Express* staff. He did not want stories getting back to Nigel. Kenneth Fleet, at that time our City Editor, was in the unhappy position of being an old friend of Broackes. In the end it cost him dearly.

As no doubt it would have cost me. When once I lunched with Victor at the Ritz we sat down for a drink before lunch and he pointed out to me that Nigel Broackes was sitting at the other corner of the room in the main hall.

As we went into lunch, Nigel rose, extended a hand to me and said, 'Hello, John. You've lost weight, haven't you?' I protested that unhappily I hadn't, and Victor and I went into lunch. He began to tell me how he'd awakened at 3.30 that morning in a panic about the prospect of the new Associated Newspapers' Sunday paper, the *Mail on Sunday*.

Then he suddenly said to me, 'When did you meet Nigel?'

I did not understand what he was saying, since it had been evident that he had been with me when we had met Nigel only half an hour previously.

'What do you mean?' I asked. 'I met him with you just a few minutes ago.'

'No, no,' he said. 'I mean when did you last meet him?'

'The last time I saw him was when you entered the House of Lords,' I replied. 'Don't you remember he was at the lunch you gave?'

As I spoke I realised that because Nigel had said that I had lost weight, Victor suspected I might have been meeting him secretly. And that might well have been curtains for me so far as Victor was concerned.

For Victor was no push-over. When James Callaghan was a senior minister in Harold Wilson's government he made a determined effort to woo every newspaperman whom he thought might be of help in his ambitions. He met with me several times and was most agreeable. But when eventually he did become Prime Minister and the *Sunday Express* continued to attack him and in the most violent terms he took the huff and would have nothing more to do with me.

But Callaghan was a wily man and did his damnedest to seduce Victor. At this time Victor was quite new to Fleet Street and also quite unsophisticated. So he was flattered beyond measure when one day his secretary told him that the Prime Minister was on the telephone. 'Could Mr Callaghan speak to Mr Matthews?'

Victor was overwhelmed. Even more so when the Prime Minister said to him 'Mr Matthews, I would like to get to know you better. Could you possibly spare me some time if I were to come and see you?' It was the most extraordinary flattery. Victor, of course, replied that there could be no question of the Prime Minister coming to see him but that he would gladly attend on the Prime Minister. And this he did. And according to Victor, Callaghan put his arms round Victor's shoulders and said, 'You know, you and I have the same sort of background. We have a lot in common.' Luckily what they did not have in common was that Victor was loyal to Margaret Thatcher. But on Callaghan's part it was a brave effort.

In a moment of engaging candour Victor told me about his early life and how as a child his ambition had been to play for Arsenal and to be a reporter for the *Daily Express*. He had had a friend older than himself who desperately wanted to become a journalist and who had in fact been offered a job on *Picturegoer* – a magazine which dealt at that time with the cinema. The other boy had desperately needed a typewriter and Victor's mother had advanced him the money to buy one. Victor was entranced and was also envious of his friend's progress.

He then told me that he had never known his father. And he

resented very much that anyone should have thought he was Jewish. Indeed one of the reasons he turned against Derek Jameson, then Editor of the *Daily Express*, was the fact that in a TV programme Jameson had indiscreetly said when asked about his boss, 'Victor Matthews? He's OK. But after all he's an Eastender like myself.' Victor thought that by that Jameson was indicating that Victor was also Jewish.

Even taking into account the occasional wart, Victor was still a most likeable man with few pretensions. And he was quite prepared to tell a story against himself. He once told me that his nineteen-year-old son Ian had come home one night wearing a very smart new blue suit. When asked where he had bought the suit, Ian replied that he had gone to a sale at the Savoy Taylors Guild and had chosen it off the peg for £50.

Victor was intrigued. The very next day he went himself to the Savoy Taylors Guild and on going downstairs into the tailoring department that very astute salesman Mr Sammy (an old friend of mine) spotted him, instantly recognised him and said, 'Good afternoon, Lord Matthews. Can I help you?'

Slightly flattered by being recognised in a shop he had never visited before, Victor explained that his son had just bought a suit there for £50. 'Ah yes,' said Mr Sammy, 'I remember him. But that's not for you, Lord Matthews. Here, come and let me show you some suits that are for you.' The result was that dear Victor went out carrying a £300 Chester Barrie suit and cursing himself for his folly.

On another occasion he was in his Rolls-Royce and caught in a traffic jam in Bond Street when suddenly he spotted in a shoe shop window a pair of crocodile leather slip-on shoes. He had always, he confessed, had an ambition to have crocodile leather slip-on shoes. So he left the car and went in to the shop where a beautifully dressed man in a black jacket and striped trousers was standing in front of the counter. Another man was up a ladder arranging shoe boxes.

'Good afternoon, Lord Matthews,' said the beautifully dressed man.

'Good afternoon,' replied Victor. 'Could I have a look at those crocodile shoes in the window?'

The beautifully dressed man looked startled. 'I don't work here,' he said. 'I'm only in buying shoes. Don't you remember me? I'm the Chairman of Barclays International. We met the other day at a cocktail party.'

Collapse of Victor. Especially when the real salesman came down from his ladder and brusquely told him, 'We've only got them in size 11 and we're not expecting any more.'

And then there were his cotton shirts which he always bought in Jermyn Street. But they were beginning to shrink, and one day going to the office he felt his shirt really tight around his throat. So he said to his chauffeur, 'I'm not going to go round with my neck tight all day. Go along to Jermyn Street and buy me another shirt.' 'Why Jermyn Street?' replied the chauffeur. 'Why don't you go to Marks & Spencer's? They do very good shirts there.'

Victor reflected for a moment. Remembering that he would only be wearing the shirt possibly for one day, he said 'OK, you go to Marks & Spencer's but make sure you get a shirt the same colour as this blue I'm wearing.'

The chauffeur duly returned with a shirt for £7.50 as compared with the £30 Victor had been paying in Jermyn Street. 'Now I only wear Marks & Spencer shirts,' a beaming Victor told me later. 'And look at this,' he said, opening his jacket. Inside was a Marks & Spencer label.

Victor told me of a secret meeting he had once had with Lord Rothermere. He did not divulge the subject discussed, but the meeting took place in the House of Lords – an ideal anonymous meeting ground for two peers who did not want to be seen together in public.

But the irony of it is that they were talking in a part of the House designated for Members only. A uniformed attendant who failed to recognise Lord Rothermere, but immediately recognised Lord Matthews, approached Lord Matthews and said politely, 'Is this a guest of yours, your Lordship?'

Squelch! It must have been a tough moment for a man whose peerage was inherited.

And it was the question of Victor's peerage that caused me to have a hiccup with him. For some time in October 1979

I received a letter from 10 Downing Street and opened it unthinkingly. It did not occur to me that it would be anything other than an official communication – probably a press hand-out. In fact it was a letter telling me the Prime Minister intended to recommend me for a knighthood. It was made clear that the information had to be kept absolutely secret. No one could be told.

This put me in a dilemma. For I knew that Victor desperately wanted an Honour. More than that he deserved one. He had done great work with Cunard and the *Queen Elizabeth II*, for example – and also in house building. I wondered how I could broach the subject without in any way breaking the confidence. But I found no way and I had the slight embarrassment at the dinner at the Ritz to celebrate my twenty-fifth year as Editor of the *Sunday Express* of having Victor make a speech in which he more or less suggested that the Prime Minister should give me an Honour. The Prime Minister, who was sitting right next to me, did not bat an eyelid.

Thereafter, I sought an opportunity of breaking the news to Victor. At one stage I said to him, 'Are you in the Honours List?' And then added hastily, 'But you wouldn't tell me if you were, would you? You would be bound to secrecy.'

But Victor just looked at me and replied, 'No, I'm not in the Honours List. I've heard not a damn thing. Are you?'

Without giving any positive indication, I suggested that I had received just a hint that I might be. Victor seemed genuinely delighted, and I believe he was. We continued on very good terms until Christmas and then he went off for nine days to the country. When he returned, I was aware that our relationship was now completely different. Something, someone, had got at him during the Christmas holiday and there was not the slightest doubt in my mind that he felt disappointed that I had received an Honour when there had been nothing for him.

There then began a critical campaign against the *Sunday Express*. I was aware that at meetings of the Executive Committee demands were being made for changes in the editorial content of the paper, but no one made a direct approach to me. Not, that is, until Victor rang me one day from Trafalgar House and asked if I would lunch with him. I had an engagement but agreed to visit him after lunch. It was a friendly enough meeting but there was no doubt that he was trying to use his power to influence the editorial policies of the *Sunday Express* and I resisted strongly.

Then at the beginning of April I received a telephone call from Gordon Reece in 10 Downing Street. Gordon said in these precise words, 'John, do you still want Victor to be on an Honours List? No need to give me an immediate reply but I can tell you for certain that he is going to be on the next one and for something more than a knighthood, providing that there is no objection to him.'

Barely half an hour later I was told that Victor Matthews wanted to see me on the third floor of the Express building where an Executive meeting was in process. I went down, whereupon Victor emerged and began criticising a paragraph which had appeared in the Kenneth Fleet column of the *Sunday Express* on the last Sunday of March. I heard him out and then said to him, 'Victor, I have just had a call from 10 Downing Street.'

I looked over my shoulder at his secretary. Victor nodded and we went into the men's room on the other side of the corridor. It was empty, and I said to him, 'Yes, I've just had a call from 10 Downing Street. I am told that you are in the next Birthday Honours List. You are going to be in it for a damned sight more than a knighthood. Provided you keep your nose clean between now and then.'

From that moment our relationship was back on the marvellously smooth level on which it had always previously been. And on Cup Final day Victor received the good news in person. Margaret Thatcher had been attending the Cup Final luncheon. So had Victor. At the end of it she drew him aside and said, 'Victor, I'm going to send you to the Lords.' He was thrilled beyond measure. She told me afterwards that she had heard I was in difficulties with Victor and implied that her granting of the peerage was her way of helping me.

But then an Honour can be a most difficult matter. For when Bernard Harris, whose leader-page articles were so often produced as Tory pamphlets, retired from the *Sunday Express* after many years of devoted and often underpaid service, I had tried my best to get him a modest OBE.

Always unsuccessfully. I asked Reginald Maudling, then Home Secretary, to put Harris's name forward. And he did so. But nothing resulted. I asked Tony Barber, then Chancellor of the Exchequer. He also tried. And again without success. In the end Harris died without any Honour from the State.

Then I discovered that I had been pursuing quite the wrong course and it was no good trying to use the influence of one's friends who happened to be members of the Cabinet. The proper procedure was through an Honours Committee which existed for almost every profession in the land. And the head of the Fleet Street Honours Committee, I discovered, was Sir Trevor Evans, who at one time had been the distinguished industrial correspondent of the *Daily Express*.

Time passed. Then at the end of February 1981 the *Sunday Express* Picture Editor, Philip Snowdon, retired. He was a man for whom I had enormous respect. His father and mother had died within months of each other when he was only about thirteen years old. He had to come to London from the North of England and had had to give up his schooling, live with an aunt and start working. He had been a prisoner of war for four years. He never earned a great deal of money and yet he never, ever complained. And he was highly respected by every other picture editor in Fleet Street and also by his staff. So when the time came for him to go, I wanted very much to see that he received some small tap on the shoulder from the community for what he had done with his life.

So I approached Sir Trevor Evans. By this stage, Trevor was nearing eighty and perhaps a little less alert than once he had been. I told him about Snowdon and asked whether it might be possible for Snowdon's name to be considered. Sir Trevor came back to me a few months later. 'Can you possibly give me the home address of that chap Jenkinson whom you recommended for an OBE?' he asked. 'The Prime Minister's office have been on to me and I don't seem to have it.'

'What man Jenkinson?' I parried.

'Isn't his name Jenkinson?' said Trevor.

'No. It is Snowdon,' I replied.

Poor Snowdon, I reflected. His OBE was on the point of being awarded to a man who did not even exist and the chances now were that he would never get anything.

But the more I reflected on what Trevor Evans had said the more I wondered whether I had stumbled on the reason why Victor Matthews had reacted so badly to my own knighthood.

For at the time I received it I had no idea of Trevor's activities in the Honours sphere. But I do vividly recollect bumping into him in Fleet Street and his congratulating me on my knighthood. 'But,' he added, 'you know it was originally meant for someone else?' Could the name on the list submitted by Evans have been that of Victor? And might the Prime Minister have changed it to mine?

A further hiccup with Victor was the Sunday Express Boat Show luncheon of January 1984.

The previous May my colleague Mike Murphy, Managing Director of Express Newspapers, had asked me to help him compile a letter to Margaret Thatcher. He was making advance arrangements for the Boat Show and very much wanted the Prime Minister to agree to open it. But in between the sending of the invitation and the Boat Show itself yawned the abyss of the general election. So he phrased his letter to make it clear that he wanted her to open the Show whether or not she was still Prime Minister. He duly received a reply saying that, unhappily, the Prime Minister had to decline, since the likelihood was that she would be abroad at the relevant time.

I thought, as a result, that it would be pointless to ask Margaret Thatcher to come to be my guest at my own Boat Show luncheon just a few days after the opening. And so when after the general election in June Nigel Lawson was appointed Chancellor of the Exchequer I asked him if he would like to come to my Boat Show do. To my pleasure, he instantly agreed. But I suddenly then thought that even if Margaret Thatcher had said no to Mike Murphy, I should still put on record my wish for her to be there at what would probably be my last Boat Show luncheon, for in 1984 I would reach retiring age.

This I did. And to my surprise I received a letter saying that she would be most happy to attend. A few days later I had lunch with Victor Matthews and he expressed his wish that I should not quit when I reached retiring age but stay on with him. Accordingly, I wrote to the Prime Minister explaining that things had changed, that it might not be my last Boat Show luncheon and offering her the chance to change her mind about coming. By return I had a letter saying that no matter whether I stayed or not she still wanted to come.

On the morning of the lunch I received a call indicating that she expected me to be there to meet her when she emerged from her car at Earls Court. This was most unusual since in previous years I had always given that job to whoever happened to be Cross-Bencher. But I did meet her and escorted her to the room in which we were having lunch. She was, as always, warm and agreeable. Even more so than on any previous year.

When after our pre-lunch drinks the time came to go to the table, she said to me, 'John, where are we sitting?' I explained to her that I had thought it better that she sit next to Victor Matthews. I did not say it was because he had asked that she should. She grimaced and replied, 'But I only came here to sit next to you.' In the event, of course, she sat next to Victor Matthews and I had Nigel Lawson on my right-hand side and Selina Scott on my left.

When the time came for speeches I stood up brandishing a copy of the 1977 Boat Show luncheon menu and reminded guests that Margaret had been coming to this affair for many years. In particular I recalled that luncheon of 1977, the lunch when I realised that Max Aitken was very ill and first became aware of the fragility of the continuing hold of the Aitken family on our newspaper group. But, I said, we had all come a long way since then. Thanks to Victor Matthews, Express Newspapers had emerged as a strong company well able to face any threat of a takeover.

I added that the government ought to keep well in mind the danger of British newspaper groups being taken over by alien interests who might feel obliged to take a line in politics which was not necessarily the best for Britain. And Margaret Thatcher too, I pointed out, had come a long way since 1977. At that time, I said, she was not even properly in command of her own party. Now, she was not just the acknowledged leader of the Tory Party and of Britain but perhaps of the free world. Reagan was floundering in his foreign policy. Andropov was ill, maybe dead. Mitterrand was in the midst of economic disaster. There was only one prominent politician in the West, Margaret Thatcher.

Normally, the Prime Minister disliked speaking at these Boat Show luncheons and usually tried to shuffle it off on to any other minister who was with her. Indeed, I had asked Nigel Lawson if he might like to say a few words. 'No chance,' he had replied. 'She wants to speak. She told me she did.'

And she did speak. But perhaps because across the table at lunch when she had asked me if it was my birthday and I had replied that I didn't want any mention of birthdays, she made an extraordinary political speech taking up the points I had made and making it clear that she was indeed prepared to act as leader of the West. Afterwards I took her to her car and I was aware that there was a great deal of warmth as she said goodbye with the words, 'You must stay on forever.'

Two days later Victor Matthews buzzed me and asked if I would go down to see him. He looked unusually serious when I entered. His first question was to ask why I had not been at the Fleet Boat Show luncheon the previous day. And he went on to say that it had been very much more important than the Sunday Express luncheon the day before that and that he had been very disappointed by my absence.

It soon became clear, however, that what had made him hopping mad had been Margaret Thatcher. He came quickly to the point. 'I felt upstaged,' he said. I replied with genuine astonishment that I had had certainly no intention of upstaging him. 'You made a political speech,' he replied. 'You spoke about me and that was wrong.'

But it was clear that the one thing that had really incensed him was the fact that after she had spoken Margaret Thatcher had stood and said, 'I ask you to rise to your feet and drink to the health of our host, John Junor', and Victor himself had been forced to rise and toast me. That rankled, and it was clear that it still rankled. For he felt that it had been he who had been host.

I pointed out that at all Sunday Express Boat Show luncheons it had always been me, as Editor of the *Sunday Express*, who had taken the host's seat. He disagreed about that and said that he had attended luncheons where it was Max Aitken who had done the speaking. I replied that he might well have done so but that they must have been Max Aitken Boat Show lunches because the *Sunday Express* luncheon had always been a separate one. He also expressed irritation that during the lunch the Prime Minister had not even appeared to be listening to what he was saying.

There were times during this conversation with Victor when I came very close to the point of saying, 'Stuff it. I'm off.' Perhaps he sensed that. Because the storm quickly passed and we ended up on terms of cordial friendship.

But there was one man with whom I was never on terms of cordial friendship during my years as Editor of the *Sunday Express*. That man was Jocelyn Stevens. He had been brought in by Max Aitken in the 1960s and soon he had supplanted Johnnie Coote as Managing Director of Beaverbrook Newspapers, first under Max and then under Victor Matthews. Legend had it that on his deathbed Jocelyn's grandfather had been more or less swindled out of his ownership of the *Evening Standard* by a young and ruthless Lord Beaverbrook. I sometimes wondered whether during his years as a Beaverbrook chief executive Jocelyn was not exacting family vengeance.

After Max had suffered his stroke and was no longer a real force to be reckoned with, there was an abortive management *putsch* against Jocelyn. I never did discover who started it. It took place in 1977 when Jocelyn was on a skiing holiday. The first whiff I had of the plot was on the first Saturday night of Jocelyn's holiday when Max's son, young Maxwell Aitken, now Lord Beaverbrook and then manager of the *Sunday Express*, suddenly almost hissed at me, 'We've got to get rid of him.' 'Get rid of who?' I asked, genuinely puzzled and also slightly alarmed lest he was speaking about his father whom he had been visiting in Cowes that very afternoon.

'Why, Jocelyn, of course,' he replied.

That reply staggered me for one good reason. Until that moment young Maxwell had been Jocelyn's stoutest defender and indeed only the previous week he had stalked out of my room in anger when I had criticised Jocelyn. His sudden conversion bewildered me. But in the coming week all the plans were made ready. Peter Hetherington, our Finance Director, was to take over from Jocelyn. He would be sitting in Jocelyn's chair when Jocelyn returned from holiday and would give Jocelyn the hard tidings that he had been sacked by Max in his absence.

Jocelyn was due to return from holiday on the Monday. On the Saturday night before leaving for home after the second edition I looked into young Maxwell's office to say goodnight and also to make sure that there had been no change in the plan.

'No, it's all going ahead as planned,' he said, but then added something which made me feel uneasy all weekend. He was looking musingly at the telephone on his desk. 'Do you realise,' he said, 'that if anyone were to pick that up and warn Jocelyn the whole plot could come crashing down?' During the weekend someone did just that. Jocelyn survived and the conspirators were routed. Except for young Maxwell who was promoted.

Jocelyn came from the same sort of social circle as Max and I do believe he was genuinely fond of Max. But with Victor Matthews he had absolutely nothing socially in common. Victor was the sort of man who once he arrived home from the office at night would think nothing of sending his chauffeur to fetch fish and chips for his wife and himself. So there was some speculation as to whether Jocelyn could survive for long in the new climate. In fact he survived brilliantly and soon had Victor eating out of his hand.

My first insight into how he did it came one day when I was sitting in Victor's office and he was bemoaning the fact that his brand-new Dupont lighter did not work. 'Could you give me a light?' he asked me as he pulled out yet another of the sixty or so Silk Cut cigarettes he smoked every day. I was just about to lean over the desk with a light when suddenly the door was thrown open and Jocelyn in a highly excited state burst in. He was carrying in his hand the faulty Dupont and he was saying, 'I've got it working, Chairman, I've got it working!'

Victor would have been less than human if he had not been flattered by that sort of attention coming from a man who moved in the very top social circles, and who was not only rich in his own right but whose live-in lover was Charles Clore's daughter. But Jocelyn's biggest trump card was Princess Margaret. Jocelyn and the Princess had been friends for years and she always seemed prepared to turn out whenever Jocelyn invited her to an *Express* function. That meant, of course, that Lord and Lady Matthews met her too. Could anyone really blame Victor for being dazzled?

If I did not like Jocelyn the feeling was mutual. Victor once told me that at a recent Executive Committee meeting Jocelyn had been urging my replacement, and that he, Victor Matthews, had said, 'Let's get this clear. John Junor is staying. And I am fed up with you bringing up this subject at every meeting. Unless you stop bringing it up, then either you or I will have to go.'

As it happened, it was Jocelyn Stevens who first got the chop. According to Victor Matthews it happened in this way. Trafalgar House had decided to demerge Express Newspapers into a new and separate public company called Fleet. It turned out to be a brilliantly successful manoeuvre but at the time it was bitterly opposed by Jocelyn who thought it simply meant that the newspapers were being abandoned by Trafalgar. Again according to Victor, Jocelyn went to see Nigel Broackes and pleaded for the plan to be scrapped. He even suggested that if only Victor were removed and he, Stevens, ran the Express group then the newspapers could soon be making really big money for Trafalgar.

That was something Victor would not take – not even from someone who could mend his lighters. That night Victor rang me at home to tell me that Jocelyn had been sacked.

On the *Daily Express*, meanwhile, the procession of editors continued. Roy Wright, who had succeeded Alastair Burnet in the Max Aitken era, was sacked by Victor Matthews in 1977. It was a decision which Victor took sadly, partly because he did not like sacking people, partly because he liked Wright and identified with him and his non-graduate background a good deal more than he did with many of the other people around him. When he broke the news to Wright and had agreed the terms of the financial settlement, Wright said that he supposed he must see his lawyer.

'Why bother with a lawyer?' said Victor. 'You have my handshake on our agreement. I will not go back on it.' Nor would he have done. He was a man who, having given his word, kept it.

Derek Jameson, reputedly put forward by Charles Wintour and without the prior agreement of Jocelyn Stevens, was next in the Editor's chair. He was a real comic and made people fall off their chairs laughing at his jokes. And he told them everywhere. Denis Healey when Chancellor of the Exchequer in Jim Callaghan's government once invited Victor Matthews to bring Derek and myself plus our City Editors to 11 Downing Street to lunch just before he went into purdah prior to the Budget. The first thing Derek did on arrival was to tell a couple of *risqué* jokes. They went down with Denis Healey like a lead balloon. Happily, Derek has since gone on to find his real vocation as a proper full-time comedian.

Next in the chair was Christopher Ward, a talented young man who had written a column in the *Daily Mirror* and who had a penchant for wearing long overcoats of the style much favoured by Chicago gangsters in the 1930s. It was during his brief tenure of the job the *Daily Express* had the wonderful scoop about the intruder in the Queen's bedroom. It was afterwards said that he had not been in the office when the story came in late at night and that the decision to print had been taken by his deputy, Ted Dickinson. Ward was soon followed in 1980 by a long-time servant of the *Express*, an amiable, placid giant of a man called Arthur Firth, a splendid technical journalist who was liked by everyone. But alas he wasn't much good as an editor.

Then in 1983 came Larry Lamb, years after he had first been offered and turned down the job. His row with Murdoch and his departure from the *Sun* had been earth-shattering news in Fleet Street. Humble reporters still looked up at him in awe. The stories about him were legendary. It was said that while he was no longer Editor but was still on the *Sun*'s payroll while Murdoch decided what to do with him, he had continued to live the most lavish of lives on expenses. One lunch bill from the Connaught for just two people amounted to over £350, so I was told by Bruce Matthews, then Managing Director of News International. On investigation it was discovered that Larry had ordered a bottle of claret costing more than £100 and had so liked it that when it was finished he had ordered the same again.

But whatever magic Larry had had on the *Sun* he failed to produce on the *Daily Express*. The staff around him were far from happy. Jean Rook still spits in anger at the mention of his name. Kenneth Fleet, in his own right a name just as big as Larry Lamb's, would open his *Daily Express* in the morning and find that the page he had worked on the previous day had been changed by Larry during the night and without consultation.

Then came the miners' strike and the quite extraordinary front page of the *Daily Express* in which the lead story was an imaginary speech by Arthur Scargill – a speech in which he confessed all his mistakes and shortcomings. As a feature it might have got by but as the lead story of a serious newspaper it was lamentable. There was a board meeting that day and at it Victor Matthews in the mildest possible terms suggested that it had been a mistake to have run the story. Larry took deep offence at this and the day ended with his flouncing out of the office and giving the impression that he would never return. But in the end he did come back, there was a reconciliation with Victor and he remained as Editor until after Victor himself had gone and there was a new Chairman, David Stevens.

There was another thing that puzzled me about Larry. After leaving the *Sun* he had a longish spell in Australia before returning to seek work in this country. We had lunch at about this time and he asked me to fill him in on the new personalities who had risen to the top of the Tory Party during his absence. Who, for example, was Cecil Parkinson and what was he like? I told him. A month or so later, by which time Larry had been appointed *Express* Editor, the Sara Keays story erupted at the Blackpool Tory Conference and one newspaper whose reporter happened to be in the same Blackpool restaurant gave what purported to be a verbatim account of what Parkinson had said to the people with whom he had been dining – one of whom was Larry Lamb. When other newspapers quizzed Larry as to whether the account was accurate, Larry confined himself to saying, 'Mr Parkinson is an old friend.' It made me wonder just what constituted old.

Yet perhaps they very quickly had become firm friends. For some time later, on 6 March 1984, I took Parkinson to lunch at the White Tower. When we went in we found David Frost and a guest in one corner of the room, Alastair Burnet and Andrew Neil, the Editor of the *Sunday Times*, in a second and Larry Lamb and a guest in a third. Parkinson waved a greeting to all three and then said to me of Andrew Neil, 'If that young man stays as Editor of the *Sunday Times* until he is old he will never get another interview with Margaret Thatcher. She is furious about what he did to Mark.' He was referring, of course, to the smears which had been made concerning Mark Thatcher's part in the Oman cementation deal.

Apparently Margaret Thatcher had given Andrew Neil an interview on the basis that, unlike the *Observer*, the *Sunday Times* was not seeking to suggest that Mark had been using influence to make money. But after the interview Neil had gone back to the office and either had himself telephoned or had someone else telephone Mark in America. 'We've just spent two hours with your mother in Downing Street,' Mark Thatcher was told. 'Will you give us the facts on the Oman deal?' And Mark, unsuspecting, had admitted that he had indeed received a fee.

Parkinson then surprised me by telling me that Larry Lamb, who had just arrived back from a month's holiday, had spent part of the time in Parkinson's holiday home in the Bahamas. 'Do you let out your holiday home?' I asked. Parkinson shook his head. The implication was that Larry had had it free. So perhaps they had become very good friends indeed.

Why did Larry's magic fail at the *Daily Express*? How could a man with so much talent as he had demonstrated at the *Sun* fail at the other end of the Street? It may be that Larry had become too arrogant. He certainly did give the impression that he could walk on water. I just wonder whether, rather like Christiansen and Beaverbrook, he had only been any good while he had

Rupert Murdoch as a proprietor and that without Murdoch he was lost.

One of the wonderful advantages of being editor of a national newspaper is that you can lunch with almost anyone you like. Including the most beautiful women. Like Anna Ford.

Anna is quite delightful. The first time we lunched, I discovered we shared a mutual dislike for the then Bishop of Southwark, Mervyn Stockwood. My dislike was political. Hers was more personal. She told me that when her father was a vicar, they had Mervyn Stockwood as an overnight guest and Stockwood had left his shoes out for Anna's mother to clean. That was something for which Anna never forgave him.

We also shared a dislike for Esther Rantzen's husband, Desmond Wilcox, who had been Anna's boss at the BBC. Wilcox, she told me, was angry at Anna's decision to leave the BBC and join ITN.

'What did he say?' I asked.

She looked me straight in the eye. 'He told me I was a stupid fucking cow.'

But even if Anna did not flinch from using such robust language, underneath it all she was as soft as marshmallow. I had the feeling that her first love was men and work came second. Timothy Aitken, then boss of TV-AM, once told me that when he had to tell Anna that she was sacked, she broke down and he ended by liking her enormously. There was no back-biting, no bitterness, just tears. Angela Rippon, on the other hand, Aitken told me, took a much tougher line when it was her turn. He doubled up his fist and said, 'She just told me to go and get stuffed.'

Then there was my friend and discovery Selina – gorgeous, delicious Selina Scott.

She is a delightful girl, warm, compassionate and unaffected. When I first met her she was an unknown working for Grampian TV. I had gone to Aberdeen to be interviewed by her. I wrote about the interview and the next thing that happened Selina was offered a job with ITN.

Soon she was a star. I remember her telephoning me one morning to arrange a lunch. I suggested Bertorelli's in Charlotte Street.

'Oh no,' was her reply, 'we can't go there.'

When I asked her why, she told me a quite astounding story. She had gone there on her own and the manager had asked her to leave because clearly he thought she was a hooker. Selina was affronted and subsequently complained angrily to the Bertorelli head office who soothed her down, apologised profusely and said the same thing would never happen again. So she went back to the restaurant and was sitting at her table awaiting her guests when the same man who had previously kicked her out arrived on the scene and said, 'So you've sneaked in behind my back. Out you go.'

It was an extraordinary story which I would have loved to have published at the time in the *Sunday Express*, but some idiot would have been bound to think that there had to be a grain of truth in the manager's accusation when of course it was utterly ludicrous. And although the story cannot harm Selina now it might have harmed her then.

From time to time Selina has had to face temptations. There was a bizarre incident, for example, involving Kerry Packer, the Australian newspaper multi-millionaire. He was in London for an operation and said he would like to see Selina to discuss a possible TV contract. The driver of his hired limousine was at pains to tell her what an extraordinarily generous man Mr Packer was and how on occasion he would hand the driver £1000 at the end of a visit to London. On another occasion he had driven him to Heathrow Airport and had been tipped £500.

Packer offered Selina a fortune to come and work for his TV stations in Australia, if nothing else. The day after seeing him she received from him a gold Rolex watch. She sent it back to him. He in turn sent it back to her. So she sent it back again – and for the last time.

But then Selina is 100 per cent her own woman and utterly incorruptible. She is also a shrewd observer. I remember her telling me that when Princess Diana visited the ITN studios to watch *News at Ten*, all the questions she put to Selina in their animated private conversation concerned who was sleeping with whom.

She also told me that the buzz was in her society that the Queen and Princess Diana were not getting on well together. Selina does not care much for Sarah Ferguson, Duchess of York. They had been fellow guests at a country house party where Sarah had acted in the most extraordinary fashion by taking her host's Minimoke and driving incessantly up and down the drive apparently in an effort to impress Prince Andrew.

Around this time, in the early eighties, I may have played a part in the removal of Sir Maurice Oldfield from his job as head of security in Northern Ireland. He had been head of MI6 and had been called out of retirement at Margaret Thatcher's personal request.

He had been in Ulster for only a few months when Sir David McNee, the Commissioner of the Metropolitan Police, telephoned me to ask if I had read a paragraph in Auberon Waugh's Diary in *Private Eye*. McNee thought that Waugh was hinting that Oldfield was homosexual. And in fact McNee was absolutely convinced that he was. He had evidence, he told me, from a Special Branch officer who had been guarding Marsham Court, where Oldfield lived, of the tremendous number of young men who visited Oldfield's flat. He indicated to me that the hall porter, if interviewed, would sing like a bird.

McNee was terrified lest the IRA got hold of this and produced another security scandal. He confided to me that he had already informed the Secretary of the Cabinet about Oldfield's proclivities in the hope and expectation that the Prime Minister would be informed. But he was not sure if she had been. Would I help?

Two days later I had lunch with Caroline Stephens, the Prime Minister's personal private secretary. I did not tell her anything about Oldfield but I did ask if it were possible for her to get a letter from me to the Prime Minister without anyone else seeing it, for normally all mail is first seen by civil servants. 'Yes, it would be possible,' she said. I handed her a letter in which I expressed my worry lest there be a security explosion over Sir

Maurice Oldfield. She promised me that she would put the letter on the Prime Minister's bed and that no one else would see it.

Two days after that the Prime Minister's official private secretary came to see me and asked what it was all about. Had I any proof to back my allegations? I had to keep McNee out of this and I did so. I said that I had no proof of any kind but that it would be quite easy for me to get proof by sending a reporter to question the hall porter at Marsham Court and I had no doubt that sooner or later a tabloid newspaper would be doing just that. Within weeks it was announced that Oldfield would not be completing his tour in Ulster.

I received another interesting call from Commissioner McNee at the time of the late Bobby Sands's hunger strike in Belfast gaol – a hunger strike which ended in his death. McNee explained why at that time Mark Thatcher was being given so much protection by the Special Branch. Apparently there had been and perhaps still was a very serious IRA threat to his life. The IRA had plans to kidnap him and deprive him of food so that he would suffer in the same way Sands suffered.

As Caroline Stephens told me after I lunched with the Prime Minister at the White Tower in June 1981, Margaret had accepted my invitation 'because I want to do this. He is a *friend*.'

On the last occasion I had lunched with a prime minister in the White Tower it had been with Ted Heath and in a private room on the second floor of the restaurant. He had been accompanied by Donald Maitland, his Press Secretary. There was no private room on this occasion. Margaret Thatcher wanted to go into the public restaurant. And she wanted to lunch with me alone. The only proviso made by her security people was that she had to have her back against the wall, a sad reflection of the state of our society even then.

Lunch was arranged for 1.15. I arrived at 1.00 and was standing in the street outside when Margaret's car, headlights blazing, came into the kerb at 1.12 p.m. She began by apologising for the fact that she had kept me waiting and explained that because of traffic jams her car had had to take a circuitous route.

And she walked into that restaurant, straight to our table, had one whisky and water and acted in every possible way as if she were the most ordinary next-door neighbour.

There are times when one has an instinct about whether someone else likes you or dislikes you. I had already suspected that the Prime Minister liked me. Now I knew for sure. There was never even one awkward pause in our conversation. Margaret talked about her difficulties in Cabinet and she sought my advice. On almost every single issue and on every single personality I shared her view.

Ian Gilmour really had to go. 'John, he takes every chance to do me down. He is against me on every issue which comes before Cabinet.'

'You have nothing to fear from Ian,' I replied. 'He will never put the dagger into your back.' And this she accepted.

'But John,' she asked, 'why does he have Roy Jenkins to dinner?'

I explained that Roy Jenkins and Lady Caroline Gilmour had been friends for many years.

'Why then does Ian speak so unkindly about me?'

We then talked about Peter Carrington. He did of course, we both agreed, think that if he had given up his title he might have been prime minister, didn't want to be, yet still felt an ineffable sense of superiority.

We also talked about Fleet Street and about the need to keep support for the government going. 'Who should I have to Number 10, John?' I suggested Rupert Murdoch. It was vital that he should be kept feeling that he was close to the centre of things. I also suggested Victor Matthews. Margaret told me that she had invited Frank Giles, then Editor of the *Sunday Times*, and that to her consternation he had arrived with a long list of questions.

Caroline Stephens had warned me that Margaret had to be back in Downing Street by 3.00 p.m. for an important meeting. We had talked so much, we had eaten so well and I did not dare look at my watch, but I was well aware that time had slipped past in an extraordinary fashion.

'Prime Minister, don't you have to be back in Downing

Street?' I reminded her. 'So I have,' she replied. 'What time is it? I haven't a watch with me.'

It was twenty-five minutes before three o'clock. And as I wrote in my diary that evening, 'I have not the faintest idea whether she is going to succeed or not. But I become more and more convinced that she is the last hope of this country.' Caroline Stephens afterwards told me that the Prime Minister had returned to Downing Street saying, 'That was wonderful. It was like a breath of fresh air.'

That month also gave me a remarkable insight into the character of Denis Thatcher. We had been playing golf at Walton Heath with Sir Adam Thomson, the Chairman of British Caledonian, and Eric Sykes. Denis turned out to be an erratic player, but he clearly loved the game. At lunch he had perhaps a pint of beer and a glass of red wine, but by no means an excessive amount. Unlike his caricature in *Private Eye*, Denis is a most moderate drinker. There is no way in which he is ever going to risk being found over the limit driving a motor car.

And then at the end of our round when he left and we went out to his car to say goodbye, we discovered that someone, most probably a lady member, had reversed into it and created quite a bit of damage. But Denis insisted that no fuss be made and drove off without saying a dicky bird to anyone.

But then Denis Thatcher is the soul of discretion. I remember the four of us again at Walton Heath on the day when the 1987 election was announced. Denis must have known that the announcement was coming just after lunch. But he gave no indication at all. And I would never have expected him so to do. He is enormously conscious that anything he does might reflect on his wife.

And he is certainly a most modest and unassuming man. On the times I have played golf with him he invariably arrives some forty-five minutes early, having driven himself from Downing Street. I always seem to arrive long afterwards but never does that seem to fuss him. I know I will find him sitting in the lounge drinking coffee or passing the time of day with the club steward.

Denis takes tremendous pride in his wife and her achievements. He believes strongly, as she does, in what he calls the Christian ethos. But there are times when life must be extraordinarily hard for him and on occasion, as when a general election is announced, when he must feel as if he were living in a goldfish bowl. But I share the view of Alec Douglas-Home that he does a quite wonderful job.

Four months after my lunch with the Prime Minister in the White Tower I attended a party given by Denis Thatcher at 10 Downing Street for an expedition led by Chris Bonington who had climbed a mountain in China which had never previously been climbed. I did not know the name of the mountain. In my ignorance I had never even heard of the expedition. And I knew that the Prime Minister was not going to put in an appearance.

But my wife Pam and I still went along because I wanted the chance of having a few words with Denis Thatcher. I found him less than brilliantly optimistic about the government's prospects. He told me of a conversation he had had with the Minister of Health, Dr Gerry Vaughan, in which he had said to Vaughan that the Ministry of Health really ought to stop lambasting tobacco companies about the millions they were pouring into sports sponsorship. To his consternation, he discovered that almost the entire conversation had been accurately reported and appeared in the Paul Foot column in the *Daily Mirror*.

'There are times when I wonder just who our friends are,' he said to me. 'What the hell can you do if you say something in your own house, in the privacy of your own home, and it is reported in the newspapers?'

I asked him how Margaret was reacting to all the attacks that were now being made on her.

'John, she regards you as a close personal friend,' he replied. 'But I can tell you, there are times when she feels like jacking it in. You just can't have a situation when every time the Cabinet meets there are people in it who are prepared to leak everything to newspapers. Her authority is being eroded. She just doesn't know who to trust. Nothing like this has ever happened to a prime minister before, except to Eden and because he was ill.'

'But her health is good?' I asked.

'Thank God it is,' he replied.

I put the question which had been in my mind all evening and which was the reason I had gone to the reception: 'She is going to win out, isn't she?'

'You know Margaret,' he said. 'She will keep on fighting.'

But that night in 1981 I went away from Downing Street depressed. For I felt that Denis himself, although he knew that Margaret would keep on fighting, was no longer sure whether she had a chance of winning.

That feeling was reinforced when the Prime Minister invited me to drinks a few weeks later, on Armistice Sunday. I arrived fifteen minutes early but was immediately put in the lift on the ground floor, the button for the third floor was pressed and at the other end Denis Thatcher was there to meet me.

He led me into their small private sitting-room – tastefully furnished, primrose walls and a Lowry on the wall opposite the door. When we entered the Prime Minister was turning on the second bar of an electric fire built in the wall. We sat in easy chairs alongside each other, separated by an occasional table. On the right-hand side of the table was a coloured portrait of her children, Carol and Mark. She was as relaxed as she could be on a Sunday evening, but clearly she had been under great strain.

Denis fetched me whisky and told me about a horrific trip they had made to Cumnock in Scotland recently, where the local socialist MP, George Foulkes, had been told in the strictest confidence by Margaret that she intended visiting a factory there.

When they arrived they discovered the secret had been blown. There were coachloads of demonstrators, some of them hurling eggs. At one stage, when Margaret went to her car, she discovered it locked and the chauffeur absent having a cup of tea. The security implications were enormous. It was during this episode that an egg was thrown and deftly caught by one of her police bodyguards.

It had clearly all had an effect on her. She wondered just how popular she was with people. Although, as she pointed out, when she spoke to people at the Armistice ceremony earlier in the day they obviously still liked her.

But she was in despair at the attitude of some members of

the Cabinet. 'Willie, Geoffrey, Cecil and Norman I can count on, but the others, John – they are in utter funk about the election.' Heseltine, she believed, was consumed by his ambition. She felt quite boxed in.

I suggested to her that Joe Gormley would be an ideal successor to Derek Ezra as Chairman of the Coal Board and that he would take delight in defeating Arthur Scargill. Surprisingly, the idea seemed quite new to her and she was clearly fascinated by it. She told me that she was seeing Enoch and Pam Powell privately and was not unaware that he might be the ace to keep up her sleeve.

There was one other subject which fascinated both of them – especially Denis. Michael Foot's demeanour at the ceremony at the Cenotaph. Denis said that he could hardly contain his anger that Michael, then leader of the Labour Party, had turned up wearing an old battle jacket and wearing a tartan instead of a black tie.

Margaret was more practical. 'You would think that his wife would have advised him better, wouldn't you?'

In all I was there for nearly two hours. As I left Margaret kissed me and blew me a handful of kisses. Denis put me back in the lift and stayed talking on the threshold for quite a while. 'Margaret's pretty close to despair,' he warned me. Clearly at the way in which the Cabinet was still leaking secrets.

Despair? I did not believe then and have never since believed that the word is in Margaret Thatcher's vocabulary. Here is a broadcast I gave in July 1981 on *Woman's Hour* – the first of a new series. I was asked to speak for six minutes on any subject I pleased.

I chose to speak of Margaret Thatcher.

It was the first Sunday after the last general election. The scene was Chequers, the Buckinghamshire mansion which is the weekend retreat of Britain's prime ministers. The new Prime Minister, Mrs Margaret Thatcher, was giving lunch to the principal members of her Cabinet, some of them accompanied by their wives. The girls who were serving at table, all of them members of the Women's Royal

Naval Service, were perhaps just a little understandably nervous.

The main course was a leg of lamb on a salver. As one of the Wrens was threading between the guests, catastrophe arrived. The lamb skidded off, landed on Sir Geoffrey Howe's shoulder and spattered his Sunday-best suit and tie in gravy. Mrs Thatcher was instantly on her feet. She ran round the table, not to give comfort to Sir Geoffrey but to the Wren. Putting her arms around her, she said, 'Don't worry dear. Don't worry. It could happen to anyone.'

That is the first of three stories I want to tell you about the woman who is sometimes called the Iron Lady.

The second concerns her driver, George Newell, who died suddenly last March at the age of sixty-two from a heart attack. His funeral was in Eltham on a Friday in a week that had been a crisis week for the Prime Minister. The easiest thing in the world would have have been for her to send a representative. But no. She went herself. She sat in a pew comforting the widow. And she tried her damnedest to prevent the story of her kind act getting any publicity at all.

My third story concerns a young member of her staff, whose wife had left him, taking their children with her. It was three days before Christmas. He was in the depths of despair at the thought of having to spend Christmas on his own. Then the telephone rang. It was the Prime Minister. 'Are you doing anything for Christmas?' she asked. 'If not, why don't you come and spend it with Denis, Carol, Mark and myself?' For she had known the desperation of his loneliness. And cared.

I tell these stories because they run absolutely counter to the widely circulated view that Margaret Thatcher is cold and hard and unfeeling. If she cares, it is argued, how can she possibly allow 2,800,000 of our people to be unemployed? Why doesn't she change her policy?

Might the answer to that not be that she stays firm in her course because she does care, and care deeply, about the future of this country?

Until now, during all our long parliamentary history, there have been men at the top. In the last twenty-five years they have, almost without exception, made a muck of it. Everyone knows why. We have paid ourselves more and more for producing less and less. We have had ever greater armies of bureaucrats in the Town Halls, in the Health service, dispensing Social Security, forming tier upon tier of local and public service administration. Simultaneously in the factories and in the nationalised industries restrictive practices, feather-bedding and overmanning have prevented our producing the wealth necessary to finance the payment of it all.

It just could not go on.

Yet every time a male prime minister, Tory or socialist, has tried to take corrective measures and unemployment rises, the consequent public outcry and loss of support in the opinion polls has caused him to retreat in panic rather than face the risk of losing an election. Every time, the result is that we end in a worse state than that from which we started.

That is the typical way of men under pressure. It is not the way of women. Women have a far more clear-sighted view of reality. When a woman knows she is right, especially on the elementary principles of good housekeeping, nothing is likely to move her.

It is daft to imagine that the follies of twenty or thirty years can be put right in two. But if Margaret Thatcher is given time and has the courage to stick by her instinctive beliefs, then I believe that instead of becoming as so many prime ministers have become – just a footnote of history – future generations will look back on our present period and in their history essay at school will describe Margaret Thatcher as the woman who made Britain great again.

That broadcast was made nine years ago. I would not today want to go back on a word of it. And afterwards the Prime Minister was good enough to write and thank me. 'Bless you for all the nice things you say – and they came just at the right time.'

It was a warm gesture to make. But then that is the kind of gesture Margaret Thatcher always makes.

One of the great hazards facing an editor is that of ending up in court. It happened to me twice. Both were traumatic experiences. The first time was 1981 and concerned the case of a mongol baby boy who had been rejected by his parents, prescribed 'nursing care only' and allowed to die in a Derby hospital. The paediatrician in the case was subsequently brought to trial. It was a case which generated much public anger and the nation was divided into those who supported the doctor and those who thought he should go to gaol. I was not and could never be among those who supported the doctor. In my column of 18 October 1981 I wrote the following paragraph.

> In the three grim days of his short sad life, mongol baby John Pearson was given no nourishment.
>
> His parents had rejected him. So instead of being fed he was drugged. Even then we know he fought tenaciously for his life. Without a chance of success.
>
> And so he died unloved, unwanted.
>
> I blame no one. I condemn no one.
>
> And I make no comment on the case in Leicester Crown Court against child specialist Dr Leonard Arthur.
>
> Save this. The case is expected to go on for at least five weeks. Five weeks?
>
> If John Pearson had been allowed to live that long, might he not have found someone apart from God to love him?

When the judge in the case, Mr Justice Farquharson, read that little lot he went bananas and demanded that the *Sunday Express* be represented in court the next day. My first belief was that he might impose a huge fine. What had aroused his anger was something of which I had been blissfully unaware. The previous week he had cleared the court, announced that he was referring the *Daily Mail* to the Attorney-General for an article it had published on the case by Malcolm Muggeridge and warned the assembled press that any repetition of the offence

266

would have the most horrendous consequences for the news-paper concerned. The judge assumed that every newspaper would be aware of his warning. What he failed to take into account was the fact that since the jury was absent from the court no newspaper had reported the event. The result was that I was utterly unaware of it. I was subsequently charged with contempt of court. It was suggested by some authorities that I could get up to two years. I never believed that.

The two days I spent in the High Court two months later were fascinating theatre. My counsel was Robert Alexander and he was magnificent. His voice has a mesmeric quality which would charm the birds off trees and surely must have some effect on judges too. In the end I was fined £1000 but the sting was taken away by the warm, friendly comments Mr Justice Watkins made on my character and my column. *The Times* went as far as to call them 'fulsome'. My own comment on the result of the case, also quoted by *The Times*, was: 'I very much regret inadvertently having been in contempt of court but what I said I believed then, I believe now and I will believe tomorrow.'

My next appearance in court could have cost the *Sunday Express* a fortune in libel damages. The man seeking them was Mr Rolf Schild, a British businessman who with his wife and daughter had been kidnapped in Sardinia. His counsel was the man who later was brilliantly to defend Ken Dodd on charges of tax evasion, Mr George Carman. I listened in court in mounting gloom as he listed one by one the appalling indignities inflicted by the kidnappers on Mrs Schild and her daughter. I could see the jury being visibly moved and I came to the conclusion that even although I had never intended any libel they were going to end up awarding Mr Schild not only the huge amount of money he had been forced to pay to his kidnappers in ransom but also for good measure a further £200,000 as compensation for his ordeal. I was again to be saved by Robert Alexander. He told the judge he wanted to plead a point of law and asked for the jury to be removed while he did so. His submission was so eloquent and successful that the judge ruled there was no case to answer.

John Gordon had a favourite saying: 'If you're walking down

Regent Street at two o'clock in the morning and see a policeman then have no fear. Simply say "Good morning, officer" as you pass him. But if you see two policemen then turn and run.' I had always laughed dutifully when he said it. I was later to become convinced that there was more than a grain of truth in what he said.

My own attitude to the police as Editor of the *Sunday Express* was completely supportive. They represented the forces of law and order. They had to be backed.

Then came a bizarre personal experience over a completely trivial matter. The incident can best be described in a letter I wrote the following morning to the Commissioner of Police for the City of London, Mr Peter Marshall.

I wish to bring to your attention an incident which occurred in Fleet Street last night, Friday 9 October, and to complain in the strongest possible terms about the conduct of two City of London police officers – bearing on their shoulders the numbers 302 and 354.

At about 7.30 p.m. I left the Express building, entered my car – Lotus Elite, registration No. KUW 772X, which had been parked for some hours in the Express vanway – and proceeded to turn right, as I was entitled to do, into Fleet Street. I was immediately flagged down by Police Constable No. 302.

Realising that he might have thought that I had come into Fleet Street from Shoe Lane – a street from which it is illegal to turn right – I explained to him that I had in fact come from the Daily Express vanway. He refused to believe me. And incredibly kept on so doing, even when he had established my identity.

He acted with what I can only describe as dumb insolence. He asked and kept on asking how, if I had really emerged from the Daily Express vanway, I had managed to get the car there in the first place. I explained to him that it had been driven there by a chauffeur.

He wanted to know if I had been drinking and asked to smell my breath. He wanted to know who was the owner of the car, then made a call by his walkie-talkie to establish that I was telling the truth. He spent as much time as he possibly could in studying the licence disc and my driver's licence.

I had to spell my name two or three times to him. When his colleague, who was standing apart much of this time, did occasionally intervene, it was to tell me that he had perfect eyesight, had seen me turn right from Shoe Lane and that if I wanted to be difficult, then they could be difficult too.

And so they were. Their conduct was a disgrace to the police force. It made me realise for the first time how an innocent man confronted by two policemen acting in concert could be baited into losing his temper.

In the end they gave me a ticket for having committed the offence of turning right into Fleet Street – an offence which never happened and which witnesses, including the chauffeur who parked the car, will certainly testify could never have happened.

I am addressing myself in the first instance to you. But I reserve the right to give the matter further publicity. For if this can happen to me, then what in God's name is happening to people equally innocent, who do not have a newspaper column behind them?

After having sent this letter to Mr Marshall I discovered something which angered me even more. I discovered that the two constables after having given me my ticket had visited the front door of the Daily Express building and had discovered that everything I had said had been true. None the less they had still logged the offence at the police station.

As a result of my letter a Superintendent Pridmore came to see me and to apologise. I was asked if I wished to make an official complaint, but I declined since I did not wish to harm the careers of the two officers concerned.

On Sunday, 18 October I wrote about the matter in the *Sunday Express*:

At 7.30 p.m. a week last Friday I had just driven away from the office when I was stopped by two policemen less than 50 yards from the Express building and accused of having made an illegal right turn into Fleet Street.

I had in fact done nothing of the kind. But they refused even to listen to my protestations that I had just emerged from the Express building.

They swore they had seen me come out of an adjoining road.

Their attitude was as menacing as if they had just caught the Yorkshire Ripper.

One of them demanded to know if I had been drinking and asked to smell my breath.

He checked over his walkie-talkie with his control unit to see whether I was telling the truth about the ownership of my car. He spent a good deal of time checking the licence disc and my driving licence.

He apparently had difficulty in taking down my name and I had to spell it for him two or three times.

The next day I discovered that they had subsequently visited the Express building and found out that I had been telling the truth.

Yet they still went back to their police station and lodged the charge against me.

I know that only a tiny minority of police act unreasonably.

But what bothers me is that if I, who can defend myself, was handled in this way, how do you suppose inarticulate and equally innocent members of the public including blacks in Brixton and Toxteth are being treated?

I thought that that paragraph had ended the affair. I was wrong.

At 10.30 p.m. two Saturday nights later as I drove home to Dorking I found myself being chased by four tough-looking men in an unmarked car. They had drawn alongside me at the Ace of Spades underpass and made threatening gestures as I turned left for Chessington and Dorking. They tried their best to push me off the road. I went faster and faster, intent only on getting to a police station.

At one stage, at the Cherkley roundabout on the Leatherhead bypass, they succeeded in passing me and turned their car across the road in a highly skilled professional way to block my exit on the Dorking Road. I reacted by turning right and taking another road and for a minute I thought I had shaken them off.

But they were waiting for me when I rejoined the Dorking road at Mickleham and in a nightmare drive pursued me to the police station at Dorking. As I drove into the police station they drove off. An eyewitness who saw them said they were laughing. The Dorking police were sympathetic and two policemen in a patrol car followed me home. But the eight-mile drive was uneventful.

The next day I telephoned Sir David McNee, the Commissioner of the Metropolitan Police, and told him what had happened. He took the view that it was probably the act of some Saturday night yobbos out for a bit of fun. I tended to take the same view myself. But the next Saturday night at exactly the same place, the Ace of Spades, though I arrived at a different time, the same four men were waiting again, made the same threatening gestures and once again a nightmare chase ensued.

On this occasion and driving even more furiously I decided to try to find Leatherhead police station which was at least five miles nearer than Dorking. But I missed it and found to my horror that in the centre of Leatherhead I was trapped by a barrier across the road guarding a pedestrian-only precinct. I had to stop. They stopped too and two of them got out of their car and advanced towards me. I had locked the door of the Lotus but there was so much glass in the car that I expected them to smash it in. Instead they came and simply looked into the car. All this time I was blowing my air horn in a way loud enough to waken the dead but the streets were deserted. Then the men just walked away and back to their own car.

The second I arrived home I telephoned David McNee. This time he was in no doubt that what had happened to me just had to be part of an orchestrated campaign. It was impossible in the darkness of night for the same people to have found me at a different time. They just had to have been guided by radio-telephone.

The next day I spoke to the Chief Constable of Surrey, Sir Peter Matthews. He was just as concerned as McNee had been. It was arranged that on the next two Saturday nights two unmarked Surrey Police cars would follow me home at a discreet distance and that lying in the back of each car and in touch with the other by radio would be a senior officer. Matthews told me it was his intention to keep the operation completely secret from the Metropolitan Police, apart of course from David McNee, and also from the City of London police.

But an odd thing then happened during the week. A Superintendent Vernon from Scotland Yard telephoned me and said he had received a tip-off from a police informer that I had been chased two Saturday nights running by a gang of four men in a car at the Ace of Spades underpass.

Was this true?

I hesitated, mindful of the fact that no one at Scotland Yard apart from Sir David McNee was supposed to know anything about the incident, and played for time by asking him what department in Scotland Yard he was attached to. Vernon hesitated, saying he said that he was attached to the department which investigated complaints against the police. A10 I think it was called. He then added that he was concerned that my pursuers might have been the IRA and he wanted to find out if the informer's story were true so that he could take the matter further.

I suggested to Vernon that he should have a word with Sir David McNee on the matter and gave no further information. But I did report the matter to Sir Peter Matthews. He was equally disturbed and arranged for one of his men to see Superintendent Vernon and find out the identity of the informer. The officer who spoke to Vernon received no real satisfaction. He was told that the informer had been a solicitor's clerk who had picked up the gossip about me in a Fleet Street café. Since no one in my own office knew what had happened that seemed most unlikely.

The next two Saturday nights were completely uneventful. Long afterwards, I spoke to David McNee and he confided to me his view that it was 'wild boys' in the City of London Police who had been getting their own back on me for what I had done to two of their colleagues.

One further incident is worth recording. Some months later I received a letter, clearly written in anguish, from a mother concerned that her son might lose his job on the railways as a result of an unjust charge being brought against him.

The boy, who wore his hair long in the fashion of the times, had been out with another boy in an old car some Saturday night previously. They had run out of petrol on a country road but had seen a garage some hundred yards or so ahead still brightly lit up and had pushed the car to the forecourt. Then they discovered that although the lights were still on the garage was closed. They were still there by their car wondering what to do next when a police car arrived.

The officers clearly thought that the boys planned to rob the garage. When they found no evidence that any doors had been tampered with they demanded to know if they had been drinking. The driver, my reader's son, was breathalysed. The result was negative.

The officers had then searched the car and in the boot had found a straight-sided pint glass beer mug. It was covered in dust and had been in the boot for a long time.

'Where did you get this?' they wanted to know.

The next thing that happened was that the boy was charged with having stolen the beer mug from a local pub and was going to appear in court on that charge. Could I do anything to help, the mother wanted to know?

I rang the pub and spoke to the landlord. After being a little cagey at first, he opened up and confessed to me that he had been pressurised by the police into bringing a charge. But in the summer didn't youths often sit outside the pub drinking beer? Couldn't a beer mug quite easily have ended up in the boot of a car without anyone intending theft? The landlord further told me that the boy's uncle was a good customer of the pub and a long-time friend. The last thing he wanted, he said, was to embarrass him by bringing charges against his nephew.

I wrote about the matter and within days the charges were dropped. But that was not the end of the story. A week later the mother rang me to tell me that when her son left his car to walk up the garden path leading to his home, he had been set upon by four men and beaten up.

A coincidence? Perhaps.

All I can say is that the mother was so grateful for what I had done for her son that the following Christmas she sent me a rose bush which still grows in my garden.

VIII

ON FRIDAY 18 February 1983 I set off in a VC10 from RAF
Brize Norton at 0900 for Ascension Island on my way to the
150th Anniversary celebrations of British rule in the Falkland
Islands.

My invitation to attend had surprised me. To begin with I
had assumed that perhaps all newspaper editors in London were
being similarly invited. When I found that this was not so, my
next assumption was that Margaret Thatcher had arranged it
for me. As it happened the Prime Minister had nothing to do
with it. My invitation had come from Mr Des King, the owner
of the Upland Goose hotel who during the Falklands campaign
had smuggled a letter to the *Sunday Express* expressing approval
of a paragraph I had written concerning a Captain Edmond
Carlisle, the brother of a former Tory Cabinet minister, Mark
Carlisle, and a Falkland Islands landowner who had expressed
public support for the Argentines. In my column I had suggested
that I would like to put my boot in Captain Carlisle's backside.
But that if I did so I would thereafter clean my boot.

The other members of the party included Timothy Raison,
the Minister for Overseas Development, Lord Shackleton, Lady
Vickers, who as Joan Vickers had been Tory MP for Devonport,
Russell Johnston, Liberal MP for Inverness, Eric Ogden, SDP
MP for West Derby, Liverpool, Mike Shersby, Tory MP for

Uxbridge and Lord Buxton, his wife, his two daughters, Cindy and Vicky, and Cindy's girlfriend, Miss Annie Price. On the plane were also Ted Needham, the Chairman of Coalite and the Falklands Islands Company, Mr Peter King of the BBC, Lord Bishopston and a Doctor Nath – an Indian GP of Stanley, Durham, who planned to set up a fund to help the children of Stanley, Falkland Islands.

We had what was, for me, a fascinating journey. And on the way we stopped at Dakar where it was intolerably hot and humid.

On the steps of the VIP lounge in Dakar Airport I sat with Lord Shackleton and talked of many things. First of all about his father, the famous Antarctic explorer. I asked him how well he had known his father. 'Hardly at all,' he replied, I thought a little sadly. 'I was just nine when he died.' He then reflected for a moment. 'But I feel that if I had got to know him better I wouldn't have liked him very much. He was away for such long periods that I hardly knew him. My brother who was older than I am didn't like him very much either.'

We spoke about Lord Buxton, the Chairman of Anglia Television. I gained the impression that Lord Shackleton did not care overmuch for him. He said to me, 'You know when Buxton went to the House of Lords, Jim Callaghan said to me, "I thought he was one of ours?"

'And it is absolutely true that he did try to get a peerage from the Labour government. When he didn't get one, he then lobbied for one from the Tories. And when he got it he went to Margaret Thatcher and said, "Would you mind very much if I sat on the cross-benches? I feel that in my position it would perhaps be better." To which Margaret Thatcher replied, "You either sit on the Tory benches or you do not sit at all." '

We had been scheduled to arrive at Ascension Island at 8.00 p.m. local time, but in fact we were very much later, since we had an engine failure and had to return to Dakar. In the event we arrived at Ascension at 11.30 p.m. and after a brief visit to the Administrator's house on the top of the mountain for drinks, we were hurried to our sleeping quarters.

To my slight surprise, Lord Buxton, his wife, his two children and Miss Annie Price together with Lady Vickers stayed behind

to sleep in the cool comfort of the Administrator's lofty resi-
dence. The rest of us were bundled into jeeps and taken to a
hot, humid bungalow down by the harbour. There was no
air-conditioning. There was no mosquito-netting even. All the
beds were bunk beds except for a single bed in one tiny room
which, in view of his age, was given to Lord Shackleton.

We were not even offered a drink. We were asked to supply
our own towels. And in general the treatment accorded to all of
us, and especially to Lord Shackleton and to Timothy Raison,
who was, after all, a member of the government, was quite
scandalous. I have no doubt that the person who suffered most
as he lay in his uncomfortable cot was Lord Shackleton. I
would not have blamed him if he had felt bitter that up at the
air-conditioned top of the mountain was someone without any
official claim to privilege at all, Lord Buxton.

But the flight from Ascension to Port Stanley was quite
fabulous, even though the interior of our new plane, an RAF
Hercules, was entirely without comfort. There were no washing
facilities, the seats were hideously uncomfortable and the noise
almost unbearable. The flight took thirteen and a half hours. It
was enchanting.

I was on the flight deck when we refuelled. We saw the tanker
aircraft as a tiny spot on the horizon. We cruised with it until it
was above and just ahead of us. Then came the moment of
impact when the protruding rod from the nose of our aircraft
embedded itself in the drogue suspended from behind the other
plane. Half an hour later our aircraft's thirst was quenched and
we continued on our way.

Port Stanley was much as I had expected it to be. Smaller
than Tobermory. The roads were non-existent. Yet curiously
one felt at home as one would on Mull or Islay or Skye. And
the next eight days were fantastic. The Upland Goose hotel was
like a Scottish hotel, with a large Raeburn in the kitchen and
always a coffee-pot on the hob.

Of the incidents which stand out in my mind I best remember
our visit to Pebble Island. We came in by helicopter, sixteen of
us in a Sea King. Beneath us, from 100 feet, I could see the
settlement with six or seven white-boarded houses with red and

green roofs on a headland beside the sea. There was a communal peat dump. And there was also Mrs Evans, the shepherd's wife.

We had brought wine and sandwiches for a picnic but Mrs Evans would have none of it. She insisted that we have lunch in her house. A mutton stew simmered on her huge Raeburn. It was magnificent. And for sweet she produced a trifle made with tinned fruit and cream from the cows of the settlement.

Her husband, Raymond Evans, told us about their experiences under the Argentines. They and the other workers of the settlement had been locked up in a sheep-shearing shed every night for thirty-two days. 'The Argentines acted absolutely correctly,' he said. 'They regard women and children as sacrosanct. We had no problems of any kind in that way. But they were very cruel, the officers, towards the men. I saw one officer kick a man to the ground and then keep on kicking him. The soldiers hated their officers.'

We also flew to San Carlos where the British forces had stormed ashore and from where I took two stones from the beach as mementos. The British cemetery was quite the loveliest cemetery I have ever seen. The grave of Colonel H. Jones was there. But it was the one next to his which brought tears to my eyes. The inscription on the headstone simply read, 'H. Holman–Smith / 2nd Paras / Killed May 28 1982 / You will remain for ever in our hearts a hero.'

He was just nineteen.

It was as I reflected a chance remark in my column which had caused me to be privileged to visit the Falkland Islands. And it was in my column that I wrote about Port Stanley and San Carlos on my return. Yet why had I ever started writing a column at all? And just what sort of people read it?

I found out in May of 1983. For it was in that month that the new High Sheriff of Greater London, R. T. S. Macpherson, whom I had not previously met, sent me a hand-written letter telling me that he was reintroducing the traditional Sheriff's Breakfast, which was in fact a luncheon, and that as a Highlander himself he would take pleasure in the attendance of another Highlander, like myself.

It turned out to be a quite delightful occasion. Quintin Hogg was there and so was his predecessor as Lord Chancellor, Lord Elwyn-Jones, and so were Sir Kenneth Newman, the Commissioner of the Metropolitan Police, Sir Thomas Hetherington, the Director of Public Prosecutions, and the Lord Lieutenant of London. Baroness Phillips and Sir Campbell Fraser were others among the twenty-six.

What humbled me was that they all seemed to read my column. At one stage during the lunch the High Sheriff asked me about an item the previous week concerning the statistics which showed that the French were not too keen either about changing their underpants or about brushing their teeth. 'I don't remember that,' said Quintin and then after a second's reflection added, 'Oh yes I do. That was the one about the fact that the citizens of Auchtermuchty wear nothing under their kilts.'

At the end people were almost queueing to shake my hand and tell me how much they enjoyed what I wrote. I had never quite realised before the extent or quality of my readership.

So how did it start? I began to write my column not because I wanted to but because I had to. Every sensible newspaper editor constantly keeps in mind the possibility of calamity occurring and one of his star attractions being suddenly removed by accident or by illness.

The cartoonist Carl Giles is a case in point. I was utterly aware of his enormous value to the *Sunday Express*. I lived in constant terror that something might happen to him, since his health had always seemed fairly fragile. So I looked around for a replacement able to step in if the worst ever happened. My eye fell on that brilliant depicter of little girls on ponies, Norman Thelwell. I never told him what I had in mind but I began using him as an illustrator elsewhere in the paper. As it happened I need not have worried. Giles turned out to be as strong as one of Thelwell's horses and seems destined to go on for ever.

John Gordon, my predecessor as Editor of the *Sunday Express*, was a different proposition. I was well aware of the enormous contribution his column made to the success of the paper. And I was terrified about what would happen when he died. In his last two years he was a sick man. A leg had to be amputated.

But he had a lot of courage and he still staggered into the office. It was then that I began to help him by sending him each week a sheaf of memos. Each of the memos was in effect an item for his column, but by presenting them in the form of ideas he was able to convince himself that by simply altering a word or two here and there he was still writing his column.

In the weeks before Gordon's death I went to see him at his house in Croydon. I had never been there before, and because he had talked about it so grandly I had expected a mansion. Instead I found an ordinary suburban house in a street with a bus route running through it. Inside the house was freezing and if there was central heating it most certainly wasn't turned on. It occurred to me that there were not too many trappings of wealth around a man who had had such a long and distinguished career.

Fearing the worst, I redoubled my efforts to find a replacement. I approached Richard Ingrams – unsuccessfully. Then it was too late and in December 1974 John Gordon was dead. I had, therefore, to begin writing the column myself. I was strongly advised against so doing by friends whose judgement I trusted. Quintin Hogg told me that I would be tying a millstone round my neck. Bill Deedes of the *Telegraph* sighed and said that only a fool wrote for a newspaper he himself edited – although I noted that shortly afterwards he began to do the same himself.

Quintin was right about its being a millstone. Writing a column may look easy. In fact if it is any good at all it is the hardest job in the world. There should be at least five or six items in a column and each one has to say something original. There have been times on a Friday night when I have felt almost like banging my head against the wall. But then there is the magic moment when it all comes right and the effort is made worthwhile.

And why did I write about Auchtermuchty? Because I wanted a sort of Brigadoon place which had been bypassed by the modern world and in which old-fashioned virtues still persisted. I had considered using Ecclefechan as my village but decided that Auchtermuchty had a better ring to it. As indeed it has. It is one of the greatest of my pleasures to visit it occasionally on my way to play golf at St Andrews and to walk through its streets without anyone knowing who I am.

There is also the enormous satisfaction of a column which gives comfort to people in trouble whom one has never met and never will meet. I had many correspondents, some of them old or lonely or sick or even in mental hospitals, who looked upon me as a sheet-anchor, as someone to whom they could write and pour out their fears and worries and know they would get a reply in return. Indeed I was to find – and I suspect the same applies to many other columnists – that there are some readers who come to look upon you as almost their only link with the outside world.

There was John Evans, for example, a patient at Shenley Park mental hospital who although himself the gentlest of persons was convinced that everyone around him was conspiring to kill him. I felt it important to answer all his letters and to send at Christmas a card in return for the lavishly expensive one he always sent me. He was a great cricket fan and there came the day when he was allowed a trip to London to see a game at Lords. I only knew about it afterwards when the Express commissionaire told me that he had a parcel of little gifts for me which a gentleman had left in the front hall. They were from John Evans.

Then there was dear Rose Perez who wrote to me, always from an accommodation address, twice weekly for years. She would send me poems by the score, poems which she had written herself, and many of them good although all of them sad. Poor Rose also felt that the world was ganging up against her. But I felt it was important to her, as it was to John Evans, to feel that she had a friend outside, someone of power and influence. That was why I had never chucked their letters in the dustbin.

Then there were the letter writers who constantly wrote telling me what a miserable Tory lackey I was and why didn't I open my eyes to the blindingly obvious? Such a writer was Mr Ness who was always telling me that I was an idiot. And then something extraordinary happened. In my column one week I quoted a few lines from a Burns love song. It brought a response from Mr Ness. A letter written in a quite different tone from his normal tone. The song I had quoted had been the favourite song of his dearly beloved daughter who had died some years ago and my column had brought tears to his eyes. He never wrote me an angry letter again.

Which leads me to wonder: Does the Queen read the *Sunday Express*? Did she read my column? I have no doubt as to the answer to the first question. Certainly she does. But does Her Majesty like the *Sunday Express*? I am in more doubt as to how to answer that question. My strong impression is that certainly Prince Philip does not, and of course he has already made clear his dislike of the *Daily Express*.

Almost every editor in London of almost every newspaper has been to a private lunch at Buckingham Palace. Bob Edwards has a riotous account of his time there. I had to wait until my thirtieth year of editorship before I received my invitation. But when it did come it was worth it.

There were nine other guests, including Sue MacGregor of *Woman's Hour*, Brian Bevan, the coxswain of the Humber lifeboat, Mr Justice Bingham, a High Court judge of the Queen's Bench Division, an interior designer called George Freeman, the late Keith Wickenden, then Tory MP for Dorking, and Miss Ann Beckwith Smith, Lady-in-Waiting to the Princess of Wales.

We met at 12.50 in the 1844 Room, where we were given a drink and lined up to await the arrival of the Queen and Prince Philip, who came in and shook hands with each of us in turn. The atmosphere at the time was just a little strained, with Prince Philip talking at one end of the room and the Queen and most of the others at the other end. It may have been imagination but I fancied that Prince Philip was just a little bit terse with me. When I asked him about the corgis – there were two of them wandering round the room sniffing – and jocularly enquired whether they were dangerous, and if it were safe to touch them, he retorted, 'You mean are they in danger from you?'

When we went in to lunch I found that I was sitting on the Queen's left-hand side. The High Court judge was on her right. On the other side of the table, Prince Philip had Sue MacGregor on his right and Keith Wickenden on his left. On my immediate left was the coxswain of the Humber Lifeboat, Brian Bevan, a youngish man with a mass of black hair and a thin, tiny gold ear-ring in his right ear. He may have had one in his left ear too, but I couldn't see his left ear.

For the whole of the first course, which was salmon, the Queen didn't speak to me at all but addressed herself entirely to the judge on her right-hand side. I began to wonder whether she had been upset by what I had written in my column about Prince Andrew a few weeks previously. The second course, the main course, was braised ham and once again she didn't speak to me at all. Instead of becoming nervous, I found myself quite relaxed and concentrated on looking around the room and studying the other guests.

'Stuff it,' I thought. 'If she doesn't want to talk to me, then to hell with her.' I looked across the table and saw that Keith Wickenden was in precisely the same situation as me. Prince Philip was lavishing all his attention and conversation on the lady on his right, Miss Sue MacGregor. No one, but no one, was talking to Wickenden. We looked at each other and gave a slight shrug of our shoulders.

Then suddenly with the arrival of the sweet the whole luncheon was transformed. As if a bell had rung somewhere the Queen turned towards me and for the rest of the lunch ignored the judge. Simultaneously Prince Philip turned to Keith Wickenden and ignored Sue MacGregor. I came to the conclusion that it was a technique which they had adopted and which probably never varied.

But I was enchanted by the Queen. For the rest of the lunch she chatted to me as if we were old friends and in a most delightful fashion. Horse-racing provided the breakthrough. On the way to the Palace my office driver, Ray Wright, who was a very keen punter, had said to me, 'Ask her if her horse Height of Fashion is going to win the Oaks.' And this I did.

It was an inspired idea. The Queen became absolutely animated and explained that the horse's legs were possibly too long for the Epsom course but that its chances would be decided by whether the horse ran well at Goodwood.

She was also fascinating on the subject of Prince Andrew. She told me that the powers that be in the Navy had tried to keep Prince Andrew away from the Falklands and that she had insisted that he go there, partly because she knew that that was what he wanted but also because, as she said, 'His grandfather fought at Jutland. So why shouldn't he fight in the Falklands?' I was suddenly aware that she was fiercely proud of both her father and her son.

After lunch we retired to the 1844 Room again for coffee and liqueurs. I left her on her own, since I felt I had monopolised her sufficiently, and went instead to speak to Prince Philip's equerry, but the Master of the Household approached me and softly informed me that Her Majesty would like to speak to me again. When I emerged into the sunshine of the Mall after the lunch it was with the feeling that perhaps for all those years I had been wrong and that the Queen not only read but liked my newspaper.

But one thing strikes me about the Queen – and that is the enormous difference between how she acts in private and her behaviour in public. In private at that luncheon I found her a relaxed, scintillating conversationalist. Her eyes danced and she had a ready and deft sense of humour. She seemed quite different on the only public occasion on which I was presented to her and that was when I was invested with my knighthood.

I was in a long line of recipients. When it came to my turn for my minute or two with her, I suddenly became conscious of the fact that she seemed extraordinarily nervous. She had met me and chatted animatedly with me on several previous occasions. She had my name and job on the piece of paper in front of her. Yet it seemed to me that she had not the faintest idea who I was. Not because she was being rude. Simply because she was so stiff and unrelaxed. Yet she conducts these investitures so often that one would have thought she would have lost all nervousness about them long ago.

I thought at the time that it might be simply because she was feeling off-colour on that particular day. But I have since met people who have had precisely the same experience. One friend who had met her, and indeed who had shown her round his business premises only three weeks previously, was slightly surprised to find that she hadn't the faintest idea who he was or what he did. The tension she suffers on such occasions must be quite daunting.

And yet in private Her Majesty has a delightful sense of humour. I still chuckle when I remember the story told to me by the Queen's Equerry, the late Lord Plunket, about Sir Alexander McDonald who was then the boss of Distillers and who many people think acted less than generously towards the Thalidomide children.

The background of the story is Edinburgh. The Queen was there on one of her official visits and was staying in Holyrood, a palace which for many years has had its beauty hidden under the dirt and grime spewed out of Edinburgh's factories.

To clean Holyrood was going to cost a lot of money and it was suggested to the Queen that it might be a good idea to enlist the financial help of local businessmen – especially those whose industries had added to the dirt on Holyrood's walls. A lunch was arranged. Sir Alexander McDonald was invited and it was suggested to the Queen that after lunch in private conversation with McDonald she should ask him if he would care to contribute. She does not like doing this sort of thing but agreed to do so.

Afterwards she was asked what success she had had. She smiled wryly. 'Well I spoke to him,' she said. 'And I told him what we had in mind and suggested that since his company had helped to make Holyrood dirty he might want to contribute. And do you know what he replied? He looked me straight in the eye and said, "Your Majesty has a very keen sense of humour."'

Which of course she has. But there is another question, surely one of the most fascinating questions of our times: What does the Queen think of Margaret Thatcher?

There have been persistent rumours that the Queen is cool towards her Prime Minister and that on one occasion – after the American invasion of Grenada – she did not offer Margaret Thatcher a seat during their weekly audience. Even though Margaret Thatcher was utterly innocent and had not known about the invasion herself until after it had happened.

Certainly it would only be natural if the Queen were a little miffed by her Prime Minister's success. They are about the same age. When the Queen first came to the throne as a young, vibrant and beautiful woman no one had ever heard of Margaret Thatcher. The talk was all about the new Elizabethan age which had started so gloriously with the successful ascent of Everest by Hillary and Tensing. People actually believed that with a new Queen on the throne all the gloom and shortages and inefficiencies which had marked the immediate post-war years would magically disappear and that Britain would return to the greatness of the pre-war years. Alas it was not to be and instead Britain began to count less and less in the world.

Ironic then that the downward trend has been arrested not by the daughter of a king but by the daughter of a grocer. It may be that all the rumours are unfounded and that Her Majesty adores her Prime Minister. I just do not know. What I do know for absolutely certain is that the Prime Minister would do anything to protect the Queen.

I had first-hand evidence of that in 1986, the week after I had ceased to be Editor of the *Sunday Express*. It was in the middle of a dreadful period for the Prime Minister. The African countries at the Commonwealth Conference were screeching their heads off because of her refusal to support sanctions against South Africa. Then came the most savage blow of all – a *Sunday Times* article which claimed to be quoting Buckingham Palace sources when it said that the Queen was very concerned about the way the Commonwealth was being treated and also that she did not like the Prime Minister's abrasive policies, especially the ones employed during the miners' strike. It was a body-blow to Margaret Thatcher.

That week I rang her secretary, Caroline Stephens, to give her the telephone number of my new office. I also asked her how the PM was reacting to the *Sunday Times* piece. She gave me the impression that Margaret was feeling just a little bit hurt by it all. She then added, 'Why don't you ring her at Chequers on Saturday morning?' I replied that I couldn't possibly just pick up the phone and ring the Prime Minister unless I had some very good reason for so doing. But Caroline pleaded with me. 'Don't you realise that everyone who does ring her has a moan of some kind? There are times like now when she really does need cheering up. So please do ring her.'

And I did indeed ring on the Saturday morning. I made as my excuse that this was the first Saturday morning since she had become leader of the Tory Party that I had not been in charge of the *Sunday Express*. But, I assured her, I would do my damnedest behind the scenes to make sure it remained a pro-Thatcher paper. I went on to say that this very Sunday I planned to come to her defence in what the *Sunday Times* had been describing as a crisis in the relationship between her and the Queen. The newspaper had indicated that its information had been obtained largely from sources inside Buckingham Palace. I proposed demanding that the Queen should make it publicly clear that there was no truth to the story. Otherwise there would be all the makings of a constitutional crisis.

The Prime Minister's reaction was immediate. 'Please John, don't do that. The only important thing is the Queen. I don't want to see anything happen that could endanger the monarchy.'

Nor was there any doubting the anguish and sincerity in her voice. I replied that it was too late for me to change my column. But I was moved by what she had said and the way in which she had said it. I just wondered whether the Queen respected Margaret Thatcher half as much as Margaret Thatcher respected her. Or whether at the root of it all her alleged coolness towards the Prime Minister might be that old problem, feminine jealousy.

It was in November 1984 that I lunched with the Prince and Princess of Wales. In fact it was the third time I had been invited to lunch with them. On both previous occasions I had been out of the country. Now at last I was going to meet Princess Diana for the first time.

I arrived at Kensington Palace at 1.00 p.m. The security was virtually non-existent. At the police barrier I was waved through the moment I gave my name. No one asked for proof of identity. No one asked to search my car for hidden explosives in the way carried out both at Chequers and Buckingham Palace.

A smiling, relaxed footman greeted me and led me upstairs to a large first floor sitting-room. It was tastefully but not ostentatiously furnished. A grand piano, surmounted by framed photographs of people I did not instantly recognise, stood beside a large window which overlooked the front door at which I had emerged from my car.

There were four doors in the room. And I heard one of them click shut as I stood by the window surveying the courtyard. Two minutes later I heard a woman's voice say, 'I'm so sorry we have kept you waiting.' They came into the room through the door which I had previously heard click. It was clear they had been awaiting my arrival in the adjoining room. The Prince looked much more slight and frail than I had expected. The Princess looked even more beautiful than her photographs. There was a warmth and lustrous quality about her eyes which was quite enchanting.

She sat on a settee and motioned me to take an armchair beside her. The Prince joined her on the settee and asked if I would like a drink. I replied no. The Princess did not have a drink either. The Prince had a tomato juice.

'Not a Bloody Mary?' I asked.

'No, I can't take alcohol in the middle of the day.'

He seemed, I thought, just a little offhand to begin with. Could it even possibly have been nerves?

I reminded him that the last time we had met I had congratulated him on the interview he had given on the BBC to Jack deManio. And how, when I had done so, he had looked at me piercingly and said, 'Are you saying that because you really believe it? Or because you think that is what I want to hear?' On that occasion, I pointed out, just two days after he had given the interview I had replied, 'The fact that I am reprinting the interview word for word in the *Sunday Express* answers that question. I would not be reprinting it if I did not think it was first class.'

The offhandedness began to disappear. The Prince remarked that he hoped Princess Diana would begin to give interviews. But then he added, 'Perhaps not just yet. It might be wise to wait until she has more experience.'

'Oh yes,' she joined in to say. 'I just hate the sound of my own voice, I can't bear it. When I launched that new liner last week I just couldn't believe it when I heard myself afterwards. It just didn't sound like me.'

The Prince laughed. 'I felt exactly the same way. I just couldn't believe that yakkety-yak voice was mine. So upper class.'

I suggested that perhaps all women have the same difficulty in as much as they all have higher-pitched voices and perhaps speak too quickly. Mrs Thatcher, I said, had the same difficulty until Gordon Reece persuaded her to drop her voice an octave and to speak more slowly. And I suggested also that she had had the original difficulty, like Ted Heath, of speaking with an assumed, artificial, upper-class accent.

'She is a bit like a school ma'am, isn't she?' the Prince said, laughing.

I remarked on the fact that the only newspaper in the room was a copy of *The Times*.

'Yes,' he replied. 'It's the only newspaper I read. I can't bear to read the others. They make me so angry when they write things about me and about my wife which are so completely untrue.'

'But there is a danger there,' I suggested. 'For if you don't read other newspapers how can you know what is being said about you?' The Prince agreed and admitted that he was indeed informed as to what other newspapers did say about him.

We went in to lunch. A round table set for three with me sitting between the Prince of Wales on my right and Princess Diana on my left. The lunch was simple. Fish and mushrooms in cheese followed by plums and *crème brûlée*.

'These plums are from Highgrove,' said Prince Charles. 'They were bottled there.'

'And that's *crème brûlée*,' said Princess Diana. 'It's hard on top. You will have to hit it with your spoon.' I did and the *crème brûlée* was as delicious as the plums.

As the meal progressed the Prince became more and more relaxed. He drank no wine. Nor did she. I had one glass of hock. He asked my advice on how to handle public relations. So many idiotic stories appeared, he said, like the one which suggested that Dr Armand Hammer was going to be godfather to Prince Harry. Or that Princess Anne had been snubbed by not having been invited to be a godmother. I suggested that he should bypass the Buckingham Palace press office and that when he wanted to deny a story, with or without an offficial denial, he should arrange for an editor he trusted like Charles Douglas-Home of the *Times* or Bill Deedes of the *Telegraph* to be telephoned and asked to put right the mistake. The Prince spoke at length about his passion for giving some training to the youth of the country, some discipline. He bemoaned the collapse and the inadequacy of the Church.

Throughout our conversation Princess Diana was silent until finally I turned to her to embrace her in the conversation. Immediately he apologised. 'Darling, I'm so sorry, I've done all the talking. Did you have something you wanted to say?' She looked slightly tremulous and nodded. Then she poured out to me her resentment about the way in which it was suggested in newspapers that she was influencing her husband and turning him against shooting and hunting.

Prince Charles broke in. 'I'm angry about that too. Because my wife is doing nothing of the kind. My wife actually likes hunting and shooting. It is I who have turned against it.'

The time simply slipped by. I moved my chair a fraction away from the table. They both rose. 'We'll come downstairs with you,' said Diana. And that is indeed what they did. Down to the front door where standing in the hall awaiting them was an old man with side-whiskers.

'Hello Dickie,' said the Prince. Sir Richard Attenborough was clearly their next appointment.

It was pouring with rain outside. The Prince tried to offer me an umbrella but I thrust it aside. My driver, Ray Cobb, was quite unaware that there in the porch just six feet away from him was the young man who would one day be King of England. As we drove back to Fleet Street I reflected that Charles was a serious, perhaps too serious, young man, obsessed with the idea of serving the nation, in some danger of overwhelming his wife and in even greater danger of boring her.

There is one other thing which worried me then and which still does today. The way in which Prince Charles keeps losing members of his personal staff. People of the calibre of Edward

Adeane whose father Sir Michael I had known and formed a slight friendship with during his long and distinguished career as the Queen's Private Secretary.

I had never met Edward but I had spoken to him once or twice on the telephone when he was fixing up for me to have lunch at Kensington Palace with Prince Charles and Princess Diana. It had come as a shock to learn so soon afterwards that he was quitting the Royal Service. Especially disconcerting were the sensational tabloid stories that it was because he could not get on with Princess Diana.

I had telephoned to say how sorry I was and as a result of that telephone call we lunched in January 1985.

He walked into the White Tower at the same moment as our former Ambassador to the United States, Nico Henderson. Each looked slightly surprised to see the other. But I imagine it was Henderson who was the more disconcerted. They had seen each other before lunch in Pall Mall, never realising that they were going to the same restaurant. 'We could have shared a taxi if we'd known,' said Adeane to me. Henderson was at the next table and must have cursed his luck at so being. For he was joined by an elegant-looking blonde in her late forties, who turned out to be, although Henderson did not introduce us, the widow of the late American Ambassador to Britain, David Bruce.

There was not the slightest doubt that Adeane was enormously saddened by his decision to quit Prince Charles's service. It had, of course, nothing to do with Princess Diana whom he liked very much indeed and got on with very well indeed. He had been delighted with a paragraph in my column in which I had exculpated her from any responsibility for his resignation.

'I don't know if Prince Charles read your paragraph,' he said, 'but I made sure that she saw it. It was good to know that at least one person got it right, although one small paragraph in the *Sunday Express* doesn't outweigh the damage done by the great double-page spreads in all the popular newspapers suggesting that she had something to do with my quitting.'

Why then was Adeane quitting? I did not ask the direct question. I did not have to. From his earliest years he had been trained to serve the Royal Family. His fifteen years at the Bar were only so that he could learn a bit about life outside. But clearly he had seen himself spending the rest of his life serving Charles while he was Prince of Wales and subsequently as King. And I am positive that he did serve him brilliantly and would have continued so to do.

There were some things he said which gave me a clue. Some comments I myself made perhaps sparked him off. I had said that at my lunch at Kensington Palace I had been very much smitten by the Princess but I had had my reservations about the Prince. He seemed to me, I said, to be almost making a profession of being a do-gooder.

I told him I had been slightly disconcerted by the Prince's frugality with food, the fact that he did not drink anything at all and his rather hair-shirt mentality. I also said I was slightly disconcerted to find that the person who was entering the building as I left was Richard Attenborough. Adeane did not disagree. He admitted to being disturbed at the way in which Prince Charles was always willing to take up and give expression to minority viewpoints. He cited alternative medicine as an example. I felt very sorry indeed for Adeane. I thought that Prince Charles had lost a wise counsellor and a good and loyal friend. And I went away hoping that Prince Charles would not continue to lose too many people like Edward Adeane.

Another member of the Royal Family, albeit a minor one, with whom I lunched quite frequently was Angus Ogilvy. I remember in particular one lunch in June 1987 which came at a time shortly after the *Sun* had sensationally announced that Prince Edward was quitting the Marines. Angus arrived for lunch as he so often does on his bicycle, parked it neatly across the road from the Terrazza-Est, undid his cycle clips and entered the restaurant looking as if he had just stepped out of a Rolls-Royce.

He told me that Prince Edward gave no hint at all to either his father or mother that he planned to walk out of the Marines. They were shocked by his action. It was only, after all, a six-month course. If he had completed it and then opted out afterwards no one would even have noticed. As it was, Ogilvy gave me the impression that both the Queen and Prince Philip felt very badly let down.

Then there was the mystery as to how the *Sun* had come to be so accurately informed. The paper was obviously getting information from inside the Marines and in considerable detail. But the biggest mystery of all concerned the letter which Prince Philip wrote to the Marine Commandant-General in Whitehall after Edward had quit. That letter, which was marked personal and confidential, was sent from Buckingham Palace by hand. It stayed there in an out-tray for one hour.

It was inconceivable, according to Ogilvy, that it could have been tampered with there. Yet the full text of the letter subsequently appeared in the *Sun*. But if it wasn't interfered with in the Palace then someone in the Marines must have leaked it. But since the letter was marked for the eyes of the Commandant-General only how could that have happened? According to Ogilvy, Prince Philip still puzzled over the matter.

Of all the people around Mrs Thatcher I have not the slightest doubt which one, in a perfect world, I would choose as her successor. Geoffrey Howe. Denis Healey once said of him in a devastating phrase which will follow Geoffrey to the grave, 'To be attacked by Sir Geoffrey Howe is like being savaged by a dead sheep.'

And there may be just the tiniest bit of truth in that. Geoffrey is not a mauler in debate. He prefers to argue softly and reasonably. But no one should ever doubt the immense depth of his intellect or the wisdom and understanding he shows in handling both domestic and world problems. No one should ever doubt either the immense honesty and integrity and decency of the man.

I have known him for many years and in and out of office he has never changed. Always unassuming, never arrogant and always ready to listen to another point of view. And for most of the time, even though latterly he has suffered from what might be called the Crown Prince syndrome, quite amazingly loyal. In at least that one respect there is a resemblance to Reggie Maudling. I personally have never heard Geoffrey utter a disloyal word about Margaret Thatcher or indeed an unkind word about anyone else. There is perhaps one further resemblance between Howe and Maudling. Just like Maudling, Howe has little money. He has been too busy in politics, including years in Opposition, ever to have made much money at the Bar. When he was somewhat shabbily turfed out of Chevening in 1989 after being moved from the Foreign Office, he and Elspeth had only a terraced house off the Old Kent Road as something they could actually call their own.

He has family worries too. His daughter's marriage broke up some time ago and Geoffrey feels an enormous personal and financial responsibility for the welfare and education of the children. Yet there is never a hint of bitterness or unhappiness about him. He was a damned good Foreign Secretary, too. One who sometimes took big stick for things which were not his fault. The US invasion of Grenada, for example. Geoffrey told me afterwards that as late as the Sunday night before the invasion they were still being told by Washington that no action was imminent. Then the invasion came and he and the Prime Minister had egg all over their faces. Yet he had no rancour towards Reagan, whom he believed at that time to be over the top and being manoeuvred by the State Department. 'That,' he said, 'is what is really frightening. We do not know who is taking the decisions.'

It is perhaps natural if after so many years there has been a slight souring of his relationship with the Prime Minister. Even honourable ambition when thwarted can produce unpleasant by-products. And besides, as Nigel Lawson so percipiently observed, 'Geoffrey has a problem with the two women in his life, his wife and Margaret. They both dislike each other.' Yet Geoffrey's standing will always be high. In his crumpled tweed suits and scuffed Hush Puppies, the eyes gleaming owlishly behind the spectacles, he is a cuddly figure whose very presence radiates normality and reason.

One of the stories I like best about him has as its background the 1982 Tory Conference at Brighton. Unemployment was rising and the socialists were whipping it up as the key issue. The Militant Tendency had joined the fray and a right-to-work march had been organised of Welsh unemployed from the Valleys. The idea was that the march would climax with a fierce confrontation at the Conference hall. Day after day the papers were full of the progress of the march. There were huge demonstrations in many cities en route and in some towns there was violence. The police presence in Brighton was huge and Cabinet ministers had to be most closely guarded as they entered the Conference hall.

In the midst of all this Geoffrey Howe and his wife slipped out of an unguarded side-door at the end of a debate into what they expected to be an empty side-street. To their consternation a gang of the Welsh were standing on the corner. One of them pointed at Geoffrey and the whole group advanced in what seemed a most menacing manner towards them. But instead of violence, all that happened when the mob reached them was that the leader thrust out his hand and said, 'You're Geoffrey Howe, aren't you? My Auntie Megan works for you.' And so indeed she did – as housekeeper. And so instead of confrontation there was laughter and back-slapping and address-exchanging.

It is a story which typifies Geoffrey Howe. But then of course the question of succeeding Margaret Thatcher is a question for a far from perfect world. And of which no one is more keenly aware than Geoffrey, as I discovered when out of the blue in May 1988 his secretary telephoned to ask if I were free to lunch with the Foreign Secretary on the eve of his trip to Hong Kong. The suggested venue was the back room at the Garrick Club. In the event we switched to the Howard Hotel where I could be the host since I was conscious that when Geoffrey bought lunch he had to do so out of his own pocket.

There was not the slightest doubt why he wanted to see me. He was clearly running scared at the thought that he had upset Margaret and could be shifted from the Foreign Office. He protested that his reference to the need for this country to join the European Monetary System in a recent speech in Scotland had been widely interpreted as his supporting Nigel Lawson against the Prime Minister. He was utterly innocent of this, he told me, pointing out that he had made the same suggestion a dozen times before and that the first half of his speech, of which of course not a line was reported, had been devoted to saying what a wonderful Prime Minister Margaret Thatcher was.

He was also puzzled and anxious about a story going around that he and Norman Tebbit before the 1987 general election had engaged in a conspiracy to unseat the Prime Minister.

'Just who is doing this to me?' he demanded.

After Geoffrey Howe had moved on in 1983 from the Treasury to the Foreign Office, I received a curious telephone call from John Kerr. He had been Geoffrey's Principal Private Secretary as Chancellor of the Exchequer and was still doing the same job for the new Chancellor, Nigel Lawson, whom I had recently criticised strongly in my column.

Kerr began by saying that he was telephoning entirely off his own bat. He reminded me that after Lawson had been appointed I had telephoned him to find if he was moving to the Foreign Office along with Geoffrey Howe. When he had replied that he was staying in his old job I had suggested to him that he might find Nigel Lawson a completely different kind of man and that he might find working with him less enjoyable.

Kerr was explaining that quite the reverse was turning out to be true. 'He is different,' he said to me. 'But I think you should know that it was Geoffrey Howe's idea that Nigel be appointed Chancellor. And he is a good man to work with and has a lot of good ideas. Don't you think you might like to get to know him?'

The thought crossed my mind that Kerr's telephone call had possibly been initiated by Nigel Lawson himself. So I replied that I had no animosity of any kind towards Lawson and that I would very much like to lunch with him. Kerr immediately replied that he would arrange one for after my return from holiday. I like John Kerr. But I found it fascinating that Lawson should clearly have been so rattled by my criticism.

When we did meet, I found Nigel Lawson to be not at all the bumptious, arrogant character I had expected. He came into the Howard Hotel looking as if his suit were two sizes too small for him. More like a little boy lost than an intellectual snob.

As lunch went on I liked him more and more. About one thing I was convinced. No matter how his views might change in the future, at that moment he had no higher ambition than to be Chancellor of the Exchequer. Nor do I believe that subsequently his views on that score ever changed. Lawson explained to me that right from the start of his career as a financial journalist he had attended press conference after press conference with Chancellors of the Exchequer. And all along it was his ambition that one day he would be standing there as Chancellor giving the press conference rather than as a reporter taking notes. And he clearly knew his stuff. He knew as much about economics and finance as most of his advisers, and that is not a common trait in a Chancellor. He was quite single-minded about getting the economy right and pushing the country towards a lasting prosperity.

From that time we were to lunch frequently together. Then in 1986 disaster struck. The cause of the trouble was the publication in the *Sunday Express* of an interview which his wife had given to a freelance writer, Alison Coles. In the interview, which had been commissioned and published while I was on holiday, Thérèse Lawson spoke briefly about the fact that she had been pregnant before Nigel's divorce from his first wife came through. She was of course at the time Nigel's secretary.

On my return from holiday I found an angry letter from Nigel awaiting me protesting about the article. It was, he said, a shameful piece of journalism. The reporter had given an undertaking that the finished copy would be submitted to his wife for approval before publication. That promise had not been kept. What was I going to do about it? I called in the Features Editor, Max Davidson, and asked him if Lawson's accusation was right. Max vehemently denied that any undertaking of any kind had been given. I had no alternative but to stand by my staff. I wrote explaining the position to Lawson and received a curt reply indicating that our relationship was finished.

Some sixteen months later I thought I would try to break the ice and wrote him a letter suggesting that we might lunch again. In my letter I made no reference at all to our row. Within twenty-four hours his secretary was on the telephone offering a date for lunch.

It turned out to be Friday 16 October 1987, the morning after the hurricane hit the South of England. I staggered out that morning to find telephone wires wrapped round my front door and trees down everywhere. It took me three hours to drive to London and it was pure luck that it took as little as that. But I made the Howard Hotel by one o'clock. Nigel arrived on time and in great form. He was bullish about the economy and dismissed my fear that the US might go protectionist in order to save the dollar. 'I don't believe Reagan will do that,' he said. 'That's the one advantage of having an old man as President. He remembers too well what happened the last time they had protection.'

Neither of us mentioned our row until, at the very end of the lunch, I said how sorry I was that it had ever happened. I explained that I had had no part in the article's publication but equally that I had had no alternative but to support my staff. Nigel said he understood but then asked me if I would be prepared to write a note of apology to his wife Thérèse. Even though it struck me as odd that she should want an apology so long after the event, I agreed and did indeed write one.

There are some odd postscripts to that lunch. Over the weekend the world's stockmarkets crashed in the greatest disaster since 1931. And then a few weeks later Mrs Lawson was unfortunate enough to be reversed into by a London bus while stuck in traffic in her car. She was breathalysed and found to be over the limit. It was the cruellest of luck and the sensational publicity which ensued was crucifying. I wrote a paragraph of sympathy in my column of 22 November 1987 and received a warm hand-written letter of thanks from her by return. I had the suspicion then that life must be hell for her in 11 Downing Street.

The next time I lunched with Nigel I suggested that he might bring Thérèse to join us.

And he did. The venue was once again the Howard Hotel and they arrived five minutes early. Thérèse was charming but desperately insecure and nervous. She smoked incessantly. She was very grateful to me for the support I had given her. She confirmed my suspicion that she hated living in Downing Street. 'Everyone is always watching you all the time there,' she said. 'Not because they are watching you in particular but just because there are always photographers around waiting for something to happen.'

So she had moved with the children to their country home in Nigel's constituency and he was looking after himself alone in Downing Street. 'I find the microwave a wonderful invention,' he told me.

Thérèse was desperate for Nigel to give up office. Although it was most certainly not financial considerations which motivated her, I thought then how imperative such financial considerations might become. Yet as it turned out it was not the lure of big money that caused Nigel Lawson to quit so sensationally in October 1989 but hurt pride that the Prime Minister preferred the views of an unofficial adviser, Sir Alan Walters, to those of her own Chancellor.

Lawson's pride can only have been further hurt by what appears to have been his lack of social contact with the Prime Minister.

'Do you know,' he once told me, 'when Margaret comes back from Chequers on a Sunday night she never thinks of dropping in for a drink with Thérèse and me or with Geoffrey and Elspeth, or indeed with any Cabinet minister? Instead she always goes to see Charles Powell and his wife.'

Charles Powell is, of course, the Prime Minister's long-serving adviser on foreign affairs and the centre of much envy and hostility because of his influence.

Even so, when it was announced in February 1990 that Lawson was to be paid more than £100,000 a year as a non-executive director of Barclays Bank, I rejoiced that he would at last be getting a salary commensurate with his outstanding ability. For I have always thought it a nonsense that a Chancellor of the Exchequer should earn less than one-fifth of the amounts picked up by comparative nonentities in the world outside.

And some months later Cecil Parkinson said something to me which added a sad note to my lunch with the Lawsons. Cecil told me that, at a function he and his wife and the Lawsons had all attended, he had danced with Thérèse and it was a dance he would never forget.

She had said to him, 'Why are you trying to get Nigel's job?'

'But I'm not,' Parkinson replied. 'It's all just newspaper stories.'

'But they wouldn't print them if they weren't true,' demanded Thérèse.

I pointed out to Cecil that, in fact, Thérèse very much wanted Nigel to pack up the Treasury and retire to private life and so I could not understand why she had taken that line with him.

'I know,' he replied. 'It is true they are terribly hard up. The rumour in Cabinet was that in the drink-driving case Thérèse had to sell her car to pay off the fine and the barrister's expenses, but it didn't come to that. Do you know they can't afford to send their children to private schools in London? Yet, he is so independent. I let it be known through my wife that I would be prepared to buy a house for them wherever they chose and then rent it to them. So they could have a place of privacy away from Downing Street. But Nigel took it very badly. He clearly didn't want to be under any obligation to me.'

That Nigel Lawson should have indignantly spurned such an offer only confirms my view of him as someone fiercely independent and utterly incorruptible. But doesn't it also give an astonishing insight into our entrepreneurial society that Cecil, whose own father was a humble railway-line tapper, should be the one who has made it financially?

Although I was sorry to see Nigel Lawson resign as Chancellor of the Exchequer, I rejoiced at the appointment of John Major as his successor. In any other age it would be inconceivable that a man of his background would have become a Tory.

He was brought up in a squalid Brixton council flat in the sort of area where old ladies just dare not answer a knock on the door, far less go out at night. His father, who had been a circus trapeze artist, was far too old and sick to work. There was no question of extended education for John. When he was a boy of thirteen he used to walk the mile or so which separated the slums of Brixton from upper-middle-class Dulwich and look longingly at the Christmas trees in the windows of warm, comfortable, tastefully lit sitting-rooms.

That memory lives with him to this day. John Major understands poverty and he knows that behind genteel curtains there is often real poverty and real suffering among the old and sick.

I often suspect that among Tory grandees – with their background of Eton, Oxford and the Guards – there is a feeling that the present type of lower-middle-class Tory leadership, as exemplified by Margaret Thatcher and before her Ted Heath, is an aberration and that the day will come when the aristocrats and landed gentry are back in control again and most of the Cabinet will be members of White's Club. Not if men like John Major have anything to do with it. He is not a Tory. He is a Thatcherite utterly committed to the continuing reform and revolution of British society and British working practices. But in his mind it is the cause of the poor and not the rich he is fighting.

In fact I had more than a hint that John Major was going to go to the top when in April 1988 Charles Forte gave a dinner party for the Prime Minister. There were some thirty-six people there – four tables with nine people at each.

When the coffee stage was reached Charles came to me and asked if I would change places with him. Margaret Thatcher wished to talk to me. We then had a fascinating half-hour's discussion. And Margaret spoke with her usual candour. Geoffrey Howe was becoming more and more like a blancmange. Kenneth Baker was not a possible successor. He was an able enough administrator but fundamentally he was wet. She was aware of Norman Tebbit's ambitions to succeed her but spoke of him with respect and affection. She thought that Nigel Lawson wanted to go and make himself some money but she wanted him to stay in his present job. She didn't think he would make a good Foreign Secretary. And John Major? John Major she made clear was the best of the younger bunch and the man most likely to succeed her.

She was reassuring about my own future, too, if and when I left the *Sunday Express*. 'There will be something for you,' she said.

But there has not always been something for the members of the Prime Minister's Cabinet. They have all had their ups and downs. Like Peter Walker, who has been a frequent lunch companion, even though our friendship changed after Margaret

Thatcher took over from Ted Heath and even more so after she became Prime Minister.

I remember Victor Matthews phoning me one morning and inviting me to lunch in the boardroom that day. He had, he told me, rather special guests including Lord Armstrong who as William Armstrong had been Cabinet Secretary in Ted Heath's government and who, although it was kept secret at the time, had had a nervous breakdown during Heath's tussle with the miners. He was now Chairman of the Midland Bank. Another guest was to be Maxwell Joseph. When I told Victor that I already had a lunch appointment that day – with Peter Walker – he suggested that I bring him along. This I did. And I was amazed and sickened at the way in which during the lunch both Armstrong and Walker talked about Margaret Thatcher. My relationship with Walker was soured for a long time after that, although he treated me most agreeably every time we met.

Even so he seldom missed a chance of thrusting in the knife. At a time when John Moore was in charge of Social Security and was on the point of resignation because of the government's refusal to raise Child Benefit, Cecil Parkinson told me that Peter Walker had been contemplating resignation on the same issue. 'But,' Cecil went on to say, 'the very moment he realised that John Moore had been talked out of it, he abandoned his own threat of resignation. And do you know why? Because if he and John Moore had resigned together it might have done real harm to Margaret Thatcher. His own resignation he knew wouldn't.'

For my own part I had and still have the highest opinion of Peter Walker's talents, although not perhaps as high as the opinion he himself has. I cannot forget the cock-up he made as Ted Heath's Minister of the Environment when he changed the names of counties and escalated Town Hall salaries so crazily. And I find it difficult to understand how right from the beginning Mrs Thatcher has incurred the disloyalty and dislike of so many male colleagues – even when subsequent events have throughout the years proved that she was right and they were wrong on so many issues. It is hard to avoid the conclusion that there is only one reason for it. The fact that she is a woman.

During the 1983 election campaign I had commented unkindly on the TV appearances of Cecil Parkinson. I had described him as looking like a piece of 'cold boiled cod'. After the election the late Anthony Shrimsley, then head of Tory Central Office publicity, had telephoned me to say that Parkinson had been upset by my reference and had wondered if perhaps he had upset me in some way. Would I like to meet him for lunch? This I did. And very much warmed to him. I suspected that we had a lot, including a liking for the ladies, in common.

At that first lunch he told me one good story of how during the Falklands campaign and before our troops had landed, there had been the Peruvian initiative which might have produced peace but which would have meant in effect that we had conceded shared sovereignty in the islands with the Argentine.

The government had to decide whether or not we would accept. There was a Cabinet meeting to discuss the issue and it was more or less decided that we should accept and hope that the Argentinians refused – which in fact they did. But Parkinson was troubled. He did not like the idea of acceptance. When he left the Cabinet meeting he decided that he had to get in touch with Margaret. At 11.00 p.m. he telephoned Downing Street and asked if he could speak to her. He was told that she had gone to bed and had asked not to be disturbed.

He decided that the following morning he would have to say that if we agreed to the Peruvian initiative he would have to quit his Cabinet post. When the Cabinet assembled, Margaret Thatcher entered the room and immediately said, 'Gentlemen, I have spent the night thinking about this Peruvian initiative and I have to tell you that if it is your decision to accept then you will have to find another Prime Minister.'

End of a personal crisis for Parkinson.

But very soon thereafter it was the start of another. The crisis of Miss Sara Keays.

He clearly felt as a result of the scandal that he had lost forever his chance of coming through the middle as a successor to Margaret. 'Brian Walden was sure that I would succeed,' he told me at one of the many meetings we had during a time of terrible torture for him. 'At a small dinner to which he invited me, he stood up and said, "I can tell you that Cecil Parkinson is going to be the next Prime Minister of Britain." I was flabbergasted. It had never occurred to me. But after the dinner Walden said to me, "Of course you will. With Peter Walker on the left and Michael Heseltine on the right you are a natural to come through the middle."' Cecil reflected for a moment or two and then said, 'And now it's all gone.'

There were times during this period when I thought his bitterness would destroy him. No matter how hard one tried to talk about other things, Cecil would so often come back to the subject of Miss Keays. I recall a lunch the day after the *Daily Mirror* had published a picture of Miss Keays and the child and after Mrs Thatcher had announced Cabinet changes from which Parkinson was again excluded. But a glint of pride and affection came into his eyes when he spoke about the child. 'She looks so lovely,' he said.

At that meeting he told me an extraordinary story of a dinner he had had with two well-known Swiss whom he did not name – naturally. They had said to him, 'Why do you stand for it? Give us the word and we will arrange a contract.' 'A contract?' asked Parkinson. 'What do you mean?' Then suddenly aware of what they did mean, he said, 'I would never condone violence of any kind.'

He also told me about his last meeting with Margaret Thatcher. It had lasted three hours. At the end of it she took his hands in hers, one in each, kissed him on the cheek and said, 'Cecil, these have been such happy hours. We have done such a lot for the country together and we will do much more.' I strongly advised him not to give up his seat in Parliament but just to sit back and await developments.

It might have been thought that Cecil at that time had already had a bellyful of trouble. But there was more to come. He was lunching with me in the White Tower on 15 October 1986 when he received a telephone call telling him that his eldest daughter had taken a drug overdose in a street just a hundred yards away from the restaurant. He rushed away in a panic. And yet the following night when he appeared on *Question Time* with Sir

Robin Day I thought that although he looked a trifle nervous, no one on God's earth except perhaps me and his wife could have suspected the trauma he had just gone through.

But not only did his daughter survive. So did he. Thanks to his own guts and determination plus the grit and determination and loyalty of his quite remarkable wife Anne, Cecil once again found himself in office.

But still a candidate for the succession? I remember meeting Margaret Thatcher in 10 Downing Street on the afternoon of 9 April 1986. There were just the two of us. And at that time poor Cecil was still out in the cold.

We had been discussing Sir Keith Joseph and the fact that he would soon have to be replaced. Margaret did not want to lose him from the Cabinet. She wanted to keep him as Minister without Portfolio even if that meant he would receive no pay.

'He has given this country great service,' she said. 'He is the only one who really thinks the same way as I do.'

The Prime Minster then said something quite unexpected. 'But Cecil Parkinson is going to stand again and if he wins his seat in the next election then I think he should come back to the Cabinet. He thinks so very much the same way as I do and he is a source of great strength.'

I agreed. But when I pointed out that Parkinson was still absolutely obsessed with the Sara Keays affair and endlessly talked about it the Prime Minister looked quite surprised.

And when eight months later I again had a private session with the Prime Minister at 10 Downing Street, on 19 December 1986, I asked her why Parkinson had come out in support of Jim Prior and GEC in favour of continuing with Nimrod as opposed to buying the Boeing AWACS system.

Margaret held up her hands and arched her eyebrows in that typical fashion of hers.

'Because Radlett is in his constituency. And there is a big GEC factory at Radlett.' She added in exasperation, 'I wouldn't have let it interfere with me if it had been in my constituency.'

At that meeting, incidentally, we discussed Ronald Reagan and whether he could recover from the Iran-Contra scandal. It was a question she had obviously been thinking about a lot herself.

'When I went to see him after the Reykjavik Conference he looked amazingly fit,' she said. 'And you know what a disaster the Reykjavik Conference nearly was for us. It's just no good going to conferences like that unprepared. Reagan was expecting just an informal chat and Gorbachev had a complete programme all ready to discuss. We were on the very brink of giving up all nuclear weapons in Europe and do you know who saved us? Gorbachev himself. He was foolish enough to demand that the Americans abandon the Star Wars project as well. If he hadn't done that Reagan would have signed an agreement. So I had to see the President and get things put right so that the same thing could never happen again.'

'But,' I persisted, 'isn't the present crisis over the arms sales to Iran getting him down?'

'There are times when he looks so creased and worn and suddenly old,' she said. 'And he was shattered by the opinion polls which showed that only 40 per cent of the American people believed him. But that's improving, it's now over 50 per cent and so he will be feeling happier about that. But you know, John, he is an honest man. He genuinely wants to rid the world of nuclear war. And he thinks that communism is now in the dustbin. But it's not.'

Two things remain in my mind from that meeting. The first is that without Ronald Reagan and Margaret Thatcher communism would not now be in the dustbin. And that I was aware during our enormously relaxed and friendly chat that the Prime Minister was wearing a split skirt and there was just a suspicion or flash of leg.

Which leads me to ponder the perennial question: Can a leopard ever change its spots? For I cannot get out of my mind what Lord King, the Chairman of British Airways, once said to me: 'Super chap, Cecil. But do you know it's amazing – he can't come into my office without telling one of my secretaries how beautiful she is or how much he admires her hair or her dress.'

Someone else whom I first got to know at this time was the man to whom Harold Wilson, when he was Prime Minister and when trade union power and political muscle seemed to be laying down the law to the government, said 'take your tanks off my lawn, Hugh'. For Hugh Scanlon was one of the two most powerful trade union figures in Britain at that time. The other was Jack Jones of the Transport and General Workers' Union. The socialists had sent them both to the House of Lords and I had written many leaders attacking the pair of them.

I met Hugh Scanlon for the first time in September 1984 and took an immediate and instinctive liking to him. He was a member of our team in the Harry Secombe Pro-Am Golf Classic at Effingham. He was accompanied by his wife, Nora, who trudged all the way round the course with him. It took us the best part of five and half hours to complete the round.

Nora was delightful and their marriage was clearly a very happy one. I can understand why. Scanlon was gentle, modest and unassuming. He was also quite clearly terrified of driving from the first tee in front of a reasonably sized crowd. He scuffed the ball about fifty yards along the ground. But there was a warmth about him that was quite captivating. I asked him if he had retired completely or if he were still undertaking some part-time consultative jobs. No, he replied, he had retired completely. And he seldom went to the House of Lords except when there was a debate in which he had some expertise.

'What's the point of going there?' he asked me. 'When you are never going to achieve anything no matter what you say since everyone's mind is already made up.'

Some years earlier the *Sunday Express* had published a story about Scanlon's retirement on the Isle of Thanet at Broadstairs and of how a cliff was crumbling in front of the house and threatening it. 'When you published that story,' he said to me, 'I received a hundred letters, all from people expressing the hope that I might be in the house when it went over the cliff.'

Neither he nor his wife flaunted their titles. But he told me about the wife of Sir John Boyd, the General Secretary of the engineering union. Apparently Boyd's wife seldom used her title either, but once when trying to get an appointment at a hairdressing salon and knowing that the place was habitually overbooked she decided to try to secure a reservation by telephone. 'This is Lady Boyd,' she had announced. 'Could I have an appointment for tomorrow morning, please?' To which the girl at the other end said, 'Lady Boyd? Is that all one word?'

Later the same month Scanlon brought his wife to lunch with me at the Howard Hotel. They had come up specially, I afterwards discovered, from Broadstairs. He had no other engagement in London, he had a pretty small pension and the train fares must have made quite a dent in his pocket-book.

They had taken an earlier train than had originally been planned and were waiting in the foyer of the hotel when I arrived. I found myself once again, as on the first occasion when I had met him on the golf course, warming to him. He was so modest and his wife so clearly adored him.

They told me about their grandchildren. They had three. I asked what their son-in-law did. Scanlon looked at his wife as if to ask 'shall we tell him?' and received a nod. Then he explained to me that his daughter had married a Libyan.

'Not a white Libyan, you understand,' he added. 'It upset us a little at first. We have always both of us taken such a strong view about equality of the races, but even so it comes as a bit of a shock when it is your own daughter who is marrying a coloured man. But they are very happy and they have this lovely child whom we adore. There was a time when it was not going too well. They were staying with us rent-free and the husband treated her just as he would a wife back in Libya. He kept coming and going at all hours just as he pleased. I had to take him aside and have a talk with him. "You can't treat my daughter like this. You are in England now and you have to behave like an English husband." And to his credit he took heed of what I said.'

He also told me about his own background and that he had been born in Australia but had only stayed there until he was two years old. 'My father,' he said 'was an upholsterer, and he went to Australia to make his fortune. But like so many of my family the demon drink got him and he died there. My mother came back with the children to England.' He had no idea where his father was buried. He had tried once while visiting

Melbourne in Australia to find out some facts, but had gone to the wrong place and discovered nothing.

After a time, and once we were all relaxed, Scanlon made it clear to me exactly why he had agreed to make the journey to London. He told me he had an idea which he thought could end Arthur Scargill's coal strike. He explained it to me. His idea was that those pits which still had coal but which could not be economically mined should be mothballed. This would save coal for any future emergency in which we needed it and at the same time would take Arthur Scargill off the hook.

But, alas, although I did not say so to Scanlon I knew that there was little chance of Arthur Scargill getting off a hook of any kind. For a few days before, on 19 September, I had had an afternoon session at 10 Downing Street with the Prime Minister.

When I arrived, Bernard Ingham had come downstairs to meet me and warned me not to come too near since he had a chest cold which he could not get rid of. It activated his asthma, he explained. As we climbed the one flight of stairs to the Prime Minister's sitting-room he was panting quite heavily. He did not seem a very fit man.

I was slightly surprised to find that Margaret Thatcher's Press Secretary clearly intended to sit in on the discussion. And that equally clearly she expected him to do so. It was evident that Ingham was now very much part of the inner Cabinet. He intervened from time to time in our talk and it was obvious from the way the Prime Minister listened to what he had to say that she respected his judgement.

She looked remarkably calm and free from strain. That morning she had been on the Jimmy Young show and had stated unequivocally that she would never surrender to the miners and that no matter how long the strike lasted she was still intent that uneconomic pits should be closed.

I remarked that the government's strategy so far had been faultless. They had succeeded in isolating Scargill, they had also succeeded in making it manifest that what he sought was not so much better conditions for the miners as a revolution against elected authority.

Margaret nodded vigorously in agreement.

But, I went on, her real strategy had been that in time the striking miners would see the pointlessness of continuing to follow a man who sought to use them for his own political ends, and would return to work. But what if they didn't? What if through either loyalty to the NUM or because of intimidation they remained on strike, what would she do then? I pointed out that some miners and their families were actually beginning to enjoy the hardship and the sense of belonging to a besieged community.

'And how do you plan to cope with that, Prime Minister?' I asked. But from her reply it was quite clear that at that time she had no plans. Her entire policy, I realised, was based on the premise that in time the striking miners just had to see the futility of their action and the uneconomic reality of keeping open pits which were costing the country £1.3 billion a year. She was proved right, too. Just as she knew the threat Arthur Scargill posed to elected government in this country.

And then of the politicians I got to know at this time there was Norman Tebbit. And Norman Tebbit is not the sort of person to whom one warms easily. He is prickly and takes offence perhaps a shade too quickly. Nor is that just the aftermath of the Brighton bombing. He has always been that way.

In 1982, when I knew him only slightly, I invited him to be guest of honour at the Sunday Express Boat Show luncheon. On the Sunday the week before the luncheon Cross-Bencher had written what was meant to be a seasonable and funny paragraph about how even Christmas presented problems for MPs and raised the question as to how they should react if, as sometimes happens, a constituent arrives on their doorstep with some minor problem slap in the middle of their Christmas dinner.

The Cross-Bencher of that time, Henry Macrory, had written:

I report the words of the Employment Secretary Mr Norman Tebbit when once asked this vexing question.

'Well,' replied Mr Tebbit sweetly, 'naturally I'd leave the dinner table. Naturally I'd go to the front door to see him.'

And then?

'And then I'd ram the Christmas pudding in his face.'

There cannot have been many who took that paragraph as a serious statement of Mr Tebbit's intentions. It never even occurred to me that he could take offence. But he did. The following Tuesday he was on the phone to me. He wanted a complete retraction of the paragraph in the next Sunday's paper and unless he got one he would not be coming to the Boat Show luncheon.

In vain I tried to point out to him that it had been evident to everyone that the paragraph had been light-hearted. He simply kept on repeating that it was going to do him harm in his constituency. Finally I lost my cool. 'Right,' I said. 'I will print a retraction and this is what it will say: "Last Sunday we published a paragraph suggesting that Mr Norman Tebbit might throw the Christmas pudding in the face of any constituent unreasonable enough to bother him at home with a minor problem on Christmas Day. Mr Tebbit asks us to make clear that even on Christmas Day he will be happy to see any constituent at his home." ' There was a silence at the other end of the phone before he said, 'OK. You win, John.'

From that time onwards I knew that Norman Tebbit always had to be handled with care. He was so touchy, especially about having any interference with his authority. That was where things started to go wrong between him and the Prime Minister. There was never any question of his being disloyal to Margaret Thatcher. He believed and believes still in the Thatcher revolution, and after all why shouldn't he? He was one of its founders. But when in office he bitterly resented the Prime Minister seeking advice from outsiders over aspects of policy for which he had responsibility. It came to a head during the 1987 general election campaign over which as Party Chairman he was in charge.

The trouble started before the election when the Prime Minister suggested to Cecil Parkinson the possibility of her having a little private group around her on whom she could call for advice on publicity during the campaign. She had in mind people like Gordon Reece, Tim Bell and Parkinson himself. It is possible that my name was also mentioned. Parkinson's reaction was that he would do anything to help but he added, 'Have you cleared this with Norman?' The Prime Minister replied that she had not but that she would. It was the last anyone heard of the idea. Indeed as Parkinson said to me afterwards, 'When I wanted to see Margaret I had to sneak in. Tebbit can't bear anyone near her.'

I was not the only one at the time to believe that the Tory campaign of 1987 started disastrously. I watched the first week in mounting horror. While Kinnock was being brilliantly and movingly presented in skilled tear-jerking fashion, all the Tories seemed to be arguing about was what Tebbit himself had said about the unemployment figures at the time of the previous election.

After the election David Owen told me that we need not have worried, that the SDP figures showed that the Kinnock campaign was having no effect on marginal voters. But that was not how it seemed at the time. The Prime Minister clearly felt something had to be done and she did it by, in effect, taking over the campaign herself. It is now history that after the victory Tebbit announced that he did not want to be considered for further high office or to remain in the Cabinet. But it would be quite wrong to imagine that he did so out of pique.

His wife's health and his own lack of money were prime factors. His paralysed wife needs constant nursing attention and he has never had a chance to earn big money or to amass capital. The last time I lunched with him, in March 1988, there was a touch of bitterness in his voice about the low salaries paid to ministers, but since then he has not done too badly for himself. He has a clutch of directorships – British Telecom, Sears Holdings, BET, Blue Arrow and JCB. One of the companies provides him with a car and driver. He sold the serial rights of his book, *Upwardly Mobile*, to the *Daily Mail* for more than £90,000. One report suggests that he could be getting nearly £100,000 a year for his programme with the Labour MP Austen Mitchell on Sky Television. He would be getting about £100,000 for his column in the *Sunday Express* and in addition he writes for the *Times*.

He was quite frank about his future. There was now no job he wanted in politics except the job of prime minister. But, as he pointed out, he would be over sixty by the time of the next general election. 'My only chance, John, is if something goes wrong. I mean if anything happened to Margaret.' I said I thought that was unlikely. 'But John, crises come from nowhere. Look at Westland. Look at the Stock Market.'

'Is there anything outside politics that would tempt you?' I asked him. Clearly there was. For he remarked that he hoped John King of British Airways would carry on long enough to allow him to keep his options open.

And of the other contenders for the prime ministership? Geoffrey Howe, he thought, would be quite a good PM but is not capable of winning an election. And that Kenneth Baker would be capable of winning an election but would make a lousy PM. And his dislike of Lord Young showed. He talked scathingly of the Prime Minister's 'gurus of the week' and said that it must have been on the advice of such a guru that Marmaduke Hussey ever got the job of Chairman of the BBC. The way in which Margaret Thatcher clearly lost faith in his running the 1987 election still rankled with him.

Yet although I found it difficult that day and still do to warm to him, I suspect that Norman Tebbit really does have a deep sense of purpose and genuinely and passionately believes in the revolution which he and Margaret Thatcher started. Just one thing, apart from his lack of a sense of humour, troubles me about him. In the book he sold for so much money he revealed to the world that long before the Brighton bombing his wife had twice been committed to mental hospitals. I have always wondered why he chose to make that fact public. I also wonder why, the fragile state of his wife's mental health having been revealed, he chose to push her in a wheelchair in front of the TV cameras past the scene of the bombing when the Tory Conference next returned to Brighton.

Will Norman's ambitions towards British Airways ever be realised? Lord King threw a fascinating light on that four months later. Even though, thanks partly to my friendship with Sir Adam Thomson and support for British Caledonian, I had always adopted a rather hostile attitude towards John King. And I had other reasons for my antagonism. I did not like the way he had treated Don Perry whom he had taken from the *Sunday Express* to be his PR man and then had later dumped. Nor did I care over much for his social climbing. He is the only man I have seen kiss Princess Diana on both cheeks in public.

But I warmed to him when we met for lunch and found myself wondering whether I had misjudged him. He has the quick brain and sharpness of eye for detail which would have taken him to the top as a newspaper reporter.

He told me how one of his problems when he took over British Airways was the huge list of former directors and their wives entitled to free travel. One of the names on the list was a Lady Douglas.

'Who is she?' King had demanded of an aide. And was informed that she was the widow of Sholto Douglas, the wartime air chief who had been chairman many moons previously. 'But my God,' said King, 'she must be a very old lady by now.' The aide replied, 'Oh no, Sir. Sholto Douglas re-married late in life a very young lady.' King scored her name off the free list.

One of the ex-directors still on the list was Kenneth Keith. One day King received a signal from New York that Lord Keith was very, very upset because he had been down-graded first of all from first class to cabin class and then from cabin class to economy because the aircraft was full of paying passengers. It was suggested that the New York staff who had treated him in this way should be disciplined. King sent a signal to New York saying that instead he thought the staff should be complimented. They had behaved with absolute correctness. That signal became widely talked about among British Airways staff and, King believed, changed the perception of many of them as to what he was really like.

Keith's wife afterwards telephoned King and said, 'Kenneth has had an awful flight. Do you know he was sandwiched in economy between a Pakistani and a baby? Do you know what it is like to travel economy?'

'I wouldn't know,' replied King. 'I have never travelled economy. But tell me, did the Pakistani and the baby mind Kenneth sitting between them?'

King also told me of an interesting discussion he had had

with Margaret Thatcher in Downing Street. They were alone and she asked him what he thought of Sir Jeffrey Sterling of P & O. Didn't he, she asked King, have tremendous ability? King knew immediately that this meant Sterling must be being considered for a top job. So he reflected carefully before replying, 'If I may say so, Prime Minister, you ought to go out more into the country, into the shires, when you are looking for people to promote. At the moment there is a feeling that you concentrate too much in selecting your advisers from North-west London.'

'What do you mean? Do you mean because they are Jews?'

'I didn't say that,' King replied. 'You did.'

But it was what King said as we made to leave the lunch table that really surprised me. For he gave me the impression that the job he would really like in the whole world is Norman Tebbit's old job as Chairman of the Tory Party.

Even as Deputy Chairman of the Conservative Party Jeffrey Archer was never a favourite of mine. My distrust stemmed from a lunch he gave at his penthouse flat overlooking the Thames at Vauxhall. There were about sixteen people at the table. Since Archer lived alone in London the meal had been cooked and was served by one of those debs on wheels organisations.

Richard Marsh, now Lord Marsh, was one of the guests and was sitting close to both me and the host. During lunch Marsh began to talk about a book which David Jacobs had written and had been serialised in the *Daily Mail*. Jacobs' wife, who had died in the same car crash in Spain as Marsh's wife, figured largely in the book. Jacobs' dead wife had been an only child. Marsh was unhappy that her mother had not even seen the book until it was too late to change anything.

I went back to the office and forgot about the conversation entirely. But later that week on the Friday when I was reading the copy for Lady Olga Maitland's Diary, I suddenly found myself reading an account of the lunch and a word-by-word report of what Dick Marsh had said. I was surprised by its accuracy but assumed that the Diary staff must have had a tip-off from one of the other guests at the lunch.

The next Tuesday morning I had Jeffrey Archer on the

telephone bellowing his head off at me. Didn't I realise that it had been a private lunch and that conversations at lunches of that type were sacred? He went on in this vein for several minutes until I lost my temper and gave him an earful in return.

I was very upset at his attack on me. As a result I did something I have rarely done. I went to the Town Talk desk and said, 'I rarely ask this, but I would like to know the source of your item about Dick Marsh and David Jacobs last week.'

They gave me the name of the informant. I was amazed because I realised that Jeffrey Archer knew this person very very well indeed. I was convinced that Archer had telephoned me possibly to deflect the spotlight from falling on the real inform-ant. Ever since then, I decided that I would use a pair of very long tongs in my dealings with Mr Archer.

The Foreign Secretary in Jim Callaghan's government of the 1970s was a man who at the time I thoroughly detested. Dr David Owen. I disliked everything about him, from the way he tossed his hair to his policies on Africa.

But I warmed to him when he lost his temper when a student threw an egg at him while he was addressing a university meeting. He leapt from the platform and chased the student out of the hall. I warmed to him even further when he broke away from the Labour Party and set up the SDP.

I still had not met him at that time but I began to commission articles from him for the *Sunday Express*. There was one which arrived on my desk on a Saturday morning which I thought to be a poor, disjointed effort. I rang and told him so in no uncertain terms. I said I was going to publish it since it had already been advertised but that it did neither him nor the *Sunday Express* any good if he submitted articles into which insufficient effort had been put. I even voiced my suspicion that it might have been written by one of the hacks at SDP Headquarters.

He bristled. He told me that he had written every word himself and that he had put a great deal of effort into it. What exactly was wrong with it? I told him. He calmed down and the upshot was that he telephoned through a rewritten and much better article.

I then started to lunch occasionally with him and to my

surprise found that I liked him. At one of our meetings he had as a starter a seafood cocktail. The next day he telephoned me and asked, 'Were you all right after lunch yesterday?' I replied that I had been absolutely fine. He explained that he had been as sick as a dog.

I also found that David Owen was a fine raconteur. Over lunch one day at the White Tower he told me the story behind his appointment when Foreign Secretary of Peter Jay as British Ambassador to Washington. He had already decided that the then Ambassador, Sir Peter Ramsbotham, had to go – partly because he did not fit into the Washington scene and partly because James Callaghan could not stand the sight of him. In fact on one visit to Washington with Owen, Callaghan refused to stay in the Embassy rather than have anything to do with the Ambassador.

So Owen racked his brain to find a successor. Peter Jay seemed to him to be the outstanding candidate. He was young, vigorous, personable and had a first-class intellect. He raised the possibility of sending Jay with Sir Michael Palliser, the Permanent Under-Secretary at the FO. Palliser pointed out the political difficulties and said that inevitably there would be a charge of nepotism.

Owen then sat down and wrote a hand-written letter to the Prime Minister saying that he'd thought long and hard about the appointment and that one name kept coming back to his mind. The name of Peter Jay. He knew that the charge of nepotism would be brought but he still thought the appointment would be the right one. What did the Prime Minister think?

For two weeks he received not a word from the Prime Minister. But he did notice at Cabinet meetings that when Callaghan pulled a diary out of his pocket there, inside the diary, was Owen's letter concerning Jay. After three weeks Callaghan took him aside and said, 'Providing it is absolutely clear that it is your own judgement and your own appointment I cannot stand in the way.'

And when my telephone rang on my last day as Editor of the *Sunday Express*, on 19 July 1986, I received a pretty fine gesture from a man whom I had savaged so often in the past.

'I believe this is your last day as Editor,' David Owen said to me. 'I just want to tell you as an old butt of yours how much I admire your achievement. It has been quite magnificent. No one has ever done anything like it before and I congratulate you.'

Later that year, with Parliament in turmoil over the government's attempt in an Australian court to prevent publication of *Spycatcher* by the former MI5 man Peter Wright, and with the Attorney-General himself right in the middle of the rumpus, I had not expected that Sir Michael Havers would be free to lunch at such short notice as I offered. But he was. My secretary telephoned him on 2 December 1986 and we lunched at the Howard Hotel the next day.

I found him to be an interesting man but with more than his share of troubles. And not only political ones. For Havers is a diabetic and in the last year had undergone open-heart surgery. He was also skint, having given up his practice at the Bar to become shadow Attorney-General when the Tories were still in Opposition. The result was that he had never made the big money that his contemporaries had. Including his MP's salary, he told me that his total income was £40,000 a year. Not a great deal for a man of his style. And the most frightening thing of all was that he had no pension.

That was why Havers had always been so desperately keen to succeed Quintin Hogg as Lord Chancellor. A post which carries with it a pension irrespective of length of service of something like £50,000 a year. I knew that Margaret Thatcher had promised him the job. For she had herself told me so during a session with her at 10 Downing Street in September 1984.

'I love Quintin,' she had said, 'but you know he is getting old. There are still times when he is marvellous. But there are other times when his age is showing.'

I agreed and added, 'Who would you appoint in his place? Is there anyone of sufficient stature?'

'John,' she had replied, 'you and I are old friends. So I have to be honest with you. I could not possibly go beyond Michael Havers.'

But that was two years previously and the promise could always be broken and the Lord Chancellorship go up in smoke if

Havers did anything to upset the Prime Minister. And the Prime Minister was terrified of a by-election in his Wimbledon constituency and had told Havers that he must stay in the Commons until the next election.

That was why I found his stand over the *Spycatcher* affair so courageous. For the head of the Home Civil Service, Sir Robert Armstrong, had testified in open court that it had been on the advice of the Attorney-General that no action had been taken to prevent publication of *Their Trade Is Treachery*, Chapman Pincher's spy book to which Peter Wright had contributed most of the information before going on to publish his own.

And that was a lie. Michael Havers had never been consulted. It would have been easier for him to go along with the lie than risk confrontation with the Prime Minister. Yet confrontation was exactly what he chose and as a result Armstrong had publicly to correct the evidence he had previously given.

Havers told me he was still sure that he would get the Lord Chancellorship. But he was taking other precautions too, he said. He hoped that he had directorships arranged with Hanson Trust and Charles Forte if anything should go wrong. He also planned to write a book and wondered whether my daughter Penelope might be interested in working with him on it.

'I would also do one or two big cases a year at the Bar,' he added. 'I reckon all in all I could make as much as £200,000 a year.'

But even so there would be no pension. Havers did not look a fit man that day. Nor of course was he. But he had got guts. 'My doctors say I'll be all right as long as I avoid stress,' he said as we parted. And he laughed. Poor Michael. For while after the general election of 1987 he won both the Lord Chancellorship and the pension he so desperately wanted there were not to be too many laughs in his life thereafter.

I have often pondered over Michael Havers' courageous stand over the Chapman Pincher book. For when Margaret Thatcher's government took action in Australia to prevent the publication of *Spycatcher* and the giving away of secrets of the British Intelligence Services, a key point of Wright's defence was that logically the government could not or should not seek to ban

319

Wright's book when it had failed to take action to ban Pincher's book some five years previously and when Pincher's book had been written in collaboration with Wright.

Why then had the government not sought to stop Pincher's book and why had Havers as the government's law officer not been consulted? What if the government had obtained proofs of *Their Trade Is Treachery* illegally, by theft, and therefore could not possibly call on the law officer to advise them?

I don't believe the government ever did get copies of the Pincher book by theft. Nor did William Armstrong, the Managing Director of Sidgwick & Jackson, Chapman Pincher's British publishers. Nor is there the slightest doubt in my mind as to how the government did obtain proofs of the book. Sidgwick & Jackson at that time was owned by Lord Forte. I am absolutely convinced that Lord Forte, who was a personal friend of Mrs Thatcher, would never have published the book if he had thought it would offend her. It is my guess that he sought Mrs Thatcher's approval, told her what he was doing and showed her the proofs.

Ever since the moment when as a young, but not that young, MP he picked up the Mace in the House of Commons and waved it about his head, I wrote off Michael Heseltine as a possible prime minister. I still do so today. The British people may occasionally act daft but never so daft that they would want to put into a position of absolute power someone who in a moment of crisis, of exaltation or even of anger might part company with his trolley.

I was strengthened in my view when Heseltine as Minister of Defence appeared on that extraordinary occasion at RAF Molesworth dressed in a flak jacket. But the clincher was surely when he resigned over the Westland issue and in such a dramatically impulsive way that he came perilously damned close to bringing the whole government down with him. And yet when you look back on it now, what was it all about? The fact is that the whole God-damned issue didn't matter a row of beans. It was on the part of Heseltine just another massive misjudgement and another lightning-flash loss of control in a moment of temper.

Am I being unfair? Ever since his resignation Heseltine has spent vast amounts of money touring the country, speaking to local assocations, building up his popularity in the regions, being careful never to be too openly critical of the Prime Minister but always letting it be known just the same that in many respects of policy he would have acted differently and that he will always be available when a change is necessary. But I doubt very much, and no matter what vast amounts of his fortune he pours into the campaign, that he will ever lose his Tarzan image.

I had an interesting insight into how Michael Heseltine operated when he was Minister of Defence when on 12 March 1987 I was invited by the Fleet Street Royal Navy Association, an organisation which I had not even known existed, to lunch with them at the Presscala Club in order to say farewell to their retiring President, Vice-Admiral Sir Ernle Pope, and to say hello to his successor, Vice-Admiral Sir Desmond Cassidi.

Admiral Cassidi sat on my right-hand side during lunch. He was a little reticent to begin with until he learned that both he and I had been in the Fleet Air Arm as pilots. Then he began to thaw. Finally he told me how on his last day as Second Sea Lord he had a private meeting – to which as Second Sea Lord he was entitled – with the Minister of Defence.

He arrived at Admiralty House in good time for his 9.30 a.m. appointment and was just a little bit annoyed when at 9.45 a.m. a secretary, rubbing his hands in sorrow, explained that the Minister was very busy and that it might be a little time before he was able to see the Admiral. So it was indeed.

When finally Cassidi was shown into Heseltine's room, Heseltine did not even look up or invite him to take a seat.

'I'm sorry,' he said, 'but I'm already late for another appointment.'

Cassidi – and he had the air of a man who tells the truth – told me that he replied, 'I'm sorry about that Minister, but on my last day I'm exercising my statutory right to give you my views on what is wrong with the Service.' And he continued to do so for the next fifteen minutes.

Need I add that Admiral Cassidi did not like Michael Heseltine. 'How,' he asked me, 'could anyone ever regard him as a possible Prime Minister of Britain or a possible successor to Margaret Thatcher?'

When I first started in Fleet Street the newspaper proprietors belonged to another world from the rest of us. They actually owned their newspapers and they lived and travelled like royalty. In every capital city of the world they had a news bureau staffed with people ready to attend their every whim whenever they paid a state visit, in much the same way as a monarch had an embassy. In London Lord Northcliffe described the Press Club as 'the servants' hall' and that is precisely what it was.

Now only the empire of Lord Northcliffe, whose brother was once offered the crown of Hungary, survives. That it has done so is almost entirely due to the fact that the present member of the Harmsworth family in charge, Vere Lord Rothermere, is a dedicated newspaperman who actually seems to care passionately not only for the *Daily Mail* and its sister papers but also for the people who work on them. One of his journalists, Peter McKay, once said to me of him, 'He is the only man left in London with a pre-war sense of honour.'

The rest of the great families have disappeared like puffs of smoke, extinguished by escalating costs, old-fashioned technology and the rapacious demands of a Luddite machine-room workforce. The Kemsleys have gone, but then who even remembers the Kemsleys? Brave Max Aitken, crippled by illness, sold the entire Beaverbrook empire, including the *Evening Standard*, for just twelve and a half million pounds which today might be the going rate for a chain of six fish-and-chip shops. Michael Berry, Lord Hartwell, who was himself a brilliant journalist and who cared so much for the *Telegraph* group, lost control of his birthright to the Canadian financier Conrad Black for just £15 million.

Now, as I say, only Vere Harmsworth survives. Happily he seems to be doing so in astoundingly profitable fashion. When we met in his office on Tuesday 3 October 1989 he had until then always represented to me the competition. He was the owner of the *Daily Mail* group. I had worked most of my life for the *Daily Express* group. And by an odd coincidence the number of his room was 601, the number of the RAF Squadron in which Max Aitken had fought during the Battle of Britain.

We travelled in his car to the Berkeley Hotel. On the way he explained that he was having to go to Tunbridge Wells that afternoon to attend the funeral of the widow of his late Managing Director, Mick Shields. He had a black tie in an envelope ready to put on after lunch.

And he told me an amazing story. The night after Mick Shields's death he had had a vivid dream in which Mick Shields appeared and kept saying to him, 'Tell Jacqueline she must see her doctor.' All through the night in his dream Mick Shields kept saying to him, 'You won't forget. Jackie is in danger. She must see her doctor.'

In the morning Vere Harmsworth had wondered what on earth to do. It seemed crazy to take a dream seriously. So should he ignore it? Finally he had comprised and telephoned a mutual friend of Mrs Shields and had diffidently explained to her his extraordinary dream. The friend had immediately said, 'But I know the name of that doctor. He is the doctor Jackie went to when she had cancer some years ago. I think I had better telephone her.'

And she did. And Jackie went to see the doctor and found that her cancer which everyone thought was cured had come back again. It was an incredible story. There was no doubt in my mind that Vere Harmsworth was speaking in earnest seriousness.

When we arrived at the Berkeley Hotel we had the most civilised and fascinating lunch. I liked everything about him and we talked about many things. And then at the end of the lunch he said, 'Well, I suppose we had better go if I am going to get to Tunbridge Wells in time for the funeral.' Then as we walked out of the hotel into the sunshine Vere asked me to come and write for the *Mail*.

I remember every word of my reply. 'You and I are almost the last of our era,' I said. 'I took Beaverbrook's shilling and fought all my life for the Montagues. It seems strange to think that I should now want to join the Capulets. But I do. For the old battle is finished. The *Sunday Express* is no longer the paper I knew and loved. It is in completely different hands and I feel almost a stranger there.'

'I know,' said Vere. 'That's why I want you to join us.'

But what of the new men? Conrad Black I have met only once and it would be unfair to offer judgement on that one lunchtime meeting. But if I were forced to, my thumbs would go firmly down.

As for Robert Maxwell, I have known him for many years although never as an intimate. He has enormous charisma. As he enters a room you feel his presence before you even see him. But work for him? I would rather brush the teeth of a tiger. There is also the question which is never going to go away, the question as to the true ownership of the Liechtenstein-based Pergamon Holding Foundation which ultimately controls the shares of the *Daily Mirror*.

But Rupert Murdoch? Rupert is different. I have often lambasted the conduct of some of his tabloids like the *Sun* and the *News of the World*. But he has this in common with Vere Harmsworth. He may be a great financier but far more important than that he is a newspaperman who understands newspapers. There is no job on a newspaper he cannot do himself, from writing the lead story to selling a full-page advertisement.

He is also so personally unostentatious. There was the time when accompanied by his then chief executive, Alick Mackay, he arrived at the Savoy Grill for lunch with the sole of one shoe separated from the upper. Alick persuaded him to go in to the nearby Savoy Taylors Guild in search of a new pair of shoes but when Rupert discovered the price of the shoes he asked instead for a rubber band to bind sole and upper temporarily together. I remember a time when he met me at the same hotel and in pouring rain arrived by bus. He went back the same way too. There cannot be too much wrong with a man like that.

On another occasion I arrived late for a lunch with Rupert because I had to see Victor Matthews before leaving. Our conversation had lasted rather longer than I had expected. Indeed when I told Victor that I was lunching with Murdoch his eyebrows raised a little.

'I don't trust that man,' Victor said to me. 'I don't know what he's up to.'

I sensed a slight disapproval on his part that I was meeting

Murdoch at all. I explained to him that I had known Rupert for many years and that I thought Victor was judging him perhaps a little harshly. And that my infrequent meetings with Rupert were entirely social and they took place because I liked him. I pointed out to Victor that over all the years I had known Rupert, I had never heard him speak ill of anyone on the *Express*, least of all Victor.

He reflected for a moment and then said to me, 'Would you ask him a question. The other day Robert Holmes à Court said to me that Rupert had no time for me and had described me as a sewer rat. Would you find out if Rupert actually said that?'

I replied that I would ask the question, but I would bet him any money that Rupert had never said anything of the kind.

When I arrived late at the White Tower, Rupert – and I found this quite extraordinary – was almost in a nervous state. He had arrived ten minutes earlier and had thought that perhaps he had the date confused. I explained to him why I was late and asked the question straight away. Had he called Victor Matthews 'a sewer rat'? He was genuinely and utterly astounded.

'I have not even spoken to Holmes à Court in eighteen months,' he replied, 'and I don't regard him highly. I never said that about Victor Matthews.'

I suggested to him that in that case he might telephone Victor and tell him so.

We had a simple but vastly enjoyable lunch, with a bottle of house wine at my insistence instead of the lavish wine which he wanted to order from the list. I reflected that the more I saw of Rupert Murdoch, the more I liked him. There was not the slightest doubt in my mind that he was on the side of good, that his enemies were the enemies of democracy and that he was in newspapers not for the benefits which come from great wealth or indeed from the power which is attached to newspaper ownership. But simply from a driving urge to fight and win the battle against communism.

When I got back to the office, I rang Victor to tell him the answer to his question. But he already knew. Rupert had already been on the telephone and I was absolutely aware from Victor's attitude that he was taking a new and much better view of Rupert Murdoch.

Under the chairmanship of Victor Matthews, it was a joy to be a member of the board of Fleet Newspapers. It was a small board – just seven of us. There was no malice, no back-biting. We were all friends. And the company was prospering mightily.

Then on 22 June 1984 came a bombshell.

The company controlled by Robert Holmes à Court, ACC, advised Fleet that it had sold its shareholding in Fleet to Robert Maxwell. Later that day Lord Matthews saw Maxwell who told him that he would like to bid for Fleet but did not want a contested situation. But Maxwell was soon to disappear from the scene. On 13 July it was announced that he had succeeded in purchasing Mirror Group Newspapers which effectively prevented him from bidding for Fleet.

On 15 January of the following year Maxwell phoned the Fleet Managing Director, Iain Irvine, to tell him that he had sold his shares in Fleet to United Newspapers. And on 25 March United issued an announcement stating that it was seeking consent under the Fair Trading Act to proceed with a bid for Fleet. There followed a summer of tension while the Monopolies & Mergers Commission considered the United bid.

The climax came on 14 October. I had been playing golf at Walton Heath. When I came into the clubhouse after my round I was told there was an urgent message for me. My presence was required at a Fleet board meeting in London. I arrived at the meeting to find my fellow directors despondent. United had made a revised offer for Fleet and institutions had started rushing to take it. The trend was such that a surrender was inevitable. We decided to issue an announcement containing the board's recommendation to shareholders to accept the United offer.

A sad Victor Matthews left his office in Fleet Street that afternoon taking with him all the personal pictures and photographs which had adorned his walls.

Shortly afterwards I was summoned to the presence of the man who now controlled the newspaper of which I had been

Editor for more than thirty years. David Stevens. He told me that he would like me to continue as Editor of the *Sunday Express*. This I did for a further two years. In that time I cannot fault the way in which he treated me.

I was not quite so happy about the way he treated other people. He roared with laughter when he told me how when he had invited Neil Kinnock to come to lunch in the City and at the luncheon table he had specially arranged for Kinnock to be given a seat which was lower than everyone else's. I did not join in the laughter. There were other things I did not like. I did not like the treatment accorded a front hall commissionaire who failed to recognise the new Chairman and stand to attention when he entered the building. I did not like, either, the way Stevens treated Ron Hall who at that time was the Editor of the *Sunday Express* Colour Magazine.

Hall was summoned to attend a meeting in the Chairman's office on the third floor. There were about twelve other people present, including myself. Some of the others were in rank subordinate to Hall. I had no clear idea what the meeting was about but a nervous tic on the Chairman's left cheek made me apprehensive. Rightly. He proceeded to rubbish the magazine and Hall's editorship of it in a way which made it clearly impossible for Hall to continue in the job. It was a less than agreeable way in which to treat a distinguished journalist.

But Stevens was considerate enough to me and when the time came for me to move on as Editor he gave me a contract to stay on at my old salary as a columnist. He did not consult me about the choice of successor to me as Editor. But then I understood that. I would have chosen someone who would have shared my views about the future of the paper whereas he clearly wanted someone who would take the *Sunday Express* along different lines. But he did keep me fully informed about the names of the candidates being interviewed. And if I had been antagonistic to the final choice of Robin Esser I would have left the paper there and then.

It was also agreed that I would move out of the Express building in Fleet Street and take a new office in the headquarters of United Newspapers in Tudor Street, the home of *Punch* magazine. I found the new surroundings delightful. After the rush and frenetic activity of the Express building, walking into the United Newspapers office each morning was like entering a cathedral of calm and tranquillity. Yet the bustle of Fleet Street was practically on the doorstep. During the next three years David Stevens was a frequent visitor to my office. But he never sought to interfere with my column, just as he had never sought to interfere when I was the Editor of the newspaper.

Then one Saturday – 18 February 1989 – an enormous personal tragedy happened to David Stevens.

That night at 5.15 p.m. I wanted to speak to him and telephoned his home number at Chesham Mews. His wife Melissa answered. 'John,' she said, 'do you mind if I don't disturb him? He is asleep. But I am sure he will be awake by six o'clock and I will ask him to ring you.'

I apologised for disturbing her. 'You were not to know,' she told me.

That night Melissa died, and in the most extraordinary way.

As David Stevens himself told me later, 'We had gone to bed. She was eating a peach – she was always eating fruit. In the middle of the night she got up to go to the bathroom. When after a time she had not come back to bed I went to find out what was wrong and found her slumped on the lavatory seat. I extracted a piece of peach from her throat and called the doctor. When she arrived in hospital she was dead.'

It was the cruellest of blows. For there is not the slightest doubt that he was utterly devoted to his wife. Even to the extent of having made himself a figure of fun by serialising in the *Daily Express* a book Melissa had written about how a woman should make herself sexually attractive to her husband and advocating that she began the process by kissing his toes.

After a funeral service in St Brides on 27 February he flew with his wife's body to Las Vegas for burial. Her mother lived there and according to David Stevens was much upset afterwards by receiving a succession of anonymous telephone calls telling her that her daughter had been murdered. Matters were not helped by a vitriolic and cruel obituary which appeared in the *Daily Telegraph*. But such was David Stevens's strength of character that he overcame it all, even to the extent of marrying again within the year.

In many ways he is an odd mixture. He can be curiously diffident and insecure. He will hesitate before making a personal approach to a Cabinet minister and would prefer an editor to do it for him. His speeches in the House of Lords are largely written by the *Daily Express* leader writer, Derrick Hill. But his energy is enormous and although his personal share in the equity of United Newspapers is microscopic he plays the part as if he owned the entire company. The only snag from my point of view was that he knows nothing about what sells newspapers and in the three years I was with him he didn't even begin to learn.

Nor were matters helped when we all moved into our new custom-built offices on the south side of Blackfriars Bridge.

It is a magnificent building with panoramic views of the Thames.

It has fine restaurants and even a pub contained within the building. But there is just one big snag. In Fleet Street, when you came out of the front door you were in the midst of your readers. The pavements were thronged with ordinary people. When you come out of the new building you are in the midst of nothing. Even though the hustle and bustle is only a few hundred yards away on the other side of the river, the sense of isolation is extraordinary. On the top floor Stevens has built for himself the most remarkable office I have ever seen. It occupies the entire front of the building and is like a sultan's palace. Beaverbrook never had anything like it. Nor, I imagine, has any press baron.

That early summer of 1989 Stevens began to be very unhappy with Robin Esser's editorship of the *Sunday Express*. He told me about his unhappiness and I counselled him to avoid at all costs making a change of editor until he was certain he had the right replacement. I pointed out that nothing could more quickly destroy a newspaper than a succession of editors, each of them lasting no longer than a few months. I suggested that if he were unhappy with Esser he should appoint an Associate Editor and then send Esser on a longish trip abroad to see how the replacement performed in his absence. To his credit, Stevens thought that was an underhand way of doing things. He asked me if there were any names I wanted to put forward as possible replacements for Esser.

I had two names. He was interested in the first and asked if I could arrange a lunch for the three of us so that he might have a chance to measure the man I was suggesting. The lunch was arranged for 29 June 1989, the same day on which the Prime Minister was due to come down to declare the new building officially open. The lunch duly took place. I was surprised by the cursory nature of the questions which Stevens put to my nominee. No God-damned wonder. At the time he was lunching with us he had already appointed someone else Editor.

I did not care overmuch for that sort of treatment. But when a few days later I finally met the new Editor I did not care for him very much either.

I was aware that I was being totally unreasonable. But then during the thirty-two years I had edited the newspaper I had always been totally unreasonable.

I had never once taken on to the staff anyone I didn't personally like. I took the perhaps simplistic view that if I didn't like him then other members of the *Sunday Express* might not like him either. I was even less prepared to work under someone with whom I might feel uncomfortable and at odds and who in his public utterances had already conveyed the impression that until his arrival the *Sunday Express* had been a pretty poor newspaper.

And I cared least of all for working with a chairman who had utterly lost any respect I had ever had for him.

A week later the time came for me to go on holiday. In my column of 5 August 1989 I ended my last paragraph by saying: 'When you read this I will be walking barefoot on the wet sand of a Normandy beach. Humming all the while "Ae fond kiss and then we sever".

'Anyone know the next line?'

The rest as they say is history.

INDEX

All Pan books are available at your local bookshop or newsagent, or can be ordered direct from the publisher. Indicate the number of copies required and fill in the form below.

Send to: **CS Department, Pan Books Ltd., P.O. Box 40, Basingstoke, Hants. RG21 2YT.**

or phone: 0256 469551 (Ansaphone), quoting title, author and Credit Card number.

Please enclose a remittance* to the value of the cover price plus: 60p for the first book plus 30p per copy for each additional book ordered to a maximum charge of £2.40 to cover postage and packing.

*Payment may be made in sterling by UK personal cheque, postal order, sterling draft or international money order, made payable to Pan Books Ltd.

Alternatively by Barclaycard/Access:

Card No. ☐☐☐☐☐☐☐☐☐☐☐☐☐☐☐☐☐☐

Signature:

Applicable only in the UK and Republic of Ireland.

While every effort is made to keep prices low, it is sometimes necessary to increase prices at short notice. Pan Books reserve the right to show on covers and charge new retail prices which may differ from those advertised in the text or elsewhere.

NAME AND ADDRESS IN BLOCK LETTERS PLEASE:

....

Name————————————————————————

Address————————————————————————

————————————————————————

————————————————————————

————————————————————————

3/87